What others say about *Trage*

"In this last review of the season, I've tal
by Global Authors Publications, or (
writing aspirations, and I suspect there
legitimate opportunity to have your woi... ....
professionally marketed. In ***Tragedy in Tin Can Holler,*** Floridian Rozetta Mowery has turned the flowery sentimentality we have come to expect of family history on its head: she has written a memoir from hell.

"Hardscrabble doesn't begin to describe the Snopes-like existence of this family. Ms. Mowery's horrific story unfolds in the voice of a sensitive girl from a background of limited prospects, where violence and indecency were commonplace. Her earnest quest for the truth about her family plays against the ferocious characters who emerge from her research. Court transcripts, prison logs, letters, accounts of fraudulent adoptions, and the testimony of witnesses paint a picture of ravenous neglect, incest, and homicide. Here is everything you would never wish to discover about your relatives: Grandma was a hog farmer who lured mail-order husbands to her ranch and killed them, practiced prostitution, infanticide, and turned her son, Seig, the author's father, into a murderer before he reached adulthood. But reach adulthood he did, married Eliza, and fathered six children. But Seig Mowery, an epic alcoholic and philander, had a violent nature and a criminal mind. After his second incarceration, his six poverty-stricken children were removed from their emotionally broken mother and placed in an orphanage, the author among them. Following his release from prison, Seig returned to his wife, and shortly thereafter, murdered her. The second half of Ms Mowery's book is a conventional portrait of her brothers and sisters, what happened to each of them and to their children, but a story of privation and misadventure continues.

"It's difficult to explain this book's curious effect. It lifts the lid on a strain of the American experience most of us will never know, and if we did, would be reluctant to discuss. And when you think you've heard it all and seen it all, a Mohawk Carpets truck wheels out of nowhere and runs down her sister. It leaves you breathless with wonder at how bad hard luck can be. 'We have only two basic responses to life, one is fear and the other is love,' the author writes in her conclusion. In completing her project Rozetta Mowery has explored her capacities for love, taken the healthiest course to redemption, and perhaps most importantly, faced and gone beyond the cruel truths of her own and her family's past."
Tom Casey, Reviewer for South Florida Social

"Like slowly pulling an ice pick out of the heart. Rozetta Mowery holds a mirror in front of America and gives one of the most devastating real life accounts of domestic violence and its vicious cycle ever put on paper. The brutality is not just read, it is relived and the reader is there. The pain seethes through every page like an ice pick pushed inches deeper as you read along. Rosie's survival and ability to cope became an ice pick slowly being pulled out of the reader where she and we note a healing process. The book is an indictment against domestic abuse and should be among required reading for women as well as men who are drawn toward or feel trapped in abusive relationships. The fact this book was written at all is in itself a miracle. Hats off to the new voice speaking out against domestic violence!"
William Wright, Journalist and Screenwriter

"*Tragedy in Tin Can Holler* is Rozetta Mowery's account of the hard things that led to the murder of her mother by her father. The story, which spans generations and describes the decades of physical, psychological, sexual and substance abuse that culminated in that brutal murder, unspools in precise, measured language that recalls Capote's *In Cold Blood*. Mowery in unsparing in the details as she pursues the leads that will give her the answers she's sought since her mother was taken from her at age seven. Remarkably, she ends her account with a word of forgiveness, which must be a testament to the influence of a Higher Power. *Tragedy in Tin Can Holler* should perhaps be read in pieces. I raced through it in one sitting and couldn't sleep for three nights. I suspect I'll always carry this story with me. When you read something by Stephen King, you can comfort yourself with the knowledge that it's only fiction. Unfortunately, the monsters described by Mowery don't exist only between the covers of a book. They're real and they're all the more haunting for it."
Luke Osteen, Freelance Journalist

TRAGEDY IN TIN CAN HOLLER

ISBN: 978-0-9779680-6-0
Library of Congress Control Number: 2009920738
Published by Global Authors Publications

Filling the GAP in publishing

Edited by Barbara Sachs Sloan
Interior Design by KathleenWalls
Front Cover Design by Ann Ryan
Back and Spine design by Kathleen Walls

TRAGEDY IN TIN CAN HOLLER

BY

ROZETTA MOWERY

"No one knows how many lives one man touches"

Release

Not now or then, not here or there
But blown on the winds to God knows where.

Eliza and Seig bore six children together,
Separated by the death of their mother.

Seig took her life, never thinking ahead,
Of his six children, and the lives that they led.

Eliza was gone at just thirty-six years.
There is no accounting for her hopes or her fears.

Her children are the victims, they have cried the tears
That washed away the memories through all these many years.

They have lived through the sorrow and all of their fears,
But can finally feel the truth is getting near.

Their mother feels their freedom with each line of her life.
Thank God there's an end to all of their strife.

Written by: Bonnie Stoddard 01/10/07

Table of Contents

Memory Page

Dedication

Introduction

Section 1 – "The Beginnings"
Chapters 1 – 11

Section 2 – "Tin Can Holler"
Chapters 12 – 18

Section 3 – "The Tragedy"
Chapters 19 – 26

Section 4 – "What Happened to the Children"
Chapters 27 – 36

Author's Conclusion

Acknowledgements and Credits

IN MEMORY OF

    Eliza Mae Robinson Mowery. She was a loving mother, sister, grandmother, aunt and friend. Her memory will remain in the hearts of all those who loved her and continue to miss her.

DEDICATION

I dedicate my book to all my hundreds of wonderful girlfriends, past and present, near and far who helped me each and every day from childhood until the present. Thank you for the happiness and joy you shared with me; your hugs when I needed one; for listening and giving me a shoulder to cry on when I had no one else; and for your many words of encouragement that kept me going. But, most of all…thank you for caring. Many years and many miles have separated us, but I will never forget you and I will always love you. May God always bless you and keep you safe. You came into my life for a reason, even if it was only for a season.

INTRODUCTION

Did you ever wonder about your parents', grandparents' and great-grandparents' past? Did you ever wonder about the skeletons that are hanging in your family closet? Rozetta did! Her father murdered her mother in a place called Tin Can Holler when she was seven years old. Her mother's horrible death and disfigurement by the hands of her father always haunted her. She spent over twelve years of her childhood in abusive foster homes being raised by strangers who did not love her and was separated from her siblings, while her wealthy grandfather, whom she did not know, lived in a mansion and had a life of luxury. Her mother's love and spirit gave her the courage to overcome the many obstacles she faced during her lifetime. She was determined to be normal and prove that even though she came from a place called Tin Can Holler and was a foster child most of her childhood, there is hope for a better life. She promised herself that she would someday find the truth about her beloved mother's death.

Discovering why her father murdered her mother was just the tip of the iceberg. When a person brutally murders someone they proclaim to love, it makes you question that person's past and their upbringing. Rozetta had no knowledge of her father's background or his family, but her instincts told her there had to be more to the story. Uncovering the nightmarish details of her family's past transgressions, traumatized Rozetta and shocked the residents of three counties in southeast Tennessee.

Most people would not have done what Rozetta did. The family secrets would have remained with the ghosts who haunt the ridge where her grandmother disposed of her victims. Tragedy in Tin Can Holler is the story of a back woods family who did unspeakable horrors. The horrific cycle of hate and killings in her family span more than a century before she was born. It's also a story of understanding and forgiveness. She knew she could not change or erase her family history, but she owed it to her mother to find the truth, because of all the good that she had stood for when she was alive. She hopes her faith and the love she inherited from her mother is all that she will need to break the family curse, so it never surfaces again in her children, grandchildren, nieces or nephews for generations to come.

She knew in her heart that she must set the record straight. By writing her story she hopes to rectify the sins of her father, break the family curse and spread her message about the dangers of domestic violence and the horrible aftermath of what happens to the children. Even though forty-seven years had passed since her mother's death, and regardless of the cost, she knew the truth would finally set her free.

THE BEGINNINGS

CHAPTER 1

The year 1959 was an uneventful year for most people. In the life of one little 7-year-old girl, Rozetta Mowery, it was a life-altering year. Her mother's vicious murder left her with emptiness and a heart full of unanswered questions. It took her until she was 53 to find the answers and "the truth."

Rozetta was born on August 4, 1952, to Seignoyst Randolph Mowery (aka Seig Sims) and Eliza Mae Robinson at Epperson Hospital in the small town of Athens, Tennessee. She was brought home to a two-room shack on the other side of the railroad tracks to a community called "Tin Can Holler."

She was told her mother named her after Rosita Bazamba, a Spanish dancer who was famous at the time. At the age of 15 she discovered the real spelling of her name when she received her birth certificate while applying for a social security card and a learner's permit. She was in shock! All of her report cards and anything containing her name were not spelled correctly. Where had this mysterious "Rozetta" come from, or rather, where had she been all those years? It was half a century and what seemed a lifetime later before she found out the truth regarding her last name and what it should have been.

She uncovered the truth about her mother's brutal murder at the hands of someone she had loved and trusted as a small child in Tin Can Holler. This truth exposed family secrets that had been buried for decades and shocked her entire family and three small communities in Tennessee.

Rozetta's family tribulations began in Meigs County, Tennessee, a century before she was born and a long time before Tin Can Holler. Meigs County is located in southeast Tennessee. Its county seat, Decatur, is located in the middle of the Tennessee Valley. It's bordered on the west by the Tennessee River. The northern third of the county is bordered on the west by Watts Bar Lake and the rest of the county is bordered on the west by Chickamauga Lake. The lower third of the county is divided by the Hiwassee River.

Rozetta's great-grandfather was Tyre Houston Sims. He was named after his mother's father, Tyre Lawson, Sr. Tyre was the sixth child born of George Washington Sims and Caldonia Lawson, who had 10 children. George and Caldonia were married on July 15, 1844. George was 21 years old and Caldonia was 17. The family was very poor and times were grueling during the Civil War era from 1860 to 1865. The eldest son, William Henry Harrison Sims, enlisted in the 4th Tennessee Cavalry unit in Nashville at the age of 24. After he returned home, he and his wife, Mary, lived next to his family's farm in Meigs County because George gave his sons acreage from his original homestead when they became men.

George and his sons were loggers and owned a local sawmill. The illiterate children had to work on the farm or at the sawmill and were not allowed to go to school. They also farmed and raised hogs. They were a very private, close-knit family that was feared and considered evil by their neighbors. They had limited association with anyone in their small community. They only ventured to town once a month to purchase needed supplies.

Rozetta's great-grandparents, Tyre Houston Sims and Mary Jane Robison, applied for a marriage license in Meigs County, but the marriage license was never returned to the courthouse. There is no legal evidence that they ever consummated their marriage by law. Tyre was 27 years old and Mary Jane was 28. Tyre built a small cabin for his bride on the 12 acres given to him by his father. The surrounding farmlands were owned by the Lockmillers on the north, the Davises on the west, and the Fikeses on the east; to the south were Brickell Ridge and the McMinn County line. Tyre continued to work with his brothers harvesting lumber for their sawmill, raised hogs and farmed his 12 acres.

Mary Jane had a lot of health issues. These health problems caused her to have many miscarriages. On September 21, 1886, at the age of 34, she gave birth to Rozetta's grandmother, Grace Victoria Sims. Her grandmother, Grace, was their only child.

As Grace began to blossom into a young woman, her mother's health issues worsened. It is not known why she had so many health problems, but she may have had cancer. Grace had to care for her mother and do all the chores her mother had always done. She had been allowed to go to school but dropped out to care for her mother. Grace, still a child, was a big girl and looked older than her age. She was 5 feet 5 inches, with dark blue eyes and long dark brown hair, and weighed around 155 pounds. At this same time, Tyre's affection for Grace became compulsive and uncontrollable. He began to show her more attention and affection. Grace mistook this as her father's way of showing her he loved her. His demands and sexual advances increased, and Tyre began abusing Grace worse than incest and completely ignored his wife, Mary Jane. Grace became withdrawn and angry and tried to avoid his advances. Whenever she refused, he would beat her. There was no way to escape the clutches and the control of her father.

Mary Jane, although she knew what was happening to her daughter, was too weak and ill to stop it. Even in the best of health Mary Jane had never been able to stand up to Tyre, because she knew he would also beat her. Family secrets, no matter how terrible, were never spoken back then. This was an era of secrecy and those remained within the family.

CHAPTER 2

As Grace approached her late teen years she became very rebellious and began drinking. On one occasion she was seen drunk, riding her mule through the city of Decatur wearing only her gun and holster belt around her waist. In 1905, when Grace was 19 years old, she met Cleveland Smith, a married man. She could always get moonshine from him. They became drinking buddies and partners in crime. She and Cleveland Smith were arrested numerous times for trespassing, public drunkenness, carrying a pistol, public profanity, manufacturing moonshine, and lewdness. Lewdness during that time period was unmarried couples living together. Grace never served any jail time in Meigs County. She only had to pay the fines.

Because of her abuse at the hands of her father, Grace became a very vicious and evil woman with a hateful disposition. She also became a callus, fearless woman who did whatever she desired. She was charged twice in 1905 for felonious assault but was not arrested. Again, the local authorities only made her pay the fines.

Cleveland's wife, Elizabeth, divorced him, but he did not want to marry Grace and this made her very angry. She stopped seeing him and began to drink more. Once again she was arrested numerous times for public drunkenness and paid the fines. She continued her crime sprees but did so in the Chattanooga area, where she and a group of teenage boys would rob mom-and-pop stores. She would also steal other peoples' mail from their mailboxes, looking for money.

None of the local women would associate with Grace, and the local men would cross the street to avoid passing her on the sidewalk when she came to town to do her shopping. The local men said she was "meaner than a diamondback rattlesnake."

Because Grace was half German and half Italian she inherited a spirit of energy. She also may have had some type of chemical imbalance in her brain. Today she would possibly be diagnosed with hallucinations and schizophrenia. This could explain her bizarre behavior, or it could have been the moonshine. Grace certainly did not interpret the world in the same way normal people do. The abuse of her father probably enhanced the already pronounced chemical imbalance within her body and mind.

She was extremely divided. She was two different people. This was horrifying to Grace, as she did not know who she was. There were extremes of love and fear that went on within her constantly and she would rationalize what she did as love, because her interpretation of love was so warped from her abuse and her addiction to moonshine. Her left side was the victim and her right side was the aggressor. This is like a dual personality, and she probably had more than two personalities. The only remedy for this condition was to confine people to the insane asylums.

Grace, however, had a clever way with words, especially with men, and knew how to manipulate them. Grace began to travel outside Decatur in search of rich married men. She would be gone for weeks and sometimes a month or more. When she came back she always had plenty of money. With this money, she built a huge barn on the south end of the property and purchased more hogs. Her father had taught her the hog business and how to slaughter them and process the meat. She later built her own house close to the barn on the property which is now called Sims Road.

In 1909, at the age of 23, she met another married man, J. Marion Mowery, who leased the Sims family sawmill that Tyre and his brothers once operated. She did not care that Marion was a married man, because she had no self-respect and did not care what others thought. Because this type of behavior was uncommon for ladies during this time period, Grace became the gossip in the entire town of Decatur. Her reputation was ruined and Tyre was full of shame because of what his daughter had become. He knew he had created a monster but also that he could no longer abuse his daughter. She was out of his control. He had to let her go.

Grace became romantically involved with Marion. She now had her own home where he became a frequent visitor. On June 19, 1910, she gave birth to his son whom she named J. Cornelius Mowery. Eleven months later, May 4, 1911, little Cornelius was dead. He was a beautiful child and looked just like Grace. Because Cornelius was so like her, Grace in her tormented mind, could not allow this baby to grow up. The real reason for his death is unknown, but the rumor around the county was she killed Cornelius and fed him to her hogs. Grace told people he died in his sleep. No gravesite or birth and death records for Cornelius can be found.

She continued her affair with Marion Mowery and once again

gave birth to another son on February 4, 1912. She named him De-foyst Marion Mowery. Grace was now 25 years old. Marion would sneak away from his wife and other children in Cleveland, Tennessee, to spend time with Grace and Defoyst, but it was never enough for Grace.

Marion Mowery's visits were sporadic, and Grace needed money desperately! She would leave Defoyst with her parents and go out of town for weeks at a time in search of wealthy married men. She was blackmailing these married men after she had affairs with them. If they refused to give her money she would threaten to tell their wives about their extramarital affairs or kill them.

One man in Chattanooga, who was not a married man, was horrified of Grace. He had befriended her not knowing she had no intentions of being his friend. She threatened to kill him if he did not give her money. He and his family feared Grace and they always gave her money when she came to their home. She would always return home with plenty of money. These men, out of fear for their lives and the safety of their families, would pay her the money she demanded so she would leave them alone and never come back. But she always returned.

CHAPTER 3

During one of her trips to Decatur, Grace observed a very nicely dressed and handsome man. She could tell by his demeanor and proper etiquette that he was a man who apparently came from wealth. She was determined to find out more about him. She approached him with her charming personality, which she could turn on and off in an instant, and asked him who he was and where he was from. He was polite and answered all of her questions.

He identified himself as Harry Evans. He was the son of Thomas and Lillian Evans. His mother's parents were Mr. and Mrs. Thomas R. Edgemon of Meigs County. Grace learned that he and his mother owned and operated the Evans & Son Funeral Home in Athens, Tennessee. She immediately knew he came from a very prominent family. During their conversation Grace discovered that he was unmarried and owned property next to her father's 12 acres on the McMinn County line. She invited Harry to visit her the next time he came to town. Harry thanked her and said he would. Grace was excited and went home to tell her parents about meeting him. A few days later, Harry arrived at the Sims' home. Her parents thought he was a nice young man, and he soon became a family friend who visited the Sims' home often.

Grace wanted to impress Harry. She used her charm and soon began a love affair with him. Harry was generous with his money and lavished her with gifts. For the first time in her life she was treated with love and respect, or so she thought. At the age of 29 she gave birth to Harry's son, Reedstrom. Harry was beside himself, because he knew he could not let anyone know he was having an affair with this woman. He was concerned about his family's good name and did not want his reputation blemished. Grace told him not to be concerned and gave his son Marion Mowery's last name.

CHAPTER 4

Sometime in 1915, Mary Jane became very sick and her health worsened. She was ignored and neglected by Tyre and Grace and starved to death. They left her lying dead in her bed for days before notifying the authorities. Harry took care of the funeral arrangements and quickly buried Mary Jane in the local cemetery known as Whispering Pines in the Walnut Grove area of Decatur. Because few people liked the Sims family and were afraid of them, rumors about Mary Jane's death escalated throughout the entire community. The neighbors were shocked when they heard that Mary Jane lay dead in her bed for days. Two weeks after Mary Jane's funeral, the local authorities, upon hearing rumors that Tyre had killed her by breaking her neck or by poisoning her, exhumed her body and had her remains examined by a doctor. The doctor found no evidence of those allegations because her neck and spinal cord were intact. Her body was so deteriorated that further examination was impossible. They had no way of knowing what caused Mary Jane's sudden death. The rumors and the suspicions never stopped. Everyone still believed that Tyre had murdered his wife.

At the age of 63, Tyre decided to transfer to Grace the 12 acres of land conveyed to him by his father, George Washington Sims, in 1880. The responsibility of paying the property taxes and maintaining the farm was now bestowed upon Grace. She enjoyed bragging to Harry that her father had given her the farm. Grace knew she would have a difficult time running the farm and slaughtering the hogs, but she wanted to prove to her father that she could.

Her confidence plummeted and she began stealing from her neighbors. She was struggling on the farm and taking care of her two sons, Defoyst and Reedstrom. This was a heavy burden for a young female. The stress was more than she could bear, and she would drink herself into a stupor. She tried to get money from Marion to no avail. He was struggling to start his life over and refused to marry Grace.

Out of desperation, Grace decided the only thing left for her to do was prostitute herself with Marion's help. Marion would bring men from the surrounding counties to Grace's farmhouse. She did this for several months until the local authorities found out. She and Marion were both arrested and charged with lewdness and running a house of ill fame. This was the last time she was ever arrested and charged with a crime by the Meigs County Sheriff's Department. The threat of being locked up for an extended period of time apparently had its desired effect. Marion paid their fines and left Meigs County fearing further prosecution, but there was none.

Grace was plowing her fields one day when Harry Evans stopped by for a visit with Tyre. He knew this would be a good opportunity for him to check on his son, Reedstrom. Grace immediately stopped her plowing and rushed to her house. She bathed herself and wore her prettiest dress. She wanted to look her very best for Harry. Harry, who was attracted and addicted to Grace, accepted her invitation for dinner. He was ashamed of himself for being drawn back to her, because of her terrible reputation. Grace, with her charm, seduced Harry again and he could not resist her advances. She was a wild and very exciting woman. He had never experienced her terrible side, only her loving side. She wanted Harry to marry her, but he refused to talk about marriage. That was completely out of the question as was public exposure of his son. This angered her. Unbeknown to Grace, Harry had a secret dark side. On many occasions when he was lonely he would hire prostitutes from the Athens area to come to his cabin on the lake for weekends. He paid these prostitutes very well to entertain him and satisfy his fantasies. There was also much gossip and speculation among his embalmers and staff members who were employed by him. Whenever young women were brought into his funeral home he would lock himself in the room with them for hours and would not allow anyone else in the room. This would aggravate the embalmers as they needed to do their work.As the months passed and Grace needed money, she went to see Marion Mowery at the family sawmill. Grace demanded money and was given none, only promises from Marion that he would send her money later. Marion was unaware that Grace had stolen a pack of his bank checks.

On March 15, 1918, Grace gave birth to Harry's second son and named him Seignoyst Randolph. She also gave him Marion Mowery's last name to ease Harry's concerns about ruining his reputation. Grace's good side did not want to create a scandal for Harry even though everyone in the community knew of Harry's visits to her farm. Harry was often seen visiting the Sims farm, bringing Grace food, clothes, diapers and other necessities. During these visits he was becoming concerned that she was not being a good mother. His refusal of marriage brought a change in Grace's attitude toward him and the children. Grace had begun planting the evil seeds…the curse of her progeny that would be evident decades later.

CHAPTER 5

In 1918 Grace was arrested by Federal Marshals on charges of violating the postal laws of the United States by using the mail system to promote a scheme to defraud: Federal Case #4065. A $2,000 bond was posted on the promise that she would pay, and she was released. She was court ordered to appear before the Grand Jury for the eastern district of Tennessee in Chattanooga. Grace entered a "not guilty" plea, but witnesses against her proved otherwise.

Before Seig was born, Grace wrote letters to numerous companies throughout Tennessee and Alabama placing orders through ads placed in the Progressive Farmer magazine. She wrote the letters under the pretense that she was Marion Mowery and forged his name to the checks she had stolen from him months earlier. Representatives from these companies appeared to testify and presented the letters they received from her. Mr. Stubbs, an assistant cashier of the Rockwood Bank & Trust Company, testified that the checks written by Grace had insufficient funds and did not bear Marion Mowery's true signature.

Marion Mowery, her former lover and father of Defoyst, also testified against her. He stated that he did not write or authorize the writing of the letters and that the signatures on the letters were not his. He also testified that he did not draw or sign the checks for the goods she purchased and did not authorize them. He said he never gave Grace or any other living soul authority to draw checks on him or his bank account, even though Grace had drawn about $150.00 to $180.00 worth of checks on his account, which were all paid. When his account was balanced and the checks returned to him he sent those checks drawn by Grace back to the bank and told them they were not his checks, but the bank declined to refund his money. He denied the handwriting on a postal card addressed to a Mrs. J. M. Mowery, in Thomas, Alabama, and bearing the address Denver, Colorado, on May 20, 1911, which Grace presented as evidence. He admitted that he was in Denver but did not remember the date. He denied ever living with Grace as husband and wife, even though he had been arrested with Grace for lewdness in Meigs County. He stated that he never registered her at hotels or boarding houses as his wife. These assumptions led many to believe that Marion had accompanied Grace on her trips out of town and out of state, but he firmly denied it.

Grace admitted that she wrote the letters and received the goods. She claimed she had the authority to sign Marion Mowery's name to the checks and had been doing so for nine years. She stated that Marion understood that she was doing so and had honored $200.00 to different companies at the same time. She stated to the Grand Jury that Marion Mowery was using her family sawmill and was to pay the sum of $50.00 per month and she had always written his name to his checks to pay for the rent on the sawmill with his knowledge.

The Grand Jury, after hearing Grace's testimony and the testimony of the witnesses, unanimously agreed to prosecute Grace for her violating federal postal laws. She wasn't able to pay the $2,000.00 bond as promised and was arrested again by the Federal Marshalls. She was held in a Chattanooga jail until her trial date. Grace was found guilty and was sentenced to 18 months in the Missouri State Penitentiary at Jefferson City, Missouri. The Federal Marshals transported Grace to the federal prison to begin her 18-month sentence.

While in prison, Grace gave numerous depositions on behalf of her father, claiming his innocence. The Grand Jury indicted Tyre as a co-defendant because he picked up the merchandise and goods Grace had ordered. She testified under oath that her father had no knowledge of what she had done and he only picked up the goods because she told him to and to sell various items to the workers on their farm. She purchased bushels of potatoes, turnips, onion sets, seed oats, seed corn, seed peas, cane seed, seed rye, black-eyed peas, whippoorwill peas, cotton seed, 15 bushels of pure white corn for bread only, and yards of different kinds of cloth. She always had the goods shipped in Tyre's name, and shipped to various locations, so he was assumed guilty by association. She proclaimed her father's innocence because of his age and ill health. Tyre was now 67 years old and Grace was 34 years old when she began her prison sentence. She took all the blame to keep her father out of prison. The charges against Tyre were eventually dropped.

Tyre was unable to care for Defoyst, 8 years old; Reedstrom, 5 years old; and Seig, 21 months old, while Grace was in prison. Harry was highly respected in both Meigs and McMinn counties, and was known for his kindness toward helping others. He assisted Tyre in finding homes in the local community for the boys while Grace was in prison. The boys were kept by good Christian families that took pity upon them until Grace came back home after serving her prison sentence.

Because of the hostile feelings toward Tyre by his neighbors, Harry had to secure workers for the farm. At this point he feared his sons would lose their claim to the Sims property if Tyre lost possession of the property.

CHAPTER 6

W hile Grace was in a controlled, structured environment in prison, no problems were ever reported by the prison warden. She returned home in June 1921. Shortly after she returned home she was out of control again. The prison system had not changed her; it only controlled her for a short period of time. She had had plenty of time to think about what she was going to do when she returned home. She began drinking moonshine compulsively and started leaving home for weeks at a time to prostitute herself in Knoxville and Chattanooga.

She became pregnant twice and did not know who the fathers were. She did not want these babies. Soon after the first baby was born she killed it and put his body in the huge meat grinder she kept in the barn to process the hog meat, and fed him to her hogs. The second baby was born when Seig was six years old. She threatened to beat Seig if he did not hold his baby brother under the water in a washtub. After his baby brother went lifeless in the washtub he realized what she had made him do. Seig went into shock and started running away screaming. He ran to the field that was owned by Harry Evans and leased to the Robinson family. Ernest and Howard, the eldest sons of Fred and Anner Robinson, grabbed Seig and asked him what was wrong. As he stood there crying he screamed, "My momma made me kill my baby brother!"

They had heard rumors about this crazy woman, Grace and her evil family, but they comforted Seig and told him he should go back home. They knew that the Sims family was feared by everyone in the community and they did not want to get involved.

When Seig returned home his baby brother was gone. To dispose of his little body quickly, Grace carried him to the top of Brickell Ridge, behind her farm, and threw him in a deep, dark hole. It is not known whether Grace was drunk or sober when she committed these crimes, but she had no conscience or remorse. In her sick mind, she was ridding herself of problems and added hardships she did not want in her life. This was the breaking point for Seig, because he had been so badly abused by Grace prior to this. This was a determining factor in what led to him being who he was.

After this incident, Grace would not allow Seig to attend school. She feared that he would tell someone even though she threatened him if he did. Seig was glad he did not have to go to school anymore. He was a very unhappy child and would tease the girls, which made them very angry. He also had dyslexia. The teachers back then could not figure out why he was not able to read and write. This was embarrassing for Seig, because he couldn't learn the school work like all the other kids. He knew his teachers and classmates thought he was stupid and he would get angry with everyone. Just for spite, while at home during the day, Seig would climb up the big tree in his front yard and pee on anybody that came by. Seig thought this was very funny, but each time he got caught, he would get a terrible beating when he climbed down from the tree.

Grace had a plan that did not include any more children to care for. In her sick mind she did not love her three sons, but knew they could help her on the farm as they grew bigger and stronger. She wanted to buy all the land that was once owned by her grandfather George Washington Sims. She thought this would please her father and the land would remain in the family for generations.

Grace checked the property records at the courthouse in Decatur and found out that H. G. Buckelew, an unmarried man from Chattanooga, was the owner. She contacted Mr. Buckelew and told him she would like to buy his land because it was part of the original homestead once owned by her grandfather. It is unknown how she convinced Mr. Buckelew to sell his land to her, but Mr. Buckelew met Grace at the courthouse in Chattanooga to legalize the sales transaction and promissory note. Mr. Buckelew wanted $2,700 for all 400 acres. Grace gave him a down-payment of $1,200 cash and signed a note to pay three installments of $500 each for the next three years.

The atmosphere in the Sims home was filled with constant turbulence. Grace was not a good mother and abused her three sons on a daily basis. She would beat them and make them sit in the yard with hand scissors and cut the grass. She was a fanatic about her home and property. She had expensive taste for the finest and most expensive items she could purchase for her home. She wanted all the same beautiful things that she had seen in the homes of the very wealthy. She filled her home with expensive china, satin linens, silk curtains and Persian rugs in every room.

Grace was desperate for money to support her expensive and luxurious illusions of grander and maintain her desired lifestyle. When she had no food to feed her children she would wake up Defoyst, Reedstrom and Seig in the middle of the night and make them sneak to neighboring farms to steal their chickens. They were also forced to steal from their neighbors' gardens and to drink moonshine at an early age. They too became alcoholics like their mother. This was the beginning of their life of thievery.

She struggled to get the money for the payments on the land she purchased from Mr. Buckelew and got a job in a hospital for 18 months, but that was still not enough. She contacted Harry to see if he would be interested in buying the family sawmill. Harry, after seeing the realized potential of the sawmill, purchased it from Tyre. After she paid off her debt to Mr. Buckelew she quit her job at the hospital. Grace was now 43 years old.

CHAPTER 7

The Great Depression that began in 1929 and lasted until about 1939 was an economic slump in North America, Europe, and other industrialized areas of the world. It was the longest and most severe depression ever experienced by the industrialized Western world, and Meigs County was no exception. Poverty spread throughout the community like a deadly virus. Family businesses closed, farmlands were lost, and people were starving. Honest, law-abiding citizens became common thieves. They did unspeakable things to feed their families. Husbands had to leave their wives and children to go look for work in the big cities like Knoxville and Chattanooga.

Grace made Defoyst and Reedstrom leave the farm to look for work in nearby McMinn County. They dropped out of school and found meager jobs, but had to give all their money to Grace. The things she made her boys do were despicable. She trained them to be criminals, just like her. Her eldest son, Defoyst, was charged with larceny: illegal taking and carrying away of personal property belonging to another with the purpose of depriving the owner of its possession. The records did not state what his punishment was. Seig, at 12 years of age, was caught and arrested for stealing watermelons. When the judge discovered he was a juvenile, he gave him a stern warning and released him to Grace. All three of her sons were known as and referred to as the "Sims boys," children of Grace Sims, because they were constantly getting into trouble and were breaking the law, just like their mother always had.

Harry's visits continued. He was deeply concerned about the boys. He also felt the need to check on Tyre, who was now 77 years old and suffered from many ailments and had difficulty walking. Harry knew that Grace was not taking care of her father as she should. He became much tormented over what Grace was doing to the boys, tormented as in he didn't know how to do things differently. There was a lot of conflict within him. He tried to do what was best for his sons, but he didn't have the right guidance. He was very troubled and did not know what to do or how to handle it. Harry was more involved on an emotional level than anyone realized. He really did want to do what was best for his sons. Unfortunately, he had an understanding that he couldn't do anything. He was just not able. This was a period of time when child abuse was not reported. People did not betray the family secrets no matter how hard they were, and that tormented Harry. He remained in constant turmoil, because in his heart he knew things weren't right. He also protected Grace in many ways. That was one of the challenges within him. He couldn't get close to any other females, and he never married.

As the economic struggles continued to worsen around the country, Grace came up with another scheme to make money. She was now 45 years old and knew she couldn't compete with the younger prostitutes any longer. She started reading the personal ads in the local newspapers. What she decided to do filled her with excitement as it seemed to be the perfect plan. Men from all over the United States were searching for mail-order brides. She began corresponding to these men through their personal ads. The men responded with enthusiasm about the prospect of getting a bride. She was very convincing in her letters even though she had no intention of marrying any of them. These poor, unfortunate men did not know they were walking straight into Satan's den. When they arrived at the local train station, Grace was there waiting for them. She had described herself to them in her letters, so they knew what she looked like.

Before leaving her house in her horse-drawn wagon to pick up the men at the railroad station in Athens, Grace would lock her boys in the closet by the fireplace in the front parlor of her home. She installed a lock on the door that had no doorknob, so the boys could not get out. She gave them a pee pot, apple butter sandwiches and a gallon of water. She threatened to beat them if they made any noise. The three boys sat in the closet sometimes for two days before she would let them out. They could hear Grace talking to the men she brought home, and they could hear her cooking in the kitchen. Sometimes there was a lot of noise, as though she was moving things around in the room and scrubbing the floor.

Grace was vicious in her attacks on these men. She would prepare a meal for them and stir arsenic into their food before she served it to them. During that time period arsenic was readily available and almost everyone had arsenic in their cupboards. After consuming their food they would become violently ill. The men would have convulsions, muscle weakness, and confusion. If their deaths were prolonged, she would smother them or stab them with her kitchen knife. Blood stains on her hardwood floors were impossible to remove. There's a huge blood stain in the hallway by the room she used as a kitchen that has remained there all these years.

Grace would take her sewing needles and prick their faces to make sure they were dead. She would search for money and any other valuables and put them in a box she kept on a table in her parlor. The most gruesome and horrific part was to follow. Grace had a distant cousin named Clive, who was mentally and emotionally challenged. He was a large man with the mentality of a small child who could not speak. He would giggle and laugh and she would laugh with him, so he would think they were playing a game. She would make Clive drag the men to her barn by their arms and strip them of their clothes. They would place the naked bodies on a wooden bench. All the while, Clive thought they were just playing a game. He did not know or realize that she had killed these men and was using him to help her to dispose of their bodies.

Grace, being an expert slaughtering hogs, was not frightened by the sight of blood. She would take a hatchet and chop off their heads. There were several pits dug on her property where Grace buried the hog carcasses and skulls. Occasionally, she would throw the human skulls in with the hog skulls and cover them with lye to keep the smell down. She and Clive would take a two-man handsaw and cut the bodies in half. In order to keep Clive's attention she would laugh at him and continue making it look like a game she was playing. She would throw the mutilated bodies into her big wheelbarrow and cover them with an old blanket. Directly behind her barn was a steep hill known as Brickell Ridge. She and Clive would take turns pushing the wheelbarrow until they reached the top. This was an exhausting endeavor because the area was full of trees and the terrain was very steep. When they reached the top of the ridge, Grace would dump the bodies into a deep, dark hole. It was like a bottomless pit.

The hole is a natural formation that Tyre had shown to her when she was a child. Many people in the area knew about the deep hole, but it was so deep and dark, no one could see the bottom. Many other people in the area used it to discard their animal carcasses, so the foul odor coming from it was not uncommon or caused anyone to be suspicious. When Grace's sons were little boys and would play on the ridge, she would warn them to stay away from the hole.

Grace had used Clive to help her kill many other men. Years before, whenever she desperately needed help running the farm, she would hire transients looking for work. When they became angry because she could not pay them, she would poison them in the same matter and dispose of their bodies. Grace made her sons dig other deep holes near her barn to bury all the clothes, shoes and hats that belonged to these men.

Grace would also wear gray coveralls and a wide brimmed hat so she would look like a man. When Clive could not help her, she would throw the bodies over her mule and cover them with a blanket. She would walk her mule to the deep hole on Brickell Ridge or to different locations on her property and dig a hole and bury them. She buried several bodies in a wooded area on the ridge in front of her home near a large boulder, which was part of her 412 acres.

Grace was drawing a lot of suspicion from her neighbors who wondered what happened to all the men she was seen bringing to her farm, but were never seen leaving. Family members of these men came to the house looking for them. Seig overheard Grace telling these family members that they had a disagreement or a fight and they left. Seig knew she was lying because she made him bury their belongings. When the man who would have been victim number 13 managed to get away from her, she knew she couldn't take another chance on being caught. Grace killed and robbed 12 men before she changed her methods. She did not want any more men coming to her home.

In her next scheme, she promised the men who were looking for a mail-order bride that she would come to them if they would send her money for traveling expenses. Five men believed her and sent her money. Two of the men were from Montana. The others were from Arizona, Michigan and Massachusetts. The man who escaped from her reported her to the authorities, and the FBI began to watch Grace. They followed her to the post office in Decatur and surrounding counties, where she would retrieve letters and money from the postmasters. Because of her prior conviction and prison sentence for mail fraud, the FBI suspected she was doing something illegal.

Their investigations began at the local post offices and telegraph companies. The postmaster for Decatur provided proof of registered letters received by Grace and from whom. The manager of the Postal Telegraph Company in Chattanooga also provided evidence of payments to Grace. The FBI contacted these men and got the evidence they needed to arrest Grace. Once again, the FBI, along with Federal Marshalls, went to Grace's home and arrested her for violating U. S. Postal laws. They searched her home for any kind of evidence and only found evidence of mail fraud. She was transported to the Hamilton County Jail in Chattanooga. Her bond was set at $1,500. She did not have the bond money but promised to pay, so the judge released her.

CHAPTER 8

Grace was indicted in federal court on five counts of Violation of U.S. Postal Laws in a scheme to defraud men on a pretense of marrying each of them: Federal Indictment #6974. She would write to each of the men, after having obtained their addresses, and suggest and request that they forward her money. The money was to defray certain expenses incident to trips and journeys for the purpose of visiting them and discussing marriage. She had no intention, whatsoever, of marrying any of them. The Grand Jury unanimously agreed to prosecute her.

Orders were sent to the Federal Marshall's office to pick up Grace and place her in the Knoxville County jail after the bonding agents filed a report against her for failure to pay the bond they posted for her. Grace had not been feeling well for over a year, so while in jail she requested to see a doctor. During her medical exam Grace was informed of numerous health problems including high blood pressure and organic heart disease. The staff doctor also informed Grace that it was a very serious condition and could be life-threatening.

Grace was taken before the federal judge again. This time she used a different bonding agent with another promise to pay and was released. Grace knew she would be found guilty of the federal charges and feared that her health would deteriorate rapidly due to her heart problems.

After giving it much thought, Grace went to the Meigs County Courthouse in Decatur and included an indenture to her original property deed. She conveyed all her property, which consisted of 412 acres, to her three sons, with certain conditions, which included life estate on her property and living in the lifestyle to which she had become accustomed. Her three sons must provide her with all necessities of life, including any medical attention and nursing care she may require during her sickness. They must also pay for her funeral expenses. After her death, all of her property would be conveyed to Defoyst, Reedstrom and Seig, which they would share equally.

Grace now faced the reality of what she dreaded the most. She must speak to her father and her three sons and inform them of what she had done and what she expected from each of them. She also knew that it was time to tell her sons, Reedstrom and Seig that Harry Evans was their natural father, not Marion Mowery. She reassured Defoyst that J. Marion Mowery was his natural father and that he lived in Cleveland, Tennessee. Tyre, who was now 80 years old, did not look surprised. He told Grace he already knew that Harry was their father because they both looked like Harry. Reedstrom and Seig demanded to know why she had not told them about Harry before. She explained the secrecy surrounding her past romance with Harry and his desire to keep it a secret because of his public image in the surrounding communities and the funeral home business he owned with his widower mother. The boys thought that was a lame excuse but now understood why Harry would visit them and bring them food and gifts. She told the boys to respect Harry's wishes and to keep this information a secret. Harry may have known about some of the murders and used that information as a threat against Grace if she ever revealed to anyone that Reed and Seig were his sons.

Grace told them about the indenture that she added to her property deed and what she expected them to do for her because she had some very serious health problems with her heart. This news did not upset the boys, but Tyre became very concerned about his lovely daughter's well-being. He worried about the medical care that Grace desperately needed and may not get if she was found guilty and sentenced to prison again. Defoyst, Reedstrom and Seig promised to take care of their mother and Tyre promised to help them. Reedstrom was angry that he could not have his real father's last name; he did not want to have J. Marion Mowery's last name. He legally changed his name to Sims. Seig wanted to change his name to Sims, but he did not have the money, so he kept Mowery.

Grace was desperate to get the money she needed to post her bond. She was an excellent quilt maker, something her mother had taught her when she was a young girl. She thought she could sell her quilts and a couple of her hogs. Unfortunately, because of the Great Depression, no one could afford to buy anything. She tried to sell her fruit, but the prices were too low. She gave her fruit away to the poor. She refused to ask Harry for help, so she made Defoyst and Reedstrom break into a local business in search of money. They were caught and arrested. The Meigs County Sheriff's Department charged both of them with larceny, and the judge sentenced them to several months in jail.

Grace was arrested because she did not pay the $1,500 to the bondsmen. Federal Marshalls placed her in the Hamilton County

Jail in Chattanooga. The federal judge refused to post another bond for her. She remained in jail until her court date, which was scheduled four days later. Grace had dreaded this day because she now had to face the five men she promised to marry. She had a court-appointed attorney, but the grand jury returned a guilty verdict because there was too much evidence against her. Federal Judge, George C. Taylor sentenced Grace to five years in the Federal Industrial Institution for Women in Alderson, West Virginia. Federal Marshall Randy R. Worley took Grace into his custody and transported her to the prison warden. Grace was 48 years old when she went to prison for the last time.

CHAPTER 9

Defoyst, 22 years old; Reedstrom, 19 years old; and Seig, 16 years old, must now take care of the farm, the hogs and their elderly grandfather, Tyre. Defoyst took the leadership role and instructed Reedstrom and Seig with the chores that needed to be done. This wasn't very difficult as they had done this before Grace went to prison. She made them do everything and threatened to beat them if they didn't. She also taught them to like moonshine. They were arrested numerous times for public drunkenness and only had to pay the fines. Seig was different, probably because he was abused the worst by Grace. He was an angry young man filled with hate. He hated himself and lived with the guilt of drowning his baby brother. He became very defiant and resented any kind of authority. He did not know how to love, since he had never felt love from anyone.

After being caught and charged with housebreaking and larceny, Seig was committed to the State Training and Agricultural School for two years. This school was a branch of the Brushy Mountain State Prison for juveniles and was located in Meigs County. During these two years, Seig escaped twice and went back to the farm. The longest time he managed to elude the authorities was 2½ months. He was eventually caught when the neighbors saw him and notified the local sheriff's department. He was picked up and returned to finish his sentence. After completing his sentence, he was discharged and released to return home.

Life at the Sims' home was much calmer and remained that way while Grace was in prison. Both Defoyst and Reedstrom got married. Seig took care of the chores around the farm and looked after Tyre. During the summer of 1937, while working in the garden, Seig noticed a pretty girl riding a horse down the road by the barn. He had not seen her before and wondered who she was. She also saw Seig and thought he was very handsome. For several weeks the two of them exchanged only glances until the pretty young girl waved at Seig and he waved back. The next time she came by on her horse he was determined to find out who she was. When he saw her coming down the road, he motioned with his hand for her to stop. He said, "Hello," and asked her what her name was. She told Seig it was Eliza Mae Robinson and her family worked on the farm next to the McMinn County line which was owned by Harry Evans.

Eliza kept spitting, and Seig asked her what she was chewing. She loved her chewing tobacco and offered him a strip of the raw tobacco she had in her pocket. He gladly accepted a strip and started chewing. He asked her if she had two older brothers and she answered, "yes." Seig immediately knew it was her older brothers he ran into when he was 6 years old after Grace made him drown his baby brother! He told Eliza that his name was Seig as he stood there petting her horse.

Eliza came to see him every day and they would go on picnics to the river, both riding her horse. Eliza was 14 years old and Seig was 19. She thought he had the most gorgeous blue eyes she had ever seen, and he thought she was beautiful. She also sensed that he had a dark side, although she did not question him about it immediately. Eliza was much more loving and affectionate than Seig, because he did not know how to show affection. Eliza did not yet know about the horrible abuse inflicted upon Seig by his mother. Seig only told her that his mother was in prison. She did not realize that he was a very cold, hard-hearted person. Eliza was the complete opposite of Seig, because she had come from a very loving family. She was very friendly, outgoing and talented. She surprised Seig one day when she showed up with her guitar. She picked her guitar and sang lots of funny songs for him, a few of her very own. He liked her cheerful personality and enjoyed her company because she made him laugh. He very seldom had anything to laugh about because his life was so miserable. They became friends and continued to see each other until harvest time came to an end.

Eliza's parents were Anner and Fred Robinson. This was Anner's second marriage. Her first husband, John Robinson, who was not related to Fred, died suddenly at a very young age. She had four children by John: Ernest, Howard, Minnie and Lucy.

Ernest was the runt of the family. He was not very big and was an easygoing fellow. He liked his whiskey and drank a lot. He was a navy man and was crippled in the war. He never married and lived off his military pension. Ernest was an outdoorsman who loved to hunt and take his nephews with him. He would go to the creeks and hunt mud turtles. He was good at catching the mud turtles and would always come home with a sack full.

Howard was the biggest of all the children. He was a huge, big barrel-chested guy and wore overalls 99 percent of the time. He wouldn't take anything from anybody and would knock your head off if you made him mad. Howard was a bootlegger for most of his life. He did this when he lived in the country and in the city of Athens when he lived on Front Street in the old Depot Hill area. People would go down the set of steps that led to the sidewalk and would go to his backdoor to buy moonshine whiskey. He would sell pints, half-pints or even just a shot of moonshine if that's all they wanted.

He made runs into the mountains to buy the moonshine. He had a '56 Ford and outran the police on the country roads. He would load his '56 Ford with gallon jugs full of moonshine. There were lots of bootleggers back then on Starr's Mountain and in the Loudon County area. He would take the old Highway 11 to Loudon and cut across to get his load and would take the back roads through Monroe County to get back into McMinn County. He would back his '56 Ford right at his backdoor and unload it. He would take the gallon jugs and pour their contents into smaller pint bottles. He went to jail many times, but he had the local officials paid off and was always released.

When Howard was in his early forties he had a life-changing religious experience and stopped bootlegging. He turned his life around and got a job with the State of Tennessee. He built a brush-harbor (outdoor church) out of brush and saplings. Sometimes they would have church every night of the week and it would be full of people. He strung lights and got benches and chairs for the people to sit on. The entire Robinson family attended church there and brought all their children. Howard would cook between church services on Sunday mornings, and all the families would bring covered dishes of food to share with everyone.

Minnie married and had seven children. She lived on a farm in the Pond Hill area of Athens, where all the Robinson clan would go to her farm on Sunday afternoons. Everyone would congregate there and cut watermelons. They all raised hogs during those days, and Minnie's farm was set up to do the slaughtering. All the family members would bring their hogs to her farm. Everyone had a job to do during hog slaughtering time. The children would take turns stirring the lard in a big iron kettle on a fire so the lard wouldn't burn or stick to the bottom of the kettle.

Lucy married young and moved to Florida. She had five daughters and only visited the family infrequently.

Anner met and married Fred Robinson after John died, and they had four children: Mary, Eliza Mae, Edgar Lee and William whom they called Bill.

Mary also married young and had four children. Her husband worked on the construction crew for the railroad and was gone a lot. Her family lived in the Avalon Height Hills area of Athens. Mary had a hard life and suffered many heartaches.

Edgar Lee married twice and had seven children. He was a trader and a wheeler-dealer. He would buy all kinds of things from land to cars and sell them to make a profit. He also worked a lot of construction and in the chair/wood factories. Edgar Lee was a Christian man and took his children to church. He also played the guitar and sang in church as did his wife and children. They were good people and were always the same, no matter when or where you saw them. Ed enjoyed preaching or testifying any time he had the opportunity.

The youngest Robinson child was William (Bill). He was big like his dad, Fred, and also worked in the chair/wood factories. He married and had several children.

Anner and Fred were Christians and raised their children in a good loving home, but they were poor and struggled to raise eight children. Anner was a midwife and assisted in the deliveries of many births of her friends and neighbors. She was a good-hearted woman and was loved by everyone who knew her. Fred knew Harry Evans and leased the farmland from him to grow the crops needed to feed his family. The Robinson family also rented one of the many homes owned by Harry in Athens.

Eliza and Seig continued to see each other as often as possible. In January 1938, Eliza met a young soldier from Cleveland, Tennessee, at the local skating rink in Athens. He was home on leave and would soon be shipped overseas. She left the skating rink with him, and he purchased a six-pack of beer. Before the evening was over he had his way with Eliza. By the time she realized she was pregnant, he had been shipped overseas. Eliza wrote him a letter about her pregnancy and waited patiently for his reply. He answered her letter very quickly. He made it perfectly clear to Eliza that he did not want to have anything to do with her or the baby. He also told her he did not love her and did not want to marry her. He told her good-bye and good luck. Eliza was still a child and did not know what she was going to do!

CHAPTER 10

While Grace was serving her five-year prison sentence, she wrote to her father regularly. Tyre's neighbors could see him struggling to walk to the mailbox with his cane. He may have had arthritis, which made it difficult to walk, because he was bent over and could only take short baby-steps. Tyre was illiterate and could not read Grace's letters. One day he asked his neighbors' teenage daughter if she could read the letters to him. She said "yes" and would check with Tyre every day to read for him. Grace would address her letters "My Dear Father."

Defoyst and Reedstrom had gotten jobs in Athens doing whatever they could to earn money. They also took care of the farm and asked their neighbors, the White family, to check on their grandfather while they were gone. Mrs. White had befriended Grace years earlier, when she would occasionally allow Seig to play with her son. Seig tried to steal a watermelon from Mr. White when he was a young boy but got caught. Mr. White told Seig that he didn't have to steal his watermelons, all he had to do was ask for them. After that incident, Seig never stole watermelons or anything from the White family again.

Grace's health continued to worsen while in prison due to her heart disease. She was eligible for probation and made a request and a plea to Federal Judge George Taylor to release her from the probation. After much deliberation and verifying Grace's health problems from the Federal Industrial Institution for Women, her request was granted. Judge George Jackson signed the order that stated the following: "It now appearing that the subject is ill of various diseases and having made application for release from probation, it is now ordered that she be released from probation and it is now ordered that she be released from further supervision and the charges against her terminated as of January 24, 1938."

Grace served a total of three years, eight months and four days in prison. She was too weak to travel alone on the train, so Defoyst drove to the prison and picked her up.

Grace was happy to be home and was proud of her sons for taking care of her father and the farm. She was very weak and unable to care for herself. Her sons kept their promise and took care of her. For the next 18 months Tyre never left her side. He moved into her house, so he could be with her constantly.

Harry, after hearing about her early release, came by to see her and increased his visits, because he knew she was slowly dying. She had been the love of his life, but because of her wild criminal lifestyle and the terrible reputation she had created for herself, his pride would never allow him to get close to her. She told him that Reedstrom and Seig knew he was their natural father but would never tell anyone. She asked Harry to promise that he would look after her sons when she was gone. He told her he would, but it was not going to be in the way Grace wanted him to … he had other plans.

At 15 years of age, Eliza did not know what to do about her pregnancy, so she traveled to Meigs County to visit Seig. She wanted to tell him what had happened to her. She had not yet told her family about her pregnancy and thought Seig could give her some advice on what she should do, since he was five years older. Seig listened to her story and was silent for a short time while Eliza sat looking at him waiting for him to say something. His solution to her problem was to ask Eliza to marry him. Eliza started crying; she couldn't believe he or any man would want to marry her. He told her to stop crying and give him an answer. She hugged Seig and said, "yes."

Several days later, Seig introduced Eliza to his mother, Grace, and his grandfather, Tyre, and announced that he and Eliza wanted to get married very soon. Grace and Tyre were not happy about their announcement but agreed to let them live at home until they could find a place of their own, since Defoyst and Reedstrom had both gotten married and moved out of the home.

Eliza was happy she had found a solution to her problem. She thought everything would be okay, since she had known Seig for almost a year and truly cared for him. When she returned home to tell her parents of her plans to marry Seig Mowery, the roof almost came off the house. Her parents and her brothers were furious with her and warned her not to go through with the marriage. Her brothers told her about Grace making Seig kill his baby brother and all the rumors they had heard about his evil family. They told Eliza that Seig was a drunk and a thief. Eliza had no choice but to tell her entire family that she was pregnant with another man's child and that Seig offered to marry her. They remained firm on their advice to her and said she would never get their blessing or approval if she married him. Eliza discovered that Seig was illiterate on the day they applied for their marriage license and she had to read everything to him. She did not heed her family's advice and warnings about Seig and married him on May 8, 1938. On October 5, 1938, Eliza gave birth to a daughter and named her Cinderella, nicknaming her Cindy. The entire Robinson family refused to come to the Sims' home in Meigs County to visit Eliza and her new baby, so Eliza would travel with her daughter to visit them in Athens. They fell in love with Cinderella and adored her.

Seig, even though he was now married to Eliza, continued to be a very troubled young man and still committed crimes. He subconsciously hated his mother. She had created a monster within him. He was arrested by the Meigs County Sheriff's Department again and was charged with petit larceny. He was sentenced to 11 months in jail, and Eliza took Cindy to stay with her parents. Seig was released after serving only a few months, and Eliza and Cindy came back to Grace's home.

On June 19, 1939, Grace passed away in her home with Tyre and her sons by her side. Defoyst notified the local authorities and Harry Evans. Harry rushed to their house and had Grace transported to his funeral home. Harry took care of all the funeral arrangements and gave Defoyst, Reedstrom and Seig an invoice for payment. Grace was buried in the Whispering Pines cemetery next to her mother two days later. Tyre was grief-stricken and heartbroken over losing his beautiful daughter Grace, but her three sons showed no emotion as they assisted Harry in lowering her coffin into the grave they had dug for her. Defoyst, Seig, Reed and Reed's wife remained behind as Harry took Tyre back to his home. Harry was very concerned about Tyre's failing health.

Reed's wife stood in horror watching Grace's three sons laughing as they threw shovels of dirt onto her coffin. She watched them whispering and laughing amongst themselves. When they finished filling in her grave with dirt they threw down their shovels and began dancing on her grave while clapping their hands, jumping up and down and cheering. She recalled the time when Reed and his mother had a terrible argument and Reed shouted at Grace, "Mother, I am married now and have a family of my own. I am not doing any more dirty work for you!" Her many questions to Reed regarding his mother and why they were dancing on her grave went unanswered, but the vision of their bazaar behavior always remained deep in her memory. Grace's legacy of abuse, alcoholism and murder did not die with her.

CHAPTER 11

Nine days after Grace passed away, Defoyst, Reedstrom and Seig went to the courthouse and placed a lien against the property to secure a note for $237 to the Tennessee Motor Company, which was payable in eight monthly installments. C. L. Williams was the Trustee. It is not known if Grace had an outstanding debt that needed to be paid or if they purchased some type of farm equipment or automobile. Three days later, they were back in the courthouse placing another lien on the property for $1,480 to Harry R. Evans, payable in eight monthly installments. Harry wanted payment for Grace's funeral expenses and nursing care that he had paid.

Six months after Grace passed away, Tyre was also dead. He lost his will to live and died in his sleep. His neighbors said he died of a broken heart. Harry Evans took care of the funeral arrangements and buried him in the Whispering Pines Cemetery next to Grace, not his wife Mary Jane. Seig, Eliza and Cindy remained in the house but not for very long.

On March 25, 1940, Harry Evans entered the Meigs County Courthouse to see C. L. Williams and H. H. Biddle, original Trustees who had drawn up the Deed of Trusts for Defoyst, Reedstrom and Seig. The sons of Grace V. Sims were in default for the money they owed to the Tennessee Motor Company and to him. Harry paid off the note to the Tennessee Motor Company, which released its lien, and demanded the house be sold for auction to the highest bidder since they were also in default for the money owed to him. C. L. Williams and H. H. Biddle knew the "Sims boys" and probably suspected that Harry was the father of Reedstrom and Seig, as did many other people in the small community of Decatur. They knew what Harry's intentions were, and they refused to assist him with his demands for sale.

Harry Evans, himself, appointed Fred Stephenson as Substitute Trustee. The property was advertised for sale by written notice posted at the East door of the courthouse in Decatur. On April 26, 1940, the 412 acres that was originally owned by George Washington Sims was offered for sale at public auction to the highest and best bidder for cash. The property sold to Harry Evans for $1,999.89, which was the highest and best bid offered. He now owned all the land that Grace Victoria Sims desperately wanted to keep in the family. Grace paid $2,700 for the 400 acres in 1925, and Harry got 412 acres for only $1,999.89 15 years later. Harry obviously wanted the property but didn't offer to buy it from the "Sims boys" so they could have gotten a fair market price. He out-smarted them and got all their property dirt cheap.

Harry offered Seig, Eliza and Cindy a shack he owned in a place called Tin Can Holler in Athens, because he had plans for the farm. Seig and Eliza had no other place to live, so they accepted Harry's offer and moved to Tin Can Holler. Harry immediately rented the farm to another family.

Defoyst and his wife had moved to Benton, Tennessee, several years earlier and built a home there. Reedstrom and his wife lived in Athens. Reedstrom was upset about everything that had transpired and decided that Harry was not just going to walk away and pretend he did not exist. He began to hang out at Harry's funeral home all the time. He made it obvious to everyone that Harry was his father without saying a word. He knew that everybody who saw him knew he looked just like Harry. Harry would give him money to get rid of him, but Reedstrom was relentless and pestered him for money or anything else he could get from him. He badgered Harry for taking his family farm away from him and his brothers.

Harry sold 222 acres of the Sims property to Tim Womac and his wife Lillie Mae Womac for $1,000. The Womacs paid Harry $100 as a down payment. He carried the remainder of the note and charged the Womacs 6 percent interest on the balance over a nine-year period. He placed a lien on the property until the balance and interest were paid in full. When Reedstrom found out what Harry had done, it angered him even more. He was determined to get the remaining 175 acres of land…. and he did. Reedstrom must have blackmailed Harry with the threats of exposing the truth about the relationship he had for years with his mother and being the father of him and Seig. Harry Evans conveyed to Reedstrom the remaining 175 acres of Grace's land.

Seig did not hang around Harry. He was content living in the little shack in Tin Can Holler. Seig and Defoyst never knew that Harry had given Reedstrom those remaining 175 acres. Reedstrom kept the property for 2½ years before selling it to W. L. Lankford for $600. The reason why Reedstrom sold his 175 acres is unknown, but the land that Grace V. Sims wanted so desperately to remain with her heirs forever was now gone.

TiN CAN HOLLER
CHAPTER 12

T in Can Holler was located in a hollow known by the city officials as the Layman Hill area of Athens. The Mowerys lived on Cleveland Avenue. Athens is located in McMinn County, between Chattanooga and Knoxville in the foothills of the Smokey Mountains of southeast Tennessee. It was called Tin Can Holler because of the tin cans that had been thrown and littered there many years earlier. Tin cans would pop up out of the ground when there were heavy rainstorms. Most of the children went barefoot in the summertime, and cutting their feet on tin cans was a common occurrence. Tin Can Holler was known as the poorest section of Athens.

The Mowerys' tiny shack, which did have running water, was owned by a man everyone called Uncle Harry, who owned the Evans Funeral Home in Athens. Uncle Harry was a short stocky-built man, about 5 feet 10 inches, probably in his sixties and wore very thick glasses, because he had cataracts. He had white, thinning hair and drove a big black Cadillac. He never married and did not have a family of his own. Uncle Harry had a beautiful, large two-story house, which in those days was considered a mansion, that sat on a hill overlooking the city of Athens on the good side of the railroad tracks.

He also had two little houses on the back side of his property that resembled servants' quarters that he purchased in Oak Ridge, Tennessee. During World War II, those houses were used by employees who worked at the Atomic Energy Plant in Oak Ridge. He bought two of them and had them put on his property. He had electricity and water connected to each of them. Uncle Harry was a very well-known, prominent businessman in McMinn and Meigs County. He owned a sawmill and lots of rental property in those counties. He would rent his farmland to families to grow crops. He was one of the original directors of the First Farmers Bank and served as Vice President of that institution. He also owned one block of office buildings in downtown Athens, the Athens Dry Cleaning Company and a horse farm with a full staff of ranch employees who cared for his show horses and organized horse shows. People from across the state would come to Uncle Harry's horse farm to participate in his shows. Uncle Harry was a very wealthy man who had a lot of free time on his hands and drove around in his big, black Cadillac.

The Mowery children looked forward to seeing him because he would sometimes bring gifts to them and food for Eliza to cook. In a strange way, Uncle Harry was looking out for the Mowery family, although he kept his distance. His visits were sporadic, and it was a mystery as to why he would be concerned about the Mowery family, but most of the townspeople and the folks in Tin Can Holler knew why he came to visit.

Every two years or so, the size of their family increased. By 1950, Seig was 32 years old and Eliza was 27. They had been married 12 years. There were five children, and Seig wasn't making much money working as a mechanic at the local gas station. Eliza couldn't work because she had to stay home to care for all the children. In 1950, Cindy was 12 years old, Beulah Lee was 6, Billy Ray was 4 and Barbara Jean was 2, and Shelia Ann was 7 months old. Uncle Harry added another bedroom to the Mowerys' little shack, and then a kitchen from part of another house, probably from one of the houses he purchased in Oak Ridge. These rooms were connected to the original shack. The room that was added to the back of the house became the kitchen. The backdoor was over 10 feet high with no steps, so the backdoor could not be used.

Eliza was one of the most beautiful women in Tin Can Holler. She didn't need to wear makeup because she was a natural beauty. She was so poor, she couldn't afford makeup, so she would pinch her checks to add a little glow and would wear a little lipstick given to her by one of her girlfriends who also lived in Tin Can Holler. Eliza would brush her hair and dab a little vanilla flavoring behind each ear. She never owned a bottle of perfume. Eliza never complained about what she didn't have and what she wished she could have. She kept the little shack neat and tidy as did most of the mothers in Tin Can Holler.

Seig was a handsome man. He stood about 5 feet 7-1/2 inches, with dark brown, wavy hair and eyes as blue as the sky. He was an average built man and weighed 150-160 pounds. He walked like a very proud man who wasn't afraid of anybody even though he was not a big man. He was not a friendly person and did not have many friends. Most people knew he had a bad side.

The Mowery family was dirt poor as were most of the families in Tin Can Holler, but they didn't know they were poor. Charity organizations would deliver food to the neediest families in Tin Can Holler, and they always stopped at the Mowery home too. The children didn't know they were poor, and even if they had known, they wouldn't have suspected that they were actually as poor as they really were. They were used to the local churches bringing over baskets of food. At Christmas time, a big truck would bring them a turkey, oranges and apples, and gaily wrapped presents to put under the tree. They assumed the big truck stopped at everyone's home, not just theirs.

CHAPTER 13

Seig couldn't get a good-paying job because he was illiterate and had a difficult time keeping a steady job. He eventually quit his job at the gas station where he was an excellent mechanic, and worked for the Pittsburg Stove Company for a year. He was later offered a job by Mr. P. D. Wade, in Meigs County, to drive one of his dump trucks. Still, with his drinking and gambling habits, there was never enough money to support his growing family. He broke into one of the grammar schools in Athens and stole food from the kitchen cafeteria. A few days later he was arrested; Uncle Harry bonded him out.

The following weekend, he and two of his buddies broke into one of the local chicken hatcheries and stole the owner's safe. One of Seig's buddies, who was employed there, told him about the safe and all the money it contained. His buddy convinced them to break in and take the safe. This sounded very easy, and Seig needed the money. The three of them agreed to do it. They managed to get inside the old building without making a disturbance and carry the big safe to their truck. They took the safe to a wooded area outside town and tried to open it. They tried unsuccessfully for hours to open that safe. They took turns hitting it with a hammer and a crowbar, but could not get it to open. After hours of frustration and dismay they gave up and left the safe in the woods and went home.

On Monday morning, the owner, upon arriving to his place of business, realized that he had been robbed and called the police. The police questioned all the employees, who were the only other people who knew about the safe. Seig's buddy, under pressure, agreed to a lesser charge if he would cooperate and told the police about Seig and his other buddy helping him steal the safe. Seig was arrested and charged with housebreaking and petit larceny. Uncle Harry bonded Seig out again and hired an attorney to represent him. Seig now had two cases against him. In Case #1030 he was indicted for housebreaking and petit larceny. In case #1032 he was indicted for larceny.

On October 3, 1950, Seig went to trial. Judge Sue Hicks presided over the case, and twelve jurors were chosen from the local community. They were duly summoned, tried, elected, impaneled and sworn according to the law. Seig had a very good attorney, but the state had a lot of evidence against him, and his buddy testified against him to get a lesser sentence. After the jurors heard all the evidence and received the charges and instructions of the Court upon their oaths, they found Seig guilty. In both cases Seig was charged with petit larceny. The housebreaking charge was dropped. Judge Sue Hicks fixed his punishment at two years' hard labor in the Brushy Mountain State Penitentiary. This was a large prison near the town of Petros, operated by the Tennessee Department of Corrections. One of the most famous inmates to be sentenced to Brushy Mountain was James Earl Ray, the convicted assassin of Martin Luther King, Jr.. Seig was to serve not less than one year and not more than two years for these offenses. He became known as convict #43690. They took Seig away as Eliza sat in the courtroom crying. She knew there wasn't anything she could do for him and she must figure out how to take care of her five children alone.

The next day Eliza went to the local welfare office and signed up for any benefits she could get to help her support and feed her children. She started getting a check every month, but it was never enough. Eliza would have Cindy, who was only 12 years old, watch the other four children while she cleaned houses and did laundry for other families. Her friends in Tin Can Holler helped, and sometimes Uncle Harry would stop by the house with bags of groceries. She was very grateful and offered to repay them when Seig got out of prison.

Christmas came, and so did the local charities. There were gifts for the children and a large box of food for Christmas dinner. Everyone in the community knew that Eliza was having a very difficult time. The ladies from the local church would visit and bring baked goods. Eliza enjoyed their visits. She would play her guitar and sing for them. Everyone prayed together and that helped Eliza to find the strength she needed to keep going. She worked hard and was waiting for the day when Seig would be released and returned home. She would go visit him whenever she could get a friend to take her or had the money for a bus ticket. She would write letters to him every night before she went to bed.

CHAPTER 14

Octtober 3, 1951, Seig was paroled. Uncle Harry sponsored him so he could be released after one year. His parole came with many conditions and would last for 12 months. He had to send monthly reports to the Board of Pardons in Nashville. When Seig came home he went back to work as a truck driver for P. D. Wade in Meigs County. Sometimes he would bring the dump truck home and let the children climb into the back of it. They would go to the very top, then he would turn the noisy engine on. The back would start rising higher and higher, and they would hold on as long as possible then slide down and fall onto the ground. This was also a lot of fun for all the children in Tin Can Holler. Sometimes on Friday nights, when Seig got his paycheck, his children would get to ride in the back of the dump truck. He would come home, put them into the back of the truck, and he and Eliza would go shopping at White's grocery store.

When they got home with the groceries, Eliza would grate cabbage on her old handheld metal grater. She would boil hot dogs on the stove, and the children could smell them all through the house. They waited impatiently for Eliza to call them to eat and made numerous trips to the kitchen asking, "Is supper ready?" She would take their hot dogs, place them in the buns, and fill them with the coleslaw she made. This was always a favorite time. All the children would sit on the living room floor to watch "Rawhide" on television. If they were lucky they would get a moon pie and a soda pop for dessert if Seig didn't stop at the old railroad station to play craps with his buddies in one of the old, abandoned railroad cars on depot hill.

On August 4, 1952, Eliza gave birth to Rozetta. Eliza was overwhelmed and at times became very frustrated and depressed. There was never enough money and never enough food. Seig stopped working for P. D. Wade and became employed as a truck driver for F. D. Webb Rock Quarry in Athens. It was a better paying job, and there was another child to feed. He also worked as a shovel operator and a mechanic for F. D. Webb.

Eliza was a good cook and did her best with what little she had. Seig loved tomatoes and cucumbers and would grow them in 5-gallon buckets in the house. He also loved gravy, biscuits and fried potatoes. He would put his fried potatoes inside his biscuits instead of jelly or apple butter, because most of the time they had neither. They had a wood burning cook stove in the kitchen. Eliza had to cook on the wood stove during the summer and winter.

Billy had to make sure the wood box behind the stove was always full, or he would get spanked with Seig's belt. Occasionally, when Billy would forget, he would run from Seig who would be yelling, "I'll get you, you little devil." Billy would sneak back home during the middle of the night by crawling through the bedroom window. Seig would always get him the next morning and spank him for not doing his chores.

The wood stove was in the middle of the shack, and Eliza would heat water on the stove to bathe the children. She would use the same bath water for all the children. Almost all the families in Tin Can Holler used footed tubs to bathe in. During the winter months Eliza would not shampoo their hair because she didn't want them to catch a cold. She would put powder on their hair and comb it out. The children were constantly scratching their heads because of lice. They all shared the same mattresses, and head lice were a major problem. Eliza would pick the lice out of their hair and kill them by squeezing them between her fingernails.

Eliza would hand-wash the children's socks and hang them around the stove to dry, so they would have clean socks to wear to school every day. She could knit, crochet and sew by hand, and made most of their clothes from 5- or 10-pound flour sacks. Every time she bought a bag of flour she would get a free washcloth. She also made her daughters' panties from the flour sacks. She would have each of them try on the hand-sewn panties, so she could measure the elastic for their waistbands. In the summertime the children would play in the yard wearing only the panties Eliza made them.

Billy was Eliza's only son, and she spoiled him. He was out of her control most of the time and would ignore her whenever she called for him. Her neighbors could see the two of them running around in the yard in her useless attempts to catch him. When Billy got into trouble, he would climb onto the roof of their shack and sit there. Eliza and Seig would yell at him to come down. If he made the roof leak, Seig would make him stand underneath the leak, so it would hit him on the head. He was made do this many times, because he wouldn't stay off the roof.

Billy would sneak Seig's bottle of whiskey and hide in the large patch of morning glories that always grew in the backyard and drink it. He would get a butt whooping when Seig found out. Eliza pampered Billy because she always wanted him to look his best. She would comb his hair and part it on the side. She would use soap on his hair to make it lie down flat. She also taught him how to roll cigarettes when he was 8 years old. As an adult, Billy still rolls his cigarettes just the way Eliza taught him.

Billy loved pestering Eliza when she was rocking and nursing one of the younger siblings. He would run around the rocking chair and put his foot on the back of the rocker to stop Eliza's rhythm. She would squeeze her breast and squirt milk on him to make him stop. Billy would laugh so hard he would almost pee his pants. She loved for Billy to rub her feet and clean her toenails. He would use a bobby-pin she would take out of her hair.

CHAPTER 15

S eig completed his parole satisfactorily and soon started drinking again. He began stealing food, mostly from stores and local farms, and was lucky he didn't get caught. Marcella was born January 25, 1954. She was the last child Seig allowed Eliza to give birth to.

There were lots of wonderful people who lived in Tin Can Holler. The Able family had seven boys, and one was a minister. Miss Bloom, who lived on Knoxville Avenue, was also a minister. There were the Bradfords and the Bradleys. Mrs. Bradley was a midwife who helped deliver a lot of babies in Tin Can Holler. They were a very nice family. The Burkes, who lived on Howard Street, had three girls. Mrs. Burton, who didn't have much patience for the rowdy neighborhood boys, would tell them to leave her house because they didn't have good raisings. The boys would laugh and say, "Yep, we didn't get any raisins today."

The Charles family lived directly in front of the Mowery family, on Cleveland Avenue. Mrs. Charles and Mrs. Hooper would argue all the time about their kids fighting. They were always interfering with the kids and getting mad at each other. The kids didn't care; they were mad one day, and the next day they were friends again. Other families in Tin Can Holler included the Cagels, the Clayton family, the Cornetts, the Davis brothers who lived together, the Dixons, the Doughertys, the Dunns and the Flowers. Bryant and Estelle Gennoe, who were good friends with Eliza, lived at the lower end of Tin Can Holler.

The Goforths were a nice family, too, as was the Goodrich family, who had a son named Roscoe. Mr. Goodrich was a navy commander on a submarine, who would sit on his front porch and play the violin. He hired Eliza to cook and clean for his family. The Gradys were also good people. They had two children. The Hester family lived on Arwine Street. They had four boys and two girls. The Hoopers and the Howards lived there, too. The Howards had a large family of 10 or 12 children, and one of their sons was nicknamed Rooster.

Another family very well-known throughout Tin Can Holler was Mr. and Mrs. Huff, who lived on Howard Street and were very active in the local church. Mrs. Huff's mother was a very sweet woman, and she would visit other families in Tin Can Holler to have prayer meetings with them.

The King family were very friendly, and they had a son named Spunky. The Lunsford family contributed a lot to the building of homes in Tin Can Holler. Mr. and Mrs. Martin had many children and lived near the Hesters on Arwine Street. The McDonalds lived near the Mowery family on Cleveland Avenue. The McGhees were a highly respected family, too. Their daughter, Lizzie, was Eliza's best friend. The McKinneys were a well-to-do family who owned an excavating company and the nicest home in Tin Can Holler.

Other families who were friends of the Mowery family were the McMahans, the Morgans, the Moores, the Ravines, and the Richard-sons. The Newmans had several daughters and one son. The Olivers were a retired couple who lived next to the Smiths, who were also senior citizens. Miss Pammer was a nice older lady who lived alone and loved to have visits from the neighborhood children. Mr. Pruitt and his family lived at the lower end of Tin Can Holler and had four boys and two girls. Mr. Pruitt collected lots of old tires.

The Ratlidge family had lots of kids, and the Simpsons were a very nice family whom everyone loved. Mr. Simpson was always willing to give a helping hand to anyone. He was highly respected throughout Tin Can Holler. The Stevens family had two sons, the Townsend family had two sons, and the True family had five chil-dren. The Mowery family also knew the Upchurch family, the Wal-laces, the Whites, and the Wynders. The Wilcox family, who lived next to the Pruitts and behind the Smiths, was the largest family in Tin Can Holler. They had 22 children. Their son Simon was Billy's very best friend. On weekends, as soon as Billy got out of bed, he would get dressed and run out the door to hook up with Simon. They were inseparable.

Everyone knew everyone else in the holler. All the people who lived in Tin Can Holler were like one big family. Everyone shared food or whatever they had with their neighbors. The families in Tin Can Holler helped each other. Neighbors would borrow lard, flour, sugar or potatoes from each other. Eliza would send one of the older children to borrow lard or flour from the neighbors, and they would do the same. One day, Eliza put a scarf on Billy's head and made him wear her apron to their neighbor's house to borrow some lard. Billy was very embarrassed that she made him do that, but he came back with the lard. Whenever anyone got sick in Tin Can Holler, the other mothers would cook and take food to them. They would even do laundry for the other sick mothers.

Some former residents are ashamed to admit that they ever lived in Tin Can Holler. Once they were able to leave, they never wanted to talk about it or admit they had ever lived there. Many of the homes consisted of dirt floors with only a linoleum rug, and those that did have wooden floors had cracks in them. Everyone helped their neighbors and shared food and clothes. Even though most families were very poor, they were clean as was the inside of their homes.

In the spring, all the children in Tin Can Holler gathered wildflowers to give their moms on Mother's Day. Occasionally, Billy would get caught red handed with a neighbor's red roses, but he always got off with a stern warning not to do it again. The Mowery children would pick morning glories that grew wild in the field behind their shack and give them to Eliza. She loved the morning glories and roses. Once, she found a rose bush lying by a garbage can that someone had thrown in the trash. She brought it home and planted it by the front porch she built herself from lumber she found in Tin Can Holler. The rose bush grew so big, it went up the side of the porch and across the roof to the other side. Every summer there would be little roses blooming everywhere. Eliza loved to smell the roses when she walked out the front door.

There was no good side or bad side to Tin Can Holler because everyone lived there together. The children would play and run around Tin Can Holler with the other kids as if they had all the money in the world. Billy and his friends would run through the streets rolling big tires they found in the wooded area at the edge of the holler. Sometimes they would find discarded paint cans and would decorate the tires with the paint. They would put sticks inside the tires to make them wider and easier to roll. Billy loved to play Tarzan. He would run through the holler yelling like Tarzan.

Simon, who was a couple of years older than Billy and stood about 6 feet tall, was skinny as a bean pole and had green eyes and jet black hair. The two of them were together all the time, and if you saw one, you would see the other. Simon had an old bicycle that had a basket wired to the handlebars. He and Billy would go all over town looking for scrap metal they could sell at Seaton's Junk Yard to get enough money to buy smoking tobacco.

Billy and Simon loved to pull silly antics and jokes on anybody they could. One Sunday night during a prayer meeting at the church in the holler, they took a rope and tied it to the bumper of a car and then tied the other end to the wooden fence next to the church. They hid in the bushes until the prayer meeting was over to see what would happen. The car belonged to a visiting preacher who was unaware of what they had done. When the preacher got into his car and started to leave, he pulled down the entire fence. Billy and Simon had to hold their stomachs as they doubled over laughing. The preacher didn't know what to think and felt terrible that he had torn down the fence that belonged to the people who lived next to the church. He didn't have to pay for the damages, and no one ever knew who tied the rope to his car.

The kids in Tin Can Holler were very resourceful and had lots of fun even though they didn't have any store-bought toys. They also used old socks to shove into their bike tires when they needed an inner tube and didn't have the money to buy one. The boys would build wagons out of wood and old lawnmower tires. They would get excited and flip a coin to see who would be the first to ride in it down the hill. The lucky winner was not always lucky, because the wheels would usually fly off the wagon and they would flip over. The losers, of course, would stand on the hill laughing. They would eventually fix the problem with the help of someone's dad, and they would take turns until they wore the wagon completely out.

All the kids in Tin Can Holler, especially the older children, loved Halloween. This was a time when they could disguise themselves and cause all kinds of havoc in Tin Can Holler. Their favorite trick was turning over the outhouses in the backyards, which was even more fun when there were people inside them at the time. All the parents would question their children endlessly to find out who turned the outhouses over, but they would never tattle even if they knew who did it.

There was an empty lot in Tin Can Holler that was used by the neighborhood kids as a ball field. They never owned a real ball, but they made their own by collecting old socks. They would get the best sock with the least holes in it and shove all the other socks into it until it was stretched too tight to put another sock inside it.

At night the older kids would steal tires from Mr. Pruitt, who collected and sold used tires. They would gather in the ball field and burn the used tires. They would run around the big campfire acting like wild Indians. The children of Tin Can Holler had to be creative. There were no swing sets or playgrounds, because none of the families could afford to buy those things for their children.

In the wintertime, if it snowed, the kids would take the hoods off old cars and turn them upside down, tie ropes to them and use them as sleds. There were many crashes because they had no way to control where they were going. Billy and Simon's other friend in Tin Can Holler was Roscoe. Roscoe was a good kid, and they really liked him. They would get Roscoe to steal his dad's Lucky Strike cigarettes for them to smoke. Roscoe would always get into trouble with his dad, but he didn't care.

Very few of the houses had running water or indoor plumbing; instead, water was carried from a hand-pumped well and most of the shacks had an outhouse in the backyard. One day, Eliza's friend Ruby Jean, who was in her early forties and lived down the road, went outside to use her outhouse. Her outhouse was in desperate need of repair. When Ruby Jean sat down on the toilet seat, it collapsed and she fell all the way into the hole. Poor Ruby Jean screamed so hard she could have awakened the dead. Everyone ran out of their homes to see what happened. What they saw was her husband pulling her out of the nasty hole completely covered in feces. Everyone watched in horror as her husband poured buckets of water all over her. All the kids were laughing, and all the mothers were shaking their heads in disbelief as they scolded their children for laughing.

Hugh Lunsford and his brother Henry were the first of many to build homes in Tin Can Holler. Hugh's wife, Myrtle, had a stroke when she got older, but that didn't stop her. She could be seen walking around with her broom because she lost the use of one of her arms. She would swing that broom and clean better than the mothers who had two good arms. Albert and Pearl Lunsford built their shack over the creek that ran through the holler. All year long water would be running beneath their house, but it was built high enough that even when the creek would rise, it didn't come into their house. Many of the homes in Tin Can Holler were owned by individuals who lived elsewhere and rented their houses to poor families.

Most of the land in that area was once owned by the Spranklers who lived in Knoxville, Tennessee. In the late 1960s the city of Athens received a federal grant to clean up Tin Can Holler and relocate the residents to other areas of Athens. This was the urban development plan to build low-income housing in Tin Can Holler. Today, the Athens Housing Authority owns all the land and rents apartments to low-income residents and retirees.

On many occasions, the Mowery children would eat dinner at the homes of various neighbors because everyone knew them in the holler. The children in the holler would pick poke-salad for their mothers to cook. It was a popular food back then and still is today. The poorest children would collect mud turtles from the nearby creeks to eat, and everybody loved eating them. The mothers would pull them out of their shell, bread them and fry them up like chicken. They would make gravy, mashed potatoes and biscuits to go with them.

The Mowery family had an elderly male neighbor who lived about six houses up the hill from them on Cleveland Avenue. He worked in the deli at the White's grocery store. He would bring boxes of baked goods to the Mowery family and many other families in Tin Can Holler. He would give away doughnuts, pastries, pies and cakes. He was a good man, and everyone loved all the goodies he would bring them.

Mrs. King knew that Beulah loved her cornbread, and she would call for Beulah from her front yard whenever she made a big pan of cornbread. If Beulah didn't come to her house after a few minutes, she would send Spunky to get Beulah. Beulah visited with the King family a lot.

Rozetta's favorite place to visit was at the home of Bryant and Estelle Gennoe who lived in the lower end of Tin Can Holler. Everyone liked Mr. and Mrs. Gennoe, because they were good, Christian people and were highly respected in Tin Can Holler. Mrs. Gennoe was a friend to Eliza and a very sweet lady. Mrs. Gennoe was also a very good cook. Rozetta's favorite dish was her chocolate gravy. Whenever Rozetta visited Mrs. Gennoe she did not want to leave, and Mrs. Glennoe would let her stay at her home for two to three days at a time. She would become concerned that Eliza would get upset with her, and would tell Rozetta that she needed to go home. Rozetta enjoyed playing with her daughter, Dorothy, because they were the same age.

Eliza taught Franklin Gennoe, Estelle's son, how to play the guitar. Sadly, when he was a young man he was killed in a car accident. Bryant Gennoe worked for the city of Athens, taking care of all the cemeteries. Everyone in Tin Can Holler knew that Thursday night was "pie night" at the Gennoes' house. Bryant would stop at the store on his way home from work and buy all the pies the owner was going to throw out. He always got a big discount on them. He would come home with bags full of pies. Everyone would come to their house to enjoy a slice of pie.

On Friday and Saturday nights, people from the other side of town would ride through Tin Can Holler just to see what was going on, and there were always exciting things happening. There could be a revival on one side of Tin Can Holler and a street fight on the other side. The older boys were very protective of the girls who lived in Tin Can Holler. Whenever outsiders would come into Tin Can Holler bothering the neighborhood girls, the boys would chase after them, and sometimes a fight would erupt.

In the wintertime, Tin Can Holler was a dirty place, because everyone had piles of coal in their front yard and beneath their porch. Wood or coal burning stoves were used for cooking and heating the homes.

Everything was dirty with suet and dust. The roads were dirt, and dust would fly everywhere whenever an automobile passed by. Many of the mothers who had an outside faucet with a water hose would spray the dirt in the summertime to get rid of all the dust.

The houses and shacks were built very close together and separated by ditches created from the rain. In the summertime, because the houses did not have bathrooms, some of the older children would take bars of soap and wash themselves in the rain. Mud would get on everything since very few people had grass in their yards.

There was a man that everyone called the "ragman" who would come through Tin Can Holler in an old wagon collecting rags. He would ask everyone if they had any rags they could give him. No one ever knew why he was collecting old rags, but he would ride through Tin Can Holler every week. The Mowery children would hop on the back of his wagon and ride up the hill to their house and jump off.

Another man who would ride through Tin Can Holler was the "egg man." He was a middle-aged man who carried a big wire basket full of eggs that he sold to the families. He had a lot of customers in Tin Can Holler and would come whenever he had a basketful of eggs to sell. All the mothers in Tin Can Holler would warn their daughters to stay away from him. They never knew why, but they always did as their mothers told them. The mothers knew that the egg man was a dirty old man, who offered free eggs to any woman who would have sex with him. He wanted to trade his eggs for sex.

Some mothers would stand on their front porch and yell for their children to come home. Their voices would echo down the holler. The children knew they had to get home quickly before their mothers really got angry. Many of the children would get scolded for mocking the mothers who yelled for their children. The next day, the older children, while walking to or from school, would tease the younger ones about how their mothers called them to come home. All the children in Tin Can Holler attended Forest Hills School. The school was located on top of the hill on the back side of the holler, so buses were not provided.

Mrs. Davis, the school's truant officer, was a very stern woman but kind in her own way. She would visit the homes of children in Tin Can Holler who were absent from school. She would check with the parents to make sure the children were truly sick. On rainy days she would ride through Tin Can Holler in her own automobile to pick up children; she knew they couldn't and wouldn't walk to school when it was raining. Mrs. Davis would get coats and shoes from donations and store them in the school basement. She began this project because she knew a lot of the children in Tin Can Holler did not have a good pair of shoes or a winter coat to wear to school which would keep those children from attending school. She wanted to make sure every child had shoes and a coat. One day she noticed that the sole was coming off Billy's worn-out shoes. Seig only bought his children one pair of shoes per year, so one day Mrs. Davis asked Billy to accompany her to the basement. She let him pick out his favorite pair. He chose a red pair of sneakers. He was so proud of those red sneakers with the high top sides, he wore them until they fell apart.

In those days you couldn't buy chickens at the supermarket. Everyone had to go to the chicken hatchery and buy live chickens. They would build fires in their backyards and fill old washtubs with water and put them on the fires. They would grab the chickens by their heads and swing them around and around and then chop their heads off. Occasionally they would drop the chickens after chopping their head off and the chickens would run around in the backyard for a few minutes before dying. This would scare the smaller children, and they would run away screaming. The chickens were put in the hot tubs of boiling water, and the oldest children would pull out their feathers. They hated doing that, because the chicken feathers were wet and smelled terrible.

There were no screens on the windows, and in the summertime flies were everywhere. If you turned on a light in the middle of the night, the ceiling would be covered with black flies. In the Mowerys' little shack, all the children slept in the same bedroom. The mattresses were all pushed together on the floor, lining the wall. The youngest children slept in the middle. On hot summer nights many families, including the Mowerys, would drag their mattresses or blankets to their front yards to keep cool. The Mowery children would lie on their mattresses looking up at the stars searching for the Big and Little Dipper. No one had air conditioning or fans. In the summertime the iceman would come through Tin Can Holler selling blocks of ice to the families who did not own a refrigerator.

During early summer, a traveling salesman in a station wagon would visit the homes in Tin Can Holler to sell his goods from a catalog. If they could afford it, the mothers would order school clothes for their children from his catalog. He would take their orders and let them make payments to him. He returned once a month to collect his money.

Eliza was a Pentecostal Christian woman and would take the children to church on Sunday morning. She would sing and play her guitar in the church in Tin Can Holler. It was in this church that her daughters began singing together. They learned how to sing the "Lord's Prayer" and would harmonize together. Seig never went to church with them; instead he would spend his Sundays, in the summertime, stealing food from gardens in the McMinn County countryside. He would fill the trunk of the car full of corn, green beans, tomatoes and whatever else was in season at the time. Eliza would go to the tent revivals in Tin Can Holler with one of her best friends, Lizzie, and she always took her guitar.

Lizzie was a sweet little black woman who lived in Tin Can Holler. Lizzie's mom, Bessie, was a Sunday school teacher, and her brother, Blane, was a minister. Lizzie and Eliza would walk to the store together and have many long conversations about their lives. Eliza would see Lizzie on Saturday afternoons, and they would remind each other about church on Sunday morning. Eliza was a friendly lady who loved everyone, and everyone in Tin Can Holler loved her. She was a beautiful lady with a beautiful voice.

Eliza loved to sing and play her guitar for her children and all the children in Tin Can Holler. One of the songs she sang was "The Mockingbird." She was a natural born entertainer and would compose silly songs to make the children laugh. One day she sang a funny song about a tom cat woman and a tom cat man having a friendly fight. All the children started laughing because she was very funny. She was always eager to teach some of the older kids in the holler how to play her guitar. She knew how to play the spoons, too, and she'd entertain the children for hours. If she wasn't singing to pass the time, she would have the children clap their hands and she would dance the "Charleston."

CHAPTER 16

On the evening of June 5, 1954, Seig and his buddy, Junior Howard, who also lived in Tin Can Holler, were drunk and riding around town in his car, when they agreed to break in and rob a service station. Howard broke a window, and Seig helped him enter the building. They stole three cartons of cigarettes and two tires. A few days later they were both arrested and taken to jail. Uncle Harry bonded Seig out of jail and hired an attorney for him. Again, there were two cases against Seig. Case #444 was housebreaking and larceny. This was for the service station break-in. Case #414 was housebreaking and larceny and possessing stolen property. Seig denied having anything to do with Case #414. He was charged with receiving and possessing a concrete vibrating machine. Seig repeatedly denied being guilty of this offense and stated he had no knowledge of it.

Seig, at the age or 36, went to trial with Junior as his co-defendant. Judge Sue Hicks again presided. She remembered Seig being in her courtroom before and was not happy that he was back in front of her again with similar charges. Seig was first tried on Case #444 – housebreaking and larceny. Twelve jurors were chosen from the local community. After the jurors heard the evidence, argument of counsel and the charge of the Court, they retired to consider their verdict. When they returned to open court, they announced that they had found Seig guilty on both charges; housebreaking and larceny. Judge Hicks, in accordance with the finding and verdict of the jurors, sentenced Seig and Junior Howard to three years of hard labor at the Brushy Mountain State Penitentiary. She informed Seig that this was an indeterminate sentence of not less than three years and not more than three years. The jurors for Case #444 were dismissed, and a second group of jurors were brought into the courtroom for Case #414 – receiving and possessing stolen property. Seig proclaimed his innocence throughout the entire trial. He told the jurors he had been set up or lied to because he did not know the property was stolen. They did not believe him.

The jurors deliberated and came back with a verdict very quickly. Judge Hicks read their findings to the crowded courtroom. Seig was found guilty of receiving and possessing stolen property, and she fixed his punishment at 10 years of hard labor in the Brushy Mountain State Penitentiary. He was told he would have to serve no less than three years and no more than 10 years and that this case would also run consecutively with Case #444. He became known as Convict #47583.

Seig's sentence began immediately. As he stood listening to Judge Hicks reading the verdict, he turned his head to the crowd in the courtroom looking for Eliza and Uncle Harry, who were seated in the third row. As he stood there shaking his head in disbelief, they silently read his lips mouthing, "I'm sorry." The sheriff's deputies handcuffed him and led him out of the courthouse through a side door. He was not allowed to leave the courtroom to say good-bye to Eliza or any of his children. He was led out of the courtroom as Eliza sat motionless, tears flowing down her cheeks. Uncle Harry comforted her as they left the courtroom together. She had been through hell due to Seig's continued criminal activity, and now with more children to care for, it would be even harder if not completely impossible to survive without outside help. She did not know what she was going to do with seven children. Cindy was now 16 years old, Beulah was 10 years old, Billy Ray was 8 years old, Barbara Jean was 6 years old, Shelia was 4 years old, Rozetta was 2 years old and Marcella was 9 months old.

Eliza was distraught and almost in shock when she left the courtroom that day. She knew she would have to tell the children that Seig was going to be gone for a long time. Uncle Harry took Eliza home. The moment Eliza walked into the house, she started crying again. She didn't have to say anything to Cindy and Beulah. Eliza's tears told them it was bad news. They tried to comfort her. They kept telling her that everything would be okay and that they would help her. Cindy and Beulah knew they would have to help their mother because she would have to go outside the home to look for work to support her large family.

Eliza was resourceful and got several house cleaning jobs and did laundry for a couple of families around town and in Tin Can Holler. She went to the local welfare office several times and begged for more money to help her with the children. Cindy and Beulah helped with the younger siblings. There wasn't a lot of food, and sometimes there was barely enough to feed everyone; Eliza started eating less, so there would be more for the children. Her daughters learned to eat fast, because their big brother Billy would take their food from them if they ate too slowly. Christmas 1954 came and Eliza made sure her children had a Christmas tree. She went into the country and found a tree and chopped it down. Cindy helped her put it in the trunk of the car and bring it home. They made their own decorations for it. They used needle and thread to string popcorn, and Eliza saved her Prince Albert tobacco cans for them. They didn't have lights for their tree, so they drew designs on the shiny part of the tobacco cans and cut them out and hung them on their tree. Eliza would always help the children by cutting the metal cans with her scissors. They drew stars, snowmen, and candy canes. When the lights hit the metal designs at night, they would shine and reflect the light. The usual charity organizations, and Uncle Harry, came to their home and dropped off food and gifts.

The New Year came. It was now January 1955, and Eliza was still struggling. She was wearing herself down. She was too tired to play her guitar as much as she wanted and couldn't go to church on Sundays, because she ironed other people's clothes. There was little money for buying wood, so Eliza would get it from her neighbors and friends to keep the stove burning. It was a bitter cold winter. She pulled the children's mattresses from the bedroom and placed them closer to the stove, so they wouldn't freeze.

Eliza begged her family for help, and they agreed only because Seig was in prison. While Eliza worked, her brother Howard and his wife Edna helped take care of Rozetta and Marcella; her brother Bill and his wife Lily kept Shelia at their house. Shelia was very attached to Eliza and did not like staying with Bill and Lily. She would cry and run to the railroad tracks and start walking home. Lily would have to go look for her on the railroad tracks and bring her back. She was only 5 years old, but she had walked the railroad tracks with Eliza so many times, she knew exactly how to get back to Tin Can Holler. Shelia cried so hard, she literally would make herself sick and start throwing up.

As spring and summer came, Eliza cheered up and looked forward to seeing the morning glories bloom in her backyard. The rosebush she planted by the front porch also began to bloom, and the children could play outside again. The children loved to visit their neighbors, just to see what they had to eat. No one ever turned them away. All the families in Tin Can Holler knew Seig was in prison, but no one ever talked about it. Other mothers in Tin Can Holler would bring Eliza hand-me-down clothes for her children. She would wash them, and the children had fun trying them on to see if they fit. Eliza would make a game out of it especially when the younger children wanted to try on the big clothes. She said they looked like little clowns. They were hand-me-downs, but they were new clothes to the Mowery children. To make the clothes fit better, Eliza would get her needle and thread and take them up.

CHAPTER 17

October 6, 1955, was a beautiful autumn day. The Mowery children were in their backyard playing, while Eliza and Beulah sat on a quilt in the grass holding Marcella. Eliza watched as a big white car pulled into her front yard and a man and woman started walking toward her. Eliza asked them who they were and what they wanted. The man said he was from the Department of Public Welfare and introduced the woman who accompanied him as Miss Mary Flenniken, a caseworker from the Holston Methodist Home for Children. As Eliza and Beulah stood up to face them, the man told Eliza that he did not want any trouble from her or he would call the police. He told her they were there to pick up her children and take them into custody. He told Eliza to gather her children, take them inside the house and get them ready for a long trip to Greeneville, Tennessee.

Eliza could not believe what she was hearing and demanded to see their identification. She demanded to know why in God's name they were taking her children. The man showed her his identification and a court order signed by a local judge. The Department of Human Services was going to take her children from her, and there was nothing she could do about it. Miss Flenniken led the younger children into their house. Billy and Beulah asked if they had to go, too, and Miss Flenniken replied, "yes." Cindy, who was now 17 years old, was told that she could stay with Eliza, but all the other children had to go.

Eliza was getting angrier and angrier by the minute, and Cindy tried to calm her down. Cindy held Rozetta by the hand, and Beulah carried Marcella to the front of the house. Miss Flenniken was on the front porch holding the door open as they entered single file. Eliza was in shock wondering what in the world these people were doing at her house and why they wanted to take her children away. Beulah and Billy immediately started complaining. They told Eliza they did not want to go with these people. They wanted to stay home with her. Shelia started crying and hanging on to Eliza's leg. Eliza demanded to know why they wanted to take her children. The man, who was stern and not very friendly, told Eliza they had received reports about her drinking and leaving her children alone. Eliza started crying and wanted to know who those people were. He told Eliza that he could not reveal the source of his information because they were anonymous callers. Eliza always thought it was one of her neighbors across the street who called the authorities, but it was Uncle Harry!

They asked Eliza to show them how much food was in the cupboards and in the refrigerator. Eliza got very emotional because there was very little food in her kitchen. They asked her how she was feeding her children. She became very defensive and told them she always fed her children even though it was very difficult sometimes. She reassured them that her children were not going hungry.

Miss Flenniken was a nice older lady, about 5 feet 4 inches, who looked to be in her mid to late fifties. She had pretty gray hair and wore glasses. The children did not realize it at the time, but Miss Flenniken would become a very important and special person in their lives. Miss Flenniken asked to speak to Eliza in private. When they came back into the room, Eliza was much calmer. Miss Flenniken reassured Eliza that this was the best for the children and she would be allowed to see them. Miss Flenniken told Eliza she would be in contact with her and Eliza could call anytime to check on her children.

Eliza got clean clothes for the children, and Miss Flenniken helped them get dressed. Eliza cried and cried and did not want to let her children go. The man led Billy, Beulah, Barbara and Shelia to the car as Miss Flenniken carried Marcella and held Rozetta by the hand. Miss Flenniken held Marcella in her lap, and Rozetta got to sit in the middle of the front seat. Billy, Beulah and Barbara had to comfort Sheila in the back seat because she wouldn't stop crying. She said she didn't want to go with them and begged them to take her back home. The older children waved good-bye to Eliza and Cindy standing on the front porch crying. It took several hours to get to Greeneville from Athens. This was the longest trip the Mowery children had ever been on and the nicest car they had ever ridden in besides Uncle Harry's big black Cadillac. While in the car traveling to Greeneville, Miss Flenniken told the children that the younger siblings would be placed into foster homes because there weren't facilities to care for the smaller children on campus.

Miss Flenniken was a very patient woman as she calmed the children when they became squeamish and irritated sitting close to each other in the back seat. She gave all of them, except Marcella who was too young, coloring books and a box of crayons to keep them occupied and quiet.

Holston Methodist Home for Children was founded in 1895 when Mrs. E. E. Wiley, a widow, took in her first homeless child. Since then, Holston Home has helped more than 8,000 children. Holston Home is proudly affiliated with the Holston Conference of the United Methodist Church, an area that covers all of East Tennessee, the western-most 17 counties in Virginia, and a little bit of territory in north Georgia. In that area, more than 915 United Methodist Churches make up the Holston Conference. Holston Home is situated on about 150 acres of gently rolling hillside in Greeneville, Tennessee. It was referred to as "the orphanage on the hill."

The goal of Holston Home is to help children and families overcome hardships in their lives. Sometimes, children are unable to live at home, and Holston Home provides housing and care for them. But their goal is always to return children to their natural home with their parents. When that is not possible, they work very hard to find an adoption home for those children, and when that is not possible, they match children with appropriate foster parents. They always strive to do what is best for the children. Their professional staff works with families to teach them how to be good parents and to help children overcome any emotional traumas or other hardships they may have experienced.

Miss Flenniken and the Mowery children arrived at Holston Home and noticed lots of children everywhere, and most of them stopped playing to stare at them. The older children told Miss Flenniken several times during the trip to Greeneville that they were hungry, so she took them to the cafeteria on campus. They ate.. and ate.. and ate... until their bellies were about to pop. After they finished eating they were taken into a big room to meet their foster parents. The young couple who was introduced to Shelia, Rozetta and Marcella was Mr. and Mrs. Preston from Fordtown, Tennessee, which was near Kingsport. They were very nice and hugged all three girls. An older couple with a teenage daughter took Billy temporarily, until a space became available on campus. All the children hugged each other and cried because they didn't know the people who were taking them away.

It was a long time before the younger children got to see their older siblings. Christmas came, and they had lots of presents under a big, beautiful Christmas tree. They never had a Christmas tree with lights before, nor had they ever received so many wonderful gifts from Santa. Shelia, Rozetta and Marcella liked their foster parents and got plenty of food to eat. They were so used to eating fast, their foster parents were amazed at them and told them they could eat slowly because no one was going to take their food. For an unknown reason, Sheila, Rozetta and Marcella were placed in another foster home nine months later. They were sent to the home of Mr. and Mrs. Quillen in Kingsport, Tennessee, on August 9, 1956. The Quillens were a young couple who were very good to the girls. The Mowery children had not seen or heard from Eliza since they were taken from their home in Tin Can Holler on October 6, 1955.

CHAPTER 18

On February 26, 1957, Mr. Hugh Gibson, Director of Social Services for the Holston Methodist Home, received a letter from Seig, that was written by another inmate or personnel at Brushy Mountain State Penitentiary. Seig was asking about his children. Uncle Harry had visited Seig and gave him the name and address of the person to contact at the orphanage. He was concerned, because he hadn't received any answers to the letters he had written to Beulah, Billy and Barbara months before. He did not understand why the older children had not responded to his letters. He wrote the following letter:

Dear Sir:

I am writing to you in regards to my children, Beulah Lee, Barbara Jean and Billy Ray. I have written to them on several different occasions, but have had no answers from them so far. Would appreciate it very much if you would check into it and see if there is something wrong with them that they can't write. And would appreciate any information regarding the safety and health of the three little ones I have in Kingsport. Would like to know how to get in touch with them. Will appreciate any help I may receive from you in this case.

Respectfully,
Seig Mowery, 47583
Box 73, Petros, Tenn.

The Holston Home followed up with Seig's letter and request to hear from his children, and Beulah, being the oldest, was asked why she had not answered any of their father's letters. Beulah was hurt and angry about being taken from her home and away from Eliza. She was also upset because she, Barbara and Billy had not been allowed to visit either of her parents. She was counseled, and the reasons were clearly explained to her. Beulah soon began writing to Seig and Eliza. She let them know that all the children were doing fine but missed them and wanted to come home. Beulah found out that Eliza had been visiting Seig at Brushy Mountain State Penitentiary and was crying about the loss of her children. She also found out that Eliza was drinking more and was recovering from a nervous breakdown. Beulah's requests to visit Eliza continued. Seig was getting desperate to get out of prison for whatever reason he could and thought the financial responsibility and burden on the orphanage for his six children would help get him an early release, if he could get someone to write to the parole board.

On May 15, 1957, another letter written for Seig arrived at the Holston Methodist Home, addressed to the children's caseworker, Miss Mary B. Flenniken:

Miss Mary B. Flenniken,
    I am writing you in regards to my children. I don't know anything about the finance or anything. I don't even know who is paying for the children to be kept there, but I do know if I can get out who will. I have always taken care of my family until I got into this trouble. Now I am eligible for parole June 20, 1957, and I believe that you can help me a lot if you would write the parole board at Nashville and tell them about the children. I know that it will be appreciated by the kids as well as myself. I realize it is a great expense to someone and if I can make parole I will cut that expense from you all because I have the job waiting for me and I will for certain take care of my kids. Will appreciate if you write Mr. Crow at the State Office Building in Nashville for me.
Yours Truly,
Seig Mowery

Miss Flenniken did not write any letters to the parole board, but she did contact Ruth Garrett, who was the county director for the Department of Public Welfare in Athens, Tennessee. Miss Flenniken knew it was important for Eliza to connect with her children, but she did not want to place the children into a serious or dangerous situation. She needed to know if Eliza was mentally stable before allowing Beulah, Barbara and Billy to visit. She also knew that Eliza was very distraught and lonely after her oldest daughter Cindy had gotten married and moved out of her home to live with her husband. On July 11, 1957, Miss Flenniken and Mr. Barrett, the new Director of Social Services at the Holston Methodist Home, received the following letter from Mrs. Ruth Garrett:

Attention: Miss MaryB.Flenniken, Caseworker

Dear Mr. Barrett:

I discussed the possibility of the 3 oldest children visiting with their mother for a short vacation yesterday. Mrs. Mowery is now living in her home alone and would certainly have room for the children for a visit. She is not employed regularly, but has been doing some laundry work and assured me that she would be able to provide food for the children without asking for help. I had not been in the home for some time and it is possible that it was in order because of my visit. However I noticed several things such as neatness of the yard, flowers and canning which made me feel that she was doing some better. I feel sure that Mrs. Mowery would hardly be able to cope with the children on a full time basis, but I believe that she can do quite well during a short visiting period. She was less emotional yesterday and talked more sensible about the future of the children than I have ever noticed. Mrs. Mowery, however, is an unpredictable person and it would be impossible for me to be absolutely sure that things would go well. She understands that the children are coming only for a visit and must return on the date designated by your agency. She mentioned herself that it would be unwise if she ever expects to get the children back or to visit them in the home to disregard this.

I do think it will have meaning for the children and she especially wants to take them to see their father. For this reason it might be better to plan it for them to leave during the week so they could visit their father on the weekend. I do not believe it would be wise for them to spend a long vacation due to the neighborhood she lives in and her inability to control the children.

If vacation leave is granted she plans now to come after the children and either bring them back or send money for their bus tickets. Mrs. Mowery understands that you are to notify her what decision is made about this. She also understands that the decision is up to the home and we are only giving the information you asked for.

Yours sincerely,

Mrs. Ruth Garrett, County Director

After receiving the information from Ruth Garrett, Miss Flenniken began the tedious process of arranging a visit for Beulah, Barbara and Billy with their mother. She wrote a letter to Eliza to set up the visitation arrangements. On July 18, Miss Flenniken received the following letter from Eliza:

Dear Miss Flenniken,
I will answer your letter I received yesterday to let you know I got it. I am glad that the three children are getting to come home for a week. I would very much like for the other three to come with them if it is possible, but if you can't arrange for them it will be alright. But, I will be after Beulah, Billy and Barbara on the 31st of this month. If I don't come I'll send the money and they can come on the bus. Beulah knows how to get a taxi on up to the house after they get off the bus and I'll put them on the bus on Thursday, August 8th and send them back. But, if I can, I'll bring them back. By everybody working it may be that they will have to make it on the bus. I'll be there if I can or send the money a few days ahead of time, so look for one or the other. I thank you for your kindness very much.
Yours truly,
Eliza Mowery
PS: The children will be taken good care of.

Eliza wasn't able to drive to Greeneville to pick up Beulah, Barbara and Billy, but she did send the money for their bus tickets. Beulah was 13 years old, Billy was 11 years old and Barbara was 9 years old. Miss Flenniken took them to the bus depot and made sure they were safely situated on the bus before leaving them. Upon returning to her office, Miss Flenniken wrote Eliza a letter detailing the stipulations of the children's visit and reaffirmed the importance of returning them back to the Holston Home as instructed. On August 5, 1957, Miss Flenniken received an answer from Eliza:

Dear Miss Flenniken,
I will answer your letter for Beulah Lee. They got down here alright. They sure are having a good time and I am so happy to see them home. I would like to see my other three children if you will let me keep these from the 8th till Sunday, the 11th. I will bring them back and take them on to Kingsport with us to see them and let them out at the Home as we come back by after we all see Shelia, Rozetta and Marcella. If you could have them at the Home for me it would be better on me, but if you can't I could go on to Kingsport. You can write me back and let me know if it will be okay or not to keep them two more days and let me bring

59

them back and if I can see my other three children or not. They are alright and they are getting plenty of everything.
Yours very truly,
Eliza Mae Mowery

Eliza was happy to have Beulah, Barbara and Billy home for a week and they were excited to be home with her. She also took them to visit Seig at Brushy Mountain State Penitentiary in Petros. They had never been inside a prison before and all they kept asking Seig was, "When are you getting out, so we can come home?" Seig told them it would be soon. He promised them it wouldn't be much longer till they would all be together again. Eliza began to cry, and Beulah and Barbara started crying, too. She kept talking about her little ones, Shelia, Rozetta and Marcella, and how much she missed them and needed to have them with her. Seig told her he would get the family back together as soon as he was released and told her not to worry about it. She told Seig she wanted to see them but was denied because it would be too upsetting for them and her at this time. Eliza blamed Seig for all the problems she was having and the loss of her children. She told Seig it was his fault for being stupid. She was extremely upset, and they all had to leave. Beulah and Barbara comforted Eliza as they left the building. Billy was angry because Seig was locked up and he had to go back to the Holston Home.

The next day Eliza contacted Miss Flenniken and told her that Beulah, Barbara and Billy would be riding the bus back to Greeneville and what time they would be arriving at the bus depot. Eliza did not want to send them back, but she knew she would go to jail if she didn't do as she was instructed by Miss Flenniken. Miss Flenniken was waiting for them at the bus depot and greeted them with her usual smile and a big hug. She knew this was very traumatic for the three of them, especially Beulah, because she was the oldest. On the way back to the Holston Home she stopped at the Dairy Queen and bought them ice cream.

On August 14, 1957, Miss Flenniken received another letter from Seig, written by someone in the prison:

Dear Miss Flenniken,
I thought I would drop you a few lines and thank you for allowing my kids to come and see me. I thank you good people for what you have done for them. I really think they are nice and behave good now.
I am in hopes that you will give the three small kids back to my wife before she loses her mind. I know now that

it is only a matter of time before I am released from here and I do know that they will be taken care of.

There will be plenty of eats for them, and I do believe if she does not get them soon, that when I do get out, I will have to be a mother as well as their father for I don't think she can take it much longer being without them.

Miss Flenniken, the main reason I am writing you is because I received a letter from my wife and from the way it reads, I am sure she is tore to pieces over the kids and I can't blame her after all she is their mother and there is nothing in this world I want more than my wife and kids and I am sure it won't be long before I am out so I can take care of them myself.

Hoping you will consider this letter and its request. I will close.

Yours Truly,
Seig Mowery

On August 28, 1957, Seig was released on parole after serving the minimum sentence of three years. His brother, Defoyst Mowery, and Eliza were waiting for him outside the prison doors. Defoyst, a long-distance truck driver, had gotten his employer, Mr. Pryor Crowe in Benton, Tennessee, to sponsor Seig for employment. Defoyst took Seig and Eliza to his home where they would live for the next couple of months. Defoyst knew that Seig would need time to work and save his money before he could get all his children out of the orphanage home. Dave Rymer in Cleveland, Tennessee, was Seig's parole officer. Defoyst took Seig to meet him as scheduled and got permission for Seig to accompany him on his long distance trips out of state. Defoyst stood over 6 feet tall with black wavy hair and was very handsome. He was very good to Seig and Eliza and helped them as much as he could.

On September 15, 1957, 18 days after his release, Seig had someone write the following letter to Miss Flenniken at the Holston Methodist Home:

Dear Miss Flenniken:

I thought I would drop you a few lines to let you hear from me. I was glad to hear that I could get my children back at any time. But, I am getting things fixed a little better for them. As you know, my wife didn't stay home all the time. I have been working around the house and cleaning the place up but, I will be able to come after them in two weeks. I hope that every plan will work out okay. If nothing goes wrong I'll let you know the day I'll come, so that you will have time to get them all together and have them ready. We wrote Beulah Lee a letter, but she hasn't answered yet. She said something about going out in a foster home when she got back up there. I would like to know if she is still at the Holston Home with Billy and Barbara or not. I was used to having the children with us and I just can't stay home at night. We have been staying at my brothers where I work. I hope to hear from you soon.

I know it won't be over two weeks before I can come after them. I thank you for what you have done for my children, but I could come home before I did, but they got my papers all mixed up. It will sure mean a lot to have them all back home.

Yours very truly,
Mr. & Mrs. Seig Mowery
% D.M. Mowery
Benton, Tennessee
PS: Miss Flenniken, we will be up Sunday to see all the children if you can get them where I can see them. Let me know if we can see them or not.

Seig and Eliza were not able to come for a visit, and Miss Flenniken was not sure when the children would be going home. There seemed to be too many uncertainties in Seig's letters to her. On September 25, 1957, Eliza wrote Miss Flenniken the following letter trying to explain why they could not come for a visit:

Dear Miss Flenniken:
I thought I would drop you a few lines to let you know why we didn't get to come up Sunday to see the children. Seig went on a trip and didn't get back. He called me Monday night and said he couldn't make it back until Thursday of this week. I was disappointed too. I don't know hardly what to say about coming after the children. I'll call you Friday morning or Saturday if he gets back and let you know for sure if we can come Sunday or not. I could come by myself, but he thought maybe he had to come too.

My brother or brother-in-law would bring me any time after them, but I thought it would be wise to wait until I heard from Seig or until he gets back off this trip. These pictures we made when they were at home. I would like for you to give them to Beulah Lee for me for I promised her I would send her some of them. I wrote her, but she hasn't wrote me yet. Seig said maybe you were stopping the mail from getting to her and we wouldn't write her anymore that it wouldn't be long until he would come for them. If she got sore at us she would get over it. If you don't want her to have these pictures, please send them back to me.

If Seig gets back tonight some times I'll know what to tell you when I call Friday morning. Soon as we come after the children he will be leaving on Monday, but I am sure that I can manage the children okay. The oldest ones will be riding a bus to school and I'll be living next door to my Aunt before too long, so I hope you can understand what I mean. I tried to explain to you, so you will hear from me.

Eliza Mae Mowery

On October 12, 1957, the Mowery children were returned to their parents. They were taken away from Eliza on October 6, 1955, after Seig was sent to prison on October 6, 1954. They had not seen Seig in three years, and it had been two years since Eliza had seen her three youngest children. Shelia, Rozetta and Marcella were taken to the Holston Home and reunited with their older siblings. Beulah was now 14 years old, Billy was 11, Barbara was 9, Shelia was 7, Rozetta was 5 and Marcella was 3 years old. Miss Flenniken stayed with them while they waited for Seig and Eliza to arrive. Shelia, Rozetta and Marcella lived with the Quillen family for 15 months. Mr. and Mrs.Quillen had grown attached to the three little girls, especially Shelia. They wanted to adopt Shelia but were told it would be impossible, because both parents had refused to give up their parental rights. Mr. and Mrs. Quillen hugged and kissed Shelia, Rozetta and Marcella goodbye and told them they loved them with tears in their eyes as they were leaving. Shelia kept clinging to Mrs. Quillen, which made the situation very bad. Beulah carried Shelia, and Barbara led all the children to the playground.

When Seig and Eliza arrived, they saw their children on the playground. Beulah, Billy and Barbara ran to greet them. Miss Flenniken led Shelia, Rozetta and Marcella to their car. Shelia, Rozetta and Marcella did not know them. They had completely forgotten their parents! Seig and Eliza were excited to see their children and anxious to take them home. They were surprised at how much their children had grown. They thanked Miss Flenniken and the Holston Home for taking such good care of them. The children's belongings were neatly lined up inside the administration building by the front door. Miss Flenniken talked with Eliza and Seig while Beulah, Barbara and Billy loaded their belongings into the trunk of the car. Miss Flenniken hugged and kissed all of the Mowery children good-bye as they climbed into the car to leave. She had to use persuasion and assistance from Beulah and Barbara to get Shelia into the car. Shelia did not want to go with them. As they were leaving, Miss Flenniken had a sad and very concerned look on her face. The children continued to wave at her from the back window of the car until they could no longer see her.

Seig and Eliza arrived at a house on Richardson Street that their children had never seen before. Seig said Uncle Harry rented their house in Tin Can Holler to someone else after Eliza moved out. Eliza told them that Cindy married Hobart Lunsford, and she did not want to stay in the house alone. She went to live with their grandparents, Anner and Fred Robinson. Seig told the children that he and Eliza had been living with their Uncle Defoyst Mowery in Benton, Tennessee, since his release from prison and that Uncle Defoyst had gotten him a job with his employer..

All the children were glad to be home with Eliza, except for Shelia. Eliza had to give Shelia a little more attention to help her adjust. Beulah, Billy and Barbara asked Eliza to write a letter to Miss Flenniken, because they had promised to write her. On October 23, 1957, Miss Flenniken received another letter from Eliza. Neither of them knew this would be the last letter written and received from Eliza. Eliza wrote the following to Miss Flenniken:

> Dear Miss Flenniken,
> Beulah, Billy and Barbara wanted me to drop you a card to say hello. They said to tell you they missed you very much too. They are going to school and like it fine. Shelia Ann is the only one who seems not to remember us, but is beginning to understand. She likes school just fine, but talks a lot about those people who kept her. We didn't have much time when we were up to get them to say very much, but my husband and I sure was glad you all did what you did for them.
> Eliza Mae Mowery

THE TRAGEDY

CHAPTER 19

T he Mowery family lived on Richardson Street in Athens, Tennessee, for almost a year before returning to their shack on Cleveland Avenue in Tin Can Holler. Seig continued to work with Defoyst until Eliza begged him to find another job. She needed and wanted him to be home with her, because she was having a difficult time controlling all the children. Seig looked for work elsewhere and was rehired as a dump truck driver by his former employer, F. D. Webb, who owned the Webb Rock Quarry in Athens. Seig knew they could not afford to have any more children, and he did not want another child to be born. He caused Eliza to miscarry several times by poking long clothes hanger wires into her. One time he stomped her in the stomach and caused her to lose the baby. Eliza made Billy and Beulah bury several fetuses in bean cans in their backyard.

The children, especially Billy, did not like living on Richardson Street. He missed his friends in Tin Can Holler, especially Simon, and would go to his house in Tin Can Holler every day after school to eat dinner with his large family. During the summer of 1958, Uncle Harry informed Seig and Eliza that they could move their family back to the little shack in Tin Can Holler, and they were all happy to be returning home again, especially Billy. He knew he could always get plenty of food from his friends in Tin Can Holler. He was a growing young man and stayed hungry all the time.

Eliza admitted to herself and to her very close friends that she had made a mistake by marrying Seig, and she knew he did not truly love her the way a woman should be loved, because he didn't know how to show love. She knew he married her only to save her good name, but now she was trapped. She knew she couldn't care for all her children alone, and she knew there was no one who could or would help her. She remembered her family's reaction when she announced her plans to marry Seig and how upset and angry they were with her. Eliza often felt that they wanted to punish her for not listening to them. She had tried the welfare system several times while Seig was in prison, but that too was never enough to support her children. She really wanted her children to have a better life but did not know what

65

to do, so she was forced to stay with Seig. The life she had chosen seemed hopeless, not only for herself, but for her children and she wanted a better life for her children.

Many years earlier, Seig had confided in her, during one of his many drinking binges, about his mother's abuse and the truth about Uncle Harry being his real father, but Harry didn't want anyone to know he was Seig's father. She and many others had always suspected that there was something strange about Uncle Harry's kindness to the Mowery family, and after she knew the truth things became much clearer. She grew to hate Uncle Harry, because he was a very wealthy man and could have done much more to help Seig and the children, but he didn't. He knew the children were going hungry and were always in need of shoes and clothing and medical care, yet he only brought them bags of groceries occasionally to probably ease his own guilty conscious for taking away their homestead in Meigs County.

Seig also told Eliza about the men Grace killed and how she made him kill his baby brother, and that she threw the bodies into a deep hole on the ridge behind her farm. He told Eliza that his mother made him help her bury their belongings, so no one would ever find out. Seig only knew what Grace had taught him….stealing and cheating anybody, any way he could to make a few dollars.

Eliza pitied Seig, and that had a lot to do with why she stayed with him. Seig had been a victim at the hands of his mother. Eliza knew there was a good side to Seig that other people had never seen. She knew he had many obstacles to overcome and had a criminal past that limited his ability to provide for his family. Being illiterate made it even more difficult, and this angered Seig. She knew he wanted so much to be different from what he was, and he just couldn't be. He had no background, no role models. The more that was done to him, the deeper he sank within himself. He had nothing or no one to help him understand who he truly was, because all he could understand was how horrible he was, because of the things his mother made him do as a child.

Eliza always envisioned a little flower bud in Seig's heart…like a tulip poplar blossom, but he could never let it open up. She also discovered his dark side and the wrath of the hate he carried within himself with his drinking, gambling and abuse. She never envisioned that her life would have turned out as bad as it did, and it hurt her deeply to see her children suffer. Eliza didn't have the resources to provide for her children in the way she wished she could, but she tried her best to give them the love she knew they would never receive from their father. Seig was not affectionate and did not hug and kiss his children, not because he didn't love them, but because he didn't know how to express his love.

CHAPTER 20

Soon after returning to Tin Can Holler, Seig began binge drinking every weekend and riding around with his buddies even though he was on parole. He was very jealous of Eliza, so she very seldom went anywhere. Sometimes he made Eliza ride with him in the dump truck while at work, just to read the street signs for him. When Billy got older Seig would keep him out of school to ride with him. Seig was intimidated by Eliza, because she could read and write. The only way he knew how to bring Eliza down to his level was to make her drink whiskey with him. As the old saying goes, "misery loves company."

Because of his gambling habits, many times Seig would come home with only a little money left from his paycheck. Eliza would be furious and would yell at him for not putting his family's needs first. She would cry and ask him how she could feed the kids if there was no money to buy food. Sometimes, when he got angry he would leave the house and take the two youngest children with him to the local beer joint. He would sit them on the bar, so the men and women would take pity on them and give them money. He would use his own children to get back the money he lost gambling.

Eliza tried desperately to live a Christian life and raise her children in a Christian home, just like the one she was raised in. She sang Christian songs to her children, taught them how to say their prayers every night, and would help them to learn Bible verses. During their walks to and from church, Eliza would talk to her dear friend Lizzie about Seig. She told Lizzie that Seig would force her to drink whiskey so she would get drunk with him and that Seig was okay most of the time, but when he drank whisky he would always have a binge fit. Seig did not like for Eliza to associate with Lizzie because she was a black woman. With the civil rights movement and school desegregation spreading throughout the south, many people did not want to change their racist attitudes, and Seig was no different. He did not approve of Eliza's friendship with the black residents of Tin Can Holler.

One summer day Lizzie and Eliza were walking together, talking and enjoying each other's company, through Tin Can Holler returning from the local grocery store. Seig ran up to Eliza and raised his fist and started to hit her. He was very angry because she had left the house and walked to the store with Lizzie. Lizzie, protecting Eliza, stepped in front of her and told Seig that if he hit Eliza he would have to hit her too. Seig dropped his fist and swore at Eliza and told her to get home where she belonged.

Seig would get angry every weekend and would force Eliza to drink whiskey with him even though she would refuse. Every Friday and Saturday night a man would come to the house selling moonshine to Seig. They would get drunk and start fighting. This was an every weekend occurrence. The Charles family lived directly across the street from the Mowerys. Mr. and Mrs. Charles adored Shelia, and she loved to visit them. They had a large family with 10 or 12 children. Mrs. Charles would yell at Seig to stop beating on Eliza when she saw him abusing her. When Eliza drank she would get a bad temper too and fight back. When she was drunk she wasn't afraid of anybody. Once, when the police were called to their home by one of their neighbors, Deputy Bigman hit Eliza in the face with a blackjack. She had to have nine stitches. Eliza and Seig were arguing and she pushed the police officer who was trying to stop the argument. The neighbors called the police a lot because of the fighting and screaming. The local police knew Seig and Eliza very well and had many encounters with them.

CHAPTER 21

E liza's godmother was Eliza Mae Coleman Goins. Eliza's parents, Anner and Fred Robinson, named Eliza after her because they had been friends for many years. Whenever Eliza became frightened of Seig, she would go to her godmother's home for protection since there were no women's shelters during those days. Eliza Coleman took care of Eliza many times when she had been beaten by Seig. Eliza told her godmother that Seig had threatened to kill her and throw her body into a deep hole behind his mother's farm in Meigs County. She advised her godmother to look for her there if she ever came up missing. Eliza's godmother protected her and always provided a safe haven for her. She feared for Eliza and wanted desperately to help her, but when Seig sobered up Eliza would always return to him because she feared for her children.

Because of Eliza's depression, the nervous breakdown she had gone through years earlier, and Seig forcing her to drink whiskey with him, she soon turned into an alcoholic. Even though she and Seig fought a lot over drinking and he forced her to drink, the only comfort she could now find was in the liquor bottle. Many times she would walk the railroad tracks to her brother Howard's home, who was a bootlegger at that time, just to get a shot of whiskey. Many times her eldest daughter, Cindy, who was now married but also lived in Tin Can Holler with her husband, Hobert, would go looking for her and would find her passed out on the railroad tracks and would bring her home. Cindy would sober her up so she could take care of the children.

Cindy worried a lot about Eliza and became very angry at Seig's abuse of her mother, which caused Eliza to drink more, but she didn't know how to help her. She confronted Seig many times and told him to leave her mother alone and to stop abusing her. Seig's anger was out of control as was his intense jealously of Eliza and the many friends she had throughout Tin Can Holler.

Christmas 1958 was very depressing for Eliza, because there was no money for Christmas gifts for her children, only what the local charities brought them. The children always talked about all the gifts they had received from Santa while in their foster homes and this saddened Eliza, because she did not have any money to buy them gifts. She and Seig cut down a tree and brought it home for them to decorate with popcorn and anything else she could make for them.

The winter months flew by, and unbeknownst to Eliza and Seig, Beulah had met a man she wanted to marry. Beulah hated Tin Can Holler and accepted his marriage proposal soon after meeting him. She wanted out of Tin Can Holler and away from all the fighting and screaming. She was only 16 years old and begged Eliza to sign the papers, but Eliza refused. Eliza told Beulah she was too young to get married and forbade her to see her boyfriend, Randy. Beulah convinced Seig to give his consent, and in March of 1959, Beulah and Randy got married. She left Tin Can Holler with a man they knew very little about.

During late July of 1959, Eliza became deathly ill with major female problems and infections due to the many forced abortions performed on her by Seig. Cindy knew there was something seriously wrong with her mother and made her go to the emergency room. The doctor on call examined Eliza and could not believe what he saw. He questioned Eliza about her condition and asked her what she had done. Cindy spoke up and told the doctor it was not her mother who did that to herself, but her husband Seig, because he did not want anymore children. The doctor shook his head in disbelief and informed them that she needed a complete hysterectomy because of a serious infection. Her uterus was poked full of holes that had become infected and had spread to her other female organs. The doctor scheduled the surgery for the next day and immediately began giving Eliza antibiotics intravenously. The next morning Eliza underwent a complete hysterectomy and remained in the hospital for several days before the doctor released her. He instructed her not to do anything strenuous and to get plenty of bed rest for at least six weeks. Cindy took Eliza, who was very weak, and drove her home. She made her go to bed and asked Barbara Jean to help take care of her. Cindy had to take care of her own children and could not stay with Eliza. Barbara did as Cindy instructed her and stayed with her mother.

Seig did not care that Eliza was sick. He was happy when he found out that Eliza would never be able to get pregnant again and there would be no more children for him to take care of. He made Barbara cook the meals and clean while Eliza was confined to her bed. The younger children visited their neighbors just to get something to eat because there was never enough food in the house. Seig did not care that his children had turned into beggars, and beggars they were and no one in Tin Can Holler ever turned them away. Everyone knew that there was a lot of turmoil in the Mowery household and that Seig abused Eliza, because the children would tell everyone about Seig getting angry and beating Eliza. Shelia Ann was a little social butterfly and talked to everyone in Tin Can Holler and would tell them everything that happened in the home.

CHAPTER 22

O n Sunday afternoon, August 16, 1959, Seig left the house to hang out with some of his drinking buddies. Eliza was feeling a little better, so while the children played with their neighborhood friends, she decided to lie on her bed and get some much needed rest. Later that afternoon Seig stormed back into the house screaming at the top of his voice, "You God damn nigger lover!" He had been drinking and was very angry at Eliza. He went into her bedroom and continued to yell profanity at her. She woke up from her nap and was very confused as to why he was yelling at her. As she struggled to sit up in the middle of the bed Seig slapped her across the face and knocked her back onto the bed and started punching her. Eliza screamed in pain begging him to stop. She rolled herself off the other side of the bed and stood up. Crying and holding her stomach with one hand and wiping the blood off her face with her other hand, she pleaded with him to calm down. She begged him to stop hitting her and to tell her what he was angry about. She knew she had done nothing to upset him and was completely confused at his behavior toward her. She had never seen him so angry. He had the look of evil on his face, and she was very frightened.

Seig was completely out of control and continued to yell, "You're a God damn nigger lover!" Eliza yelled back at him that she didn't know what he was talking about. Seig accused her of running around in Tin Can Holler with a black man. He said someone had told him they saw her with a black man. Eliza told him that was not true and whoever told him that was a liar. Seig punched her in the face several more times, knocking her to the floor. He started yelling at her to get up, but Eliza stayed down. Seig began kicking her and grabbed her by her hair. He made her stand up and dragged her outside and threw her into the backseat of his car.

For hours Seig rode around Athens with Eliza bleeding in the backseat. He stopped at the local gas station to fill up his tank, and a man noticed Eliza lying in the backseat all beaten up and bleeding. He asked Seig what was wrong with her and he replied, "she's drunk and fell down." He finished pumping his gas and drove away very quickly. He continued to drive around Athens while drinking his whiskey from a bottle he had between his legs.

Eliza was horrified and lay trembling in the backseat wondering what he was going to do to her. She knew she had to get away from him but did not know how. His anger toward her continued to worsen as he drank more whiskey. His profanity and yelling grew louder and louder. Eliza knew from past experiences with Seig that when he went into a binge fit there was nothing she could do, so she laid very still in the backseat and did not say a word.

She feared that he was going to take her to his mother's old farm in Meigs County and throw her into the deep hole as he had threatened to do so many times before. Eliza lay motionless in the backseat looking out the back window as daylight turned into darkness. She could tell by the bumpy ride that he was no longer on the city's paved streets and was indeed going to his mother's old farmhouse. Her heart was pounding faster and faster, and her breathing became heavy. She felt as though she was smothering. As he began to slow down she could hear him mumbling to himself. The occupants of the farmhouse were home and Seig wasn't able to follow through with his plans and continued driving. Seig was very drunk from all the alcohol he had consumed. The car swerved and slid all over the road. Eliza's limp body was thrown back and forth in the back seat as he raced around the curves on the old country road in Meigs County. Several times she almost rolled off the seat onto the floorboard of the car. Eliza lay quietly not making a sound holding her arms around her stomach trying to relieve her excruciating pain. Seig was yelling and cursing when the car suddenly went off the road and slid to a stop. Eliza had no idea where they were, but she shook with fear as tears rolled down her bloody face. Seig had driven the car into a ditch on No Pone Valley Road. He clumsily climbed out of the driver's seat and staggered to the back of the car. He noticed a dirt road that led to a farmhouse in the distance, but paid no attention. His only thoughts were to get the car back on the road.

As Seig looked for broken limbs and rocks to put under his back tires, an old man who lived in the house, heard the noise and slowly walked down the road to offer assistance with his tractor. As the old man approached the car he noticed Eliza lying in the backseat covered in blood. He became very suspicious and continued walking toward Seig. Seig was startled when he saw the old man. In his drunken stupor he yelled, "Old man, you better get away from me right now" as he held up a large limb he had in his hand. The old man, after recognizing that it was Seig Sims, was overcome with fear and never said a word. He turned around, dropped his head in sadness as he walked past the car knowing that a very injured woman was laying in the backseat of the car. Seig managed to get the car out of the ditch and back onto the road as the old man turned and watched him drive away.

Thirty minutes later, Eliza could see streetlights and knew Seig had come back into the city.

After hours of driving around and drinking more whiskey, Seig, who was highly intoxicated, drove his car into Tin Can Holler near Railroad Avenue and struck a ditch near Ebb Dickson's small shanty. Ebb Dickson was one of Seig's drinking buddies. He was a bachelor who lived alone in his little shanty near the lower edge of Tin Can Holler. He was a tall, slim scruffy looking guy about 5 feet 10 inches. Everyone in Tin Can Holler knew Ebb and a lot of the teenage boys would hang out with him in his shanty. Ebb always had a pot of beans cooking on his wood stove, so Billy visited him a lot just to get a bowl of beans from him.

Seig tried several attempts to get the car out of the ditch but couldn't. He yelled at Eliza and told her he was going to get help and ordered her not to get out of the car. Eliza knew this would be her only chance to escape and slowly raised herself up to look out the windows. She recognized the area immediately and knew they were back in Tin Can Holler. She saw Seig walking away from the car carrying the tire iron he had gotten from the trunk of the car. She also knew she must get away and give Seig time to sober up and calm down from his binge fit. She found an old shirt on the floor of the car and wiped the blood off her face. She quietly opened the car door and climbed out of the backseat.

Eliza knew that Seig would come looking for her, so she climbed up an embankment by the road and hid in a wooded area next to the railroad tracks and watched for him to return. An hour or more passed as she sat on the railroad tracks, which were much higher than the road by 30 or 40 feet or more. From where she sat, she had a perfect view of the street below. She saw him return with a young man who helped him get the car out of the ditch. As the young man walked away Seig opened the backdoor of the car and realized Eliza was gone. She could hear him cursing and knew he was still very angry. She watched him jump into the car and speed down the street. He took a left at the first intersection, which was the direction toward their home in Tin Can Holler. She thought he was going home to look for her.

Eliza, still in pain, climbed down the high embankment and walked over to Ebb Dickson's shanty wiping more blood from her face. As she stood in front of the doorway propping herself up with her right hand beside the door, she left a bloody handprint from her earlier beating from Seig on the outside wall of Ebb's shanty. She knocked on the door in hopes that someone would be home. She needed a safe place to hide from Seig until he sobered up. It was now midnight and she was exhausted. She looked horrible and her blouse had been torn from Seig's earlier attack.

Her knocks on the door awakened Ebb, who had gone to bed hours earlier. As he opened the door he saw Eliza standing there holding her torn blouse. She asked him if he had a pin. Ebb invited her to come in and said he would look for one. Eliza walked over to the other side of the room and sat down on a wooden box. Ebb's friend, Glen (Coot) Lawson, was sleeping on a bed that was against the wall on the other side of the shanty. Eliza was quiet and spoke softly to Ebb, not wanting to wake up Glen, as she told him that Seig was drunk and very angry. She told him Seig had torn her blouse and that is why she needed the pin. He told Eliza that he had been with Seig earlier that afternoon drinking whiskey. She begged him not to open the door if Seig came looking for her.

Less than 10 minutes later, Seig came to the shanty. He opened the door and walked in without knocking. Seeing Eliza sitting on the box on the other side of the room he started yelling, "Where are your clothes?" Ebb couldn't understand why Seig was asking Eliza about her clothes when she was fully dressed. He struck Eliza, knocking her from the box. Eliza began screaming, "Please don't Seig, please don't!"

Glenn was awakened from his sleep and watched as Seig continued to assault Eliza. Ebb Dixon ordered Seig out of his house and yelled, "I can't have this in my house!" Seig grabbed Eliza and dragged her outside and slammed the door behind him. Ebb and Glen listened as Seig assaulted Eliza in the front yard of his home. There was a struggle and Eliza tried desperately to defend herself against Seig. Eliza's screams for help could be heard all the way to her friend Lizzie's home in Tin Can Holler.

Lizzie was awakened and ran to her front porch. Lizzie knew it was Eliza's screams but could not tell from what direction they were coming from. Many other people were also awakened by the screams. Ebb and Glen, who were only several feet away, were unnerved by her screaming, but they did open the door to help Eliza. They did not interfere or intervene to stop Seig's attack on Eliza, because they thought it was a family affair. They each stood behind the door and listened as Seig viciously murdered his helpless and defenseless wife.

Seig ripped off Eliza's blouse and hit her in the head with the tire iron he had in his pocket, knocking her unconscious. When she fell to the ground he began stomping on her frail, helpless body. There were no more screams, only the sound of someone chopping wood. He was like a madman stomping his wife and jumping on her body with all his weight. He stomped and kicked her 25 or 30 times. He smashed her face and head until her forehead caved in. Her busted eyeballs popped out and lay on her cheeks. He broke her jaws and nose and completely disfigured her. He knew no mercy for the woman who had bore him so many children and who had suffered for years from his abuse. He did what he had threatened to do so many times before. Eliza's body lay lifeless on the ground in a pool of blood....blood was everywhere. Splattered blood covered Seig's clothing and his shoes. There would be no more arguments and no more fighting. Eliza's lifelong battle with Seig was now over.

CHAPTER 23

Seig stood in silence and darkness staring down at Eliza's bloody body, realizing what he had done. He began yelling for Ebb or Glen to throw him some clothes and bring him a bucket of water. He yelled, "Eliza needs medical attention, her jaw is broken!" Glen, who had been sleeping in his underwear, threw the only thing he could find out the door......his pair of pants that he hung on a nail before going to bed. He filled a bucket full of water and carried it outside and gave it to Seig. He took the bucket of water and poured it all over Eliza's body. He then had Glen help him carry her body to the shoulder of the road. Seig picked up Eliza's torso and Glenn picked up her feet and dropped her body near his car after several unsuccessful attempts to put her into his car. Seig kept saying to Glen, "She's dead, she's sure enough dead!" As Seig got into his car to leave he told Ebb and Glen that he was going to call an ambulance and the police and said, "You boys had better scatter." Glen left the shanty, but Ebb stayed and waited for the police and ambulance to arrive.

Seig knew what he had done and that he would go back to prison for murdering his wife. He also knew he must make up a story to defend himself. He drove straight to his home on Cleveland Avenue in Tin Can Holler. The children were all sleeping, so he quietly went to the kitchen and cleaned himself up. He washed Eliza's blood off his shoes and put on a clean pair of pants and a clean shirt. He rolled up his bloody clothes and woke up Billy who was sleeping on the sofa. He handed Billy his bloody clothes and told him, "Your mammy's dead! Take these clothes and shove them down the shit hole now ... do it now!" Billy, who was still half asleep, did what his dad told him to do and did not realize what his dad had just said about his mother.

While Billy went to the outhouse to throw Seig's clothes into the hole, Seig made a couple of telephone calls. He first called the police department and spoke to Jim McSpadden, a civil defense officer who was serving a weekly shift as radio operator at the county jail.

He identified himself to Mr. McSpadden and said, "I think my wife is lying dead near the road at Ebb Dickson's house…..they have killed her….go down to Ebb Dickson's house and call me back." Seig gave him his telephone number for him to call him back. He then placed a call to his brother-in-law, Howard Robinson. He asked Howard, "Did you know Eliza Mae's dead?" Howard said, "No." Seig replied, "Yes….Ebb Dickson and Glen Lawson killer her…. some policemen called me and told me she's dead!" When Billy came back into the house Seig hung up on Howard so he could talk to Billy. He told Billy he had to leave but would be back in a little while. He told Billy to go back to bed and not to wake up the other children. Seig got back into his car and rode by Ebb Dickson's shanty twice to see if the police had arrived. The second time he passed the shanty, the police were everywhere, so he went back home and went to bed.

Eliza's brother, Howard, was very angry at Seig and called the police department for confirmation about Eliza's death. He knew that Ebb Dickson and Glen Lawson did not kill his sister. He was informed that police officers were at Ebb Dickson's home but no police officer had telephoned Seig. The police officer asked Howard if he knew who killed Eliza. Howard said, "I'll have to say that he killed her…..Seig killed her!" Howard was informed that he would be notified later to come to the morgue and identify her body.

Officers Nick Crittenden and Ruel Ware were immediately dispatched to the home of Ebb Dickson in Tin Can Holler. Several minutes later Chief Deputy Sheriff Howard Thompson and Officer W. R. Reynolds arrived on the scene to assist with the investigation. W. O. Kennedy, who was the special investigator for the attorney general's office, also arrived to survey the scene and gather the evidence. When they arrived at the shanty, they found Eliza's bloody and badly beaten body. She was lying on her back in the yard near the road. Her legs were twisted and her body was nude from the waist up, because Seig had ripped off her blouse. She was pitiful, and the officers found it very difficult to look at her. They had never seen anything like this before. They began to question Ebb Dickson who told them about Seig's attack on Eliza. When the police officers asked Ebb Dickson why he had not intervened and stopped the attack, he said, "I didn't think he would kill her and I didn't want to interfere in a family fight." Eliza's body was transferred to the county morgue.

Howard, upon hearing the horrible news about his sister, called all the family members including Cindy to tell them what the police had said about Eliza's murder. The police arrived at the Mowery home early the next morning with a warrant for Seig's arrest. They took Seig into their custody and transported him to the county jail. The children were awakened and were very frightened because they didn't understand what was happening. Cindy rushed to the house to check on the children. She was distraught but knew she had to tell the children the terrible news about their mother. She waited until she received a telephone call from her Uncle Howard, who had gone to the morgue to identify Eliza's body, before she said anything to the children. She called Beulah and asked her to come to the house immediately because she would need her help.

A short time later Beulah arrived and they waited for Howard's telephone call together. The dreaded telephone call arrived, and Cindy and Beulah sat looking at each other, neither of them wanting to hear what Howard was going to tell them about their mother. Beulah refused to answer the phone, so Cindy picked up the receiver with her shaking hands. Her voice was quivering as she said, "Hello?" Howard was angry and crying at the same time. He described the horrible condition of Eliza's body to Cindy. He cursed Seig for killing his sister and threatened to kill him for what he had done. Cindy began crying and hung the phone up. She could barely speak as she repeated to Beulah what Howard had just told her. They comforted each other so they could get the strength and courage to tell the rest of the children that their mother was dead.

Cindy and Beulah gathered all the children around them and made them sit on the floor in front of them. As soon as Cindy and Beulah started crying, the children knew something terrible had happened, because they were asking where their mother was and no one would answer them. The neighbors could hear the screaming and crying coming from the Mowery house, but this time it wasn't Eliza screaming....it was her children. Shelia ran out of the house and threw herself onto the ground while kicking and screaming, "No, no, no....mommy's dead!" Beulah ran after her and picked her up off the ground and carried her back into the house. Barbara was crying while holding Marcella, and Cindy held Rozetta in her lap to comfort her. Billy was too angry to cry and stormed out of the house as he tried to remember what his dad had said to him hours earlier.

During the police investigation and interrogation of Seig, he first denied attacking Eliza. When they arrested him he was dressed in clean clothes, but he failed to change his bloodstained socks. After denying his attack on Eliza, special investigator W.O. Kennedy asked him to explain how his socks had become stained. Seig replied, "I don't know...it's just one of those things." It was later that night, during questioning by Kennedy, Thompson and other officers that Seig finally admitted he had hit and possibly stomped Eliza. He told the investigators he had found her naked in the house with Ebb Dickson and Glen Lawson. He stated he was so mad he didn't know what he was doing.

Seig was lying, and they knew he was lying. They found a bloody shirt in his car that Eliza had used to wipe blood off her face from an earlier beating and his bloodstained shirt in the weeds in the back of his home in Tin Can Holler. His son Billy, who was half asleep, unknowingly dropped his shirt but threw his bloodstained pants into the outhouse. Billy was never questioned and never told the detectives what Seig had made him do. Seig's arraignment on murder charges was scheduled for Friday, August 21st, in Sessions Court. He was allowed to make one telephone call. He called Uncle Harry.

CHAPTER 24

The news about Eliza's vicious and senseless murder spread like wildfire throughout Tin Can Holler. Neighbors comforted each other in the loss of one of their dearest friends. Special church services and prayer meetings were held for Eliza throughout Tin Can Holler. Eliza's friends and her godmother, Eliza Mae Goins, were heartbroken but not surprised or shocked. They all feared that one day Seig would kill Eliza. They repeatedly warned her to be careful. She had always managed to escape and get away from him, but not this time. Rumors about why Seig murdered Eliza also spread like melting butter on a hot burner. People heard rumors, probably from Uncle Harry, started by Seig, that Eliza was running around with a black man and that he found Eliza in bed with Ebb Dickson and Glen Lawson. He wanted and needed sympathy to save himself from the electric chair, which is what he was sure to get if he were convicted of murder.

Billy heard all the rumors about his mother and it angered him. He walked past Ebb Dickson's shanty several times the next day. He saw Eliza's bloody handprint on the outside wall by the front door and he became angrier. He was so saddened by his mother's death but received no grief counseling. His friends, especially Simon, comforted him, but he did not know how to deal with the pain he felt in his heart. Billy felt that he needed to do something. The night before Eliza's funeral Billy decided to burn down the shanty where Eliza was killed. He got some gas and was walking down the street when he saw smoke rising up above the trees. As he got closer to the shanty it was already burning. Someone else from Tin Can Holler had already set it on fire. There were lots of people standing around, but no one tried to put the fire out. Everyone stood in silence as they watched the shanty burn to the ground.

The Mowery children were devastated and the Robinson brothers were furious over Eliza's death. They all wanted to kill Seig. Because of their threats, none of the Robinson brothers were allowed inside the jail. All of Eliza's friends came to the Mowery home to help with the children. Cindy was beside herself with sadness, grief and worry. She did not know what she was going to do with all the children. She knew she couldn't care for them all. Eliza's friends in Tin Can Holler took up a collection and purchased all the children new clothes and shoes for Eliza's funeral.

Uncle Harry's funeral home took care of Eliza's arrangements. Since there was no money for her burial expenses, and the county was paying for it, Uncle Harry kept it cheap. Eliza's funeral was scheduled for August 18th. There were many heated arguments on whether to have Eliza's coffin open or closed. The Robinson brothers were angered even more when they saw Eliza's face and demanded to have her coffin opened. They wanted everyone to see what Seig had done to their sister, while Uncle Harry insisted that it be closed. Uncle Harry did not want any further trouble from the Robinson brothers and agreed to leave the coffin open. Eliza had blood running out of her ears, and Barbara stood by her coffin with tissue paper wiping the blood away. She cried her heart out as she stood by her mother's coffin. She wanted her mother to look her very best even though the woman lying in the coffin did not even resemble her mother.

Eliza had been beaten so badly by Seig that her face did not resemble the face of a human being. The embalmer had to rebuild her face with clay. It looked like a block of cement with black stitches on the side and on her forehead. The black stitches on her face were very visible. People cried the moment they looked at her because of her ghastly appearance and because she resembled the Frankenstein monster they had seen in movies.

The funeral home was crowded with hundreds of people who came from Tin Can Holler and all the surrounding communities. The compassion and sympathy from total strangers was overwhelming. The funeral home was overflowing with tears. Flowers were everywhere and filled the room around Eliza's coffin. All of Eliza's church friends prayed with her children and asked God to give them comfort and strength. Two very polite and nicely dressed ladies that were sisters, one whom was married to Eliza's embalmer, attended her viewing. The embalmer's wife spoke to Cindy, who was very distraught and emotional about her mother's appearance. She hugged Cindy and expressed sympathy for her loss. She also sympathetically explained to Cindy that her husband did the best he could, but there was so much trauma to Eliza's face that the only thing her husband could do was pack her face with clay. She said her husband worked diligently on Eliza for two days and he too was very disappointed in her appearance. She sadly stated that her husband did the best he could. She tried to comfort Cindy.

These same two sisters, who were showing extreme kindness to all the Mowery children and only wanted to help them, picked up Rozetta and her baby sister Marcella because they wanted to see their mother and say goodbye. Both children screamed hysterically and became frightened when they saw their mother in her coffin. After seeing her mother so deformed, Rozetta went into shock and couldn't speak. All she could do was babble. The trauma of seeing her mother deformed and looking like Frankenstein, caused her to lose her ability to speak clearly.

The next day, Uncle Harry let all the Mowery children ride in his big black Cadillac to the gravesite. Eliza was buried in the Clearwater Baptist Church cemetery. This was a day that was so traumatic to the children, they had nightmares for years to come. They had never seen a dead person and had never been to a funeral. There were screams and more screams at the sight of their mother being put into the ground and covered with dirt.

After the funeral, the Mowery children returned to their home in Tin Can Holler. They walked into their home and discovered an awesome sight on their kitchen floor. They couldn't believe what they saw. There was food everywhere, in all kinds of containers; ham, chicken, beans, biscuits and cornbread, pies and cakes! The wonderful people of Tin Can Holler had come to their kitchen door, which had no steps and was 10 feet from the ground, and placed a ladder there. They had opened the door and slid the food inside onto the floor. For the next several days people continued coming to the house to say they were sorry to hear about Eliza and brought more food.

Estelle and Bryant Gennoe also came to the house. They talked to Cindy because they were concerned about the children. Bryant and Estelle, who had been friends with Eliza for many years, offered to care for Barbara, Shelia, Rozetta and Marcella until a decision was made about their long-term care. No one else offered to help Cindy. Eliza's brother, Ed, came to the house and took her guitar since he was a musician. The girls loved Estelle and Bryant and were happy to be going to their home to stay, but they did not know that it was not going to be permanent.

CHAPTER 25

Seig's court hearing was on Friday, August 21st. He was transported to the courthouse under tight security because of the threats against his life by the Robinson brothers. He appeared before Sessions' Judge Jack Johnson and the grand jury for a preliminary hearing to determine how he would be charged according to the testimonies of witnesses. Uncle Harry hired L. B. Mason as Seig's defense attorney. He was known to be one of the best criminal attorney's in the district.

The courtroom was crowded with more than 350 people who came to hear the testimonies of witnesses who proved to the Grand Jury that Seig murdered his wife in cold blood. There were testimonies from Seig's brother-in-law Howard Robinson, Ebb Dickson, Glen Lawson, Criminal Investigator W. O. Kennedy, Chief Deputy Sheriff Howard Thompson, Deputies W. R. Reynolds, Nick Crittenden and Ruel Ware, and the mortician associated with Harry Evans Funeral Home, Owen Fullen.

One by one, they were questioned by prosecuting attorney Herman Gregory. Under oath, each testified and described in detail to everyone in the crowded courtroom how Seig viciously murdered Eliza and threw her body beside the street in front of Ebb Dickson's home in Tin Can Holler. Cries were heard throughout the courtroom from Eliza's friends and neighbors who filled the courtroom.

Several women, who became hysterical after hearing the gruesome details of Seig's brutal attack on Eliza, had to be escorted from the courtroom. Friends, neighbors and strangers sat in disbelief that someone could do these things to another human being.

Mason addressed the Grand Jury entering a motion that first and second degree murder charges be dropped. He said Seig could not be guilty of the two charges because if he committed the attack, it was in the heat of passion, claiming that Seig had reasonable cause to be mad. He stated that any man would be mad if he found his wife in a bedroom with two men at midnight, let alone her being there undressed! He insinuated that Eliza was sleeping with Ebb Dickson and Glen Lawson to get sympathy from the Grand Jury and asked that bond be no greater than $2,500.

Gregory insisted to the Grand Jury that Seig be held without bond on first-degree murder charges, noting "in the twinkling of an eye there can be premeditation." He stated that Seig had a chance to compose himself when Ebb Dickson ordered him from his house, but Seig dragged Eliza into the yard and stomped her to death. He also stated that the coroner's report indicated a blow to the head with a blunt instrument.

Judge Johnson said the court could find no indication of premeditation and could not hold Seig to the Grand Jury without bond on first degree murder, adding if anything, the evidence indicated second degree murder and set his bond at $10,000. He also announced to the Grand Jury that the six Mowery children would be placed in temporary custody of the welfare department.

Uncle Harry did not post Seig's bond because Seig had been released on parole August 28, 1957, and had two years, eight months and 11 days remaining. When his parole officer heard the news about Seig's arrest he contacted the parole board. Seig had violated the conditions of his parole and a retake order was issued from the Board of Pardons, Paroles and Probation office. Seig was immediately returned to Brushy Mountain State Penitentiary on August 28, 1959.

On October 6, 1959, under tight security due to continued death threats against his life, Seig was transported back to the McMinn County Courthouse and indicted by the Grand Jury in criminal court. Again, the courtroom was overflowing with people from throughout Tin Can Holler. The same witnesses presented their evidence again. Seig stood in silence listening to the charges. They unanimously agreed that he unlawfully and feloniously did willfully, deliberately, premeditatedly and maliciously assault Eliza with a deadly weapon and of his malice aforethought kill and murder her. The crowd in the courtroom and Eliza's family members were overjoyed that the Grand Jury had decided to charge Seig with premeditated murder and that he would be facing the death penalty if convicted.

On February 8, 1960, Seig was transported back to court once again under tight security. Twelve white male jurors were chosen. Gregory and Mason locked horns in a court drama that was shrouded with mystery. Seig's attorney cross examined all the witnesses and attacked their characters. This was Seig's only defense. His attorney wanted to discredit all the witnesses for the prosecution. He repeatedly criticized the character of Howard Robinson, Ebb Dixon and Glen Lawson, calling Robinson a self-confessed bootlegger.

Eliza's character was also attacked. Stories of her running around with a black man in Tin Can Holler and Seig finding her alone with Ebb Dickson and Glen Lawson in the bedroom of Ebb's shanty helped to gain sympathy from the all white male jurors. There was considerable conflict in testimony as to how Eliza was dressed at the time she was murdered. In a dramatic performance during his closing arguments, Attorney Mason made a point of the fact that "a situation like that wouldn't lead to peace and tranquility." He told the jurors he wasn't sure what happened up there that night. "I don't know how I would feel if I found my wife in the bedroom with another man, and I don't know how I would react. I'm sure you gentlemen don't either!"

Gregory, in his closing argument, insisted that Eliza was kicked to death by Seig after a blow to her head with a blunt instrument, which was never located. He showed them Eliza's bloody blue jeans and bloody bra and emphasized that Seig attempted to wash the blood off his own body. He very empathetically shouted, "Right here's your murder weapon," as he held up a pair of shoes he said Seig claimed as his own. Again, he shouted very loudly, "Oh, if these shoes could only talk!"

After hearing the closing arguments the jurors were dismissed to their chambers to decide Seig's fate. At 9:15 p.m., after only two hours of deliberation, the jurors reached a verdict and were escorted back into the courtroom. Everyone sat motionless waiting to hear the outcome. All eyes were focused on the jurors as they walked in single file and sat down. As the verdict was read, the people in the courtroom looked at one another in confusion. They were completely flabbergasted.

The jurors apparently believed the lies about Eliza's character and only charged Seig with manslaughter, even though Seig was originally indicted for premeditated murder. The judge sentenced him to from two to 10 years in the state penitentiary. His manslaughter sentence would begin immediately upon serving his previous larceny and housebreaking offense. He would have to serve the full 13 years as originally charged, for those crimes. He got a lesser sentence for killing his wife! All the angry people rushed out of the courtroom that day completely appalled at the results of Seig's trial.

CHAPTER 26

T he townspeople of Athens talked about the outcome of Seig's trial for many years. The murder of Eliza Mowery was such a traumatic episode in the lives of so many people that it was never forgotten by the residents of Tin Can Holler. Grandmothers told their grandchildren about the death of their friend Eliza Mowery during the hot summer night of August 17, 1959.

Seig was declined for parole in 1965, but a year later on August 19, 1966, he was released on parole. He violated his parole and was returned to prison on January 18, 1968, for numerous parole violations: (2) speeding, (2) D.W.I.'s, (3) P.D.'s and (1) hit and run accident. When these violations were brought to the attention of his parole officer, Arnold Johnson, he immediately reported them to the Board of Pardons. The Board revoked Seig's parole, declared him to be a parole violator and issued a warrant for his arrest.

On March 26, 1968, two months after being returned to prison, Seig tried unsuccessfully to have his verdict overturned on the idea that the original indictment listed Eliza's date of death as 8-7-59 when it should have been 8-17-59.

The Honorable S. Randolph Ayers was assigned as Seig's public defender. He claimed the typographical error was grounds enough for Seig's immediate release and there had been a grave miscarriage of law dealt to him. He stated to the court that Seig was never properly indicted. His plea to the court was the original indictment, which was for premeditated murder, but Seig was convicted of voluntary manslaughter. He claimed that within itself, it was a worthless document and should be struck from the records. Ayers argued that based on this fact ... it is impossible by "due process of law" to indict a person for one crime and then convict him of another crime, arising from the same indictment. He further stated in his appeal that it was impossible for an indictment for a crime which was allegedly committed on the 7th day of August 1959 to be in due process of law when the records clearly showed that the date of death was on the 17th day of August 1959 and that there must have been some question in the minds of the jurors that he was not guilty of murder or they never would have reduced the charge. He again called for Seig's immediate release from prison.

The townspeople had wondered the same thing. Why was Seig charged with manslaughter when he was originally indicted for premeditated murder? Were the jurors influenced by someone like Uncle Harry, or was it because Eliza had been accused of running around with a black man? All the jurors were white men, and during the late 1950s it was definitely unacceptable for a white woman to be seen in the company of a black man.

Seig's appeal was denied on April 9, 1968, and was signed by Mark Anderson, Charles Galbreath and Wayne Oliver. It was declared that the petition was filed without merit and was dismissed. Seig was informed that he would remain in prison for the balance of his sentence or until otherwise discharged in accordance with the law. His parole violation was sustained.

A year later Seig was again declined for parole, but on September 12, 1969, he was released from prison. He only served two years for viciously murdering his wife in cold blood, even though he had been in prison for over ten years for his other convictions! One Sunday morning, soon after his release, he went to a little country church in Athens and sat down quietly on the back pew. People in the church glanced at him in silence, but two deacons made a loud comment to one another, "What is Seig Mowery doing in our church!" Seig overheard their comment and slowly stood up without looking at anyone and walked out of the church. He never stepped foot in another church for the rest of his life. He completed his parole without any incidents and was released completely from the Board of Pardons on June 4, 1970.

Seig married a woman in the Athens area and settled down to a quiet life of yard selling and dealing in junk and used furniture. He would take his truck to the dump and wait for people to unload their old lamps, sofas, chairs, tables, TV's, radios, and miscellaneous household items. He rented several different old buildings on Railroad Avenue in Athens and would resale these items to the pubic. In his later years, Seig had several minor heart attacks and had to have an oxygen tank to help him breath. On his birthday, March 15, 1999 at the age of eighty-one, while in the hospital in Athens, he asked his wife to go across the street and get him a fresh cup of black coffee, which he loved. She gladly complied and returned immediately to his hospital room smiling as she handed him a large container of his favorite coffee. As he sat in his bed enjoying his coffee he looked at her very frightened and said, "I can't breathe!" He dropped dead from a massive heart attack and fell back on his pillow. He died instantly and could not be revived. He was buried in the Athens Memorial Gardens Cemetery. As of 2007, no marker or cemetery plaque had ever been placed on his grave. His children do not know where he is buried, but other family members said he was near the fence in the back of the cemetery.

WHAT HAPPENED TO THE CHILDREN?

The only thing that Eliza's children had when she was taken away from them so tragically was their happy memories of knowing how much she loved them. The memories of how their mother played her guitar and sang songs to them and walked with them to church on Sunday mornings stayed with them all the days of their lives. Her smile and the hugs they received, each time they gave her morning glories they picked from their backyard in Tin Can Holler, remained with them forever.

CHAPTER 27

C inderella (*Cindy*), Eliza's firstborn child, was 21 years old when Eliza was murdered. She had a difficult time facing the reality of what had happened to her mother and accepting the fact that she could no longer be part of her life. Eliza's bond with Cindy, as her firstborn, was the strongest. Her mother had always been her best friend. Even though she married Hobert Lunsford at the age of 19 and had two children of her own to care for, she knew in her heart that she was still Eliza's little girl. The emptiness she felt in her heart, knowing she was no longer with her, emotionally weighed heavily on her heart.

For many years it was impossible for Cindy to move on with her life. Cindy became extremely depressed and withdrawn. The daily activities of caring for her children helped her to cope, but she always thought of Eliza and how much she missed being with her. Her children recalled years later that she would cry a lot and they never knew why until they were older and Cindy told them. Cindy had three more children several years later.

Her life with Hobert was full of challenges and turmoil because of his drinking, fighting and bootlegging activities, even when the children were present. Several times they separated, and eventually they divorced, because she grew weary and exhausted from Hobert's careless attitude toward their marriage and family. Hobert was also a small-time gambler in Athens and spent a lot of time in jail for his illegal activities. Even though they were divorced, Cindy would allow him to come and go in the home. The children were never aware of the divorce.

Cindy worked in factories around the Athens area, struggling to support her five children. During the years after her divorce she never dated or looked at another man, but Hobert dated and had many one-night stands with women. Cindy became consumed with her children; they were her life. She remained friends with Hobert's family and was very close to his Aunt Marta, who became a second mother to her.

Hobert still had a lot of control over Cindy and convinced her to move away from Athens with him. They first moved to Chattanooga, where Hobert opened an upholstery shop in their home. Cindy assisted him with the business. They later moved to Ohio and Virginia where they made and sold living room furniture. Cindy had to take on a new role in her marriage when Hobert made her collect the money from customers for non-payment. On many occasions she would have to forcefully repossess the furniture from people who refused to pay. This made Cindy very uncomfortable and she would often carry a gun with her for protection. They ultimately gave this business up and moved back to Athens where they rented an apartment in the Clem Jones apartment complex on the other side of Tin Can Holler. When their financial problems began, Hobert moved the family into his parents' home in Tin Can Holler.

When Seig was released from prison, after serving only two years for murdering Eliza, Cindy became very disconcerted. She felt that he had gotten away with murder and told Hobert and her children not to have anything to do with him. She suffered from major depression, cried a lot, and began to drink heavily. She was taken to the hospital and was treated for dehydration. This was a major turning point in Cindy's life. When she was released from the hospital she knew she needed to seek guidance from the church she had stopped attending many years earlier.

Cindy went back to church and became a Christian. Cindy's strong faith in God gave her the strength she needed to survive during those difficult years, and she prayed that Hobert would change his ways. She became a very strong, determined woman and the matriarch of her family. Her prayers were soon answered and Hobert had a rude awakening. During one of his visits to a bar in Meigs County, a fight erupted with a female and several other males. Hobert was hit in the head and blacked out. He woke up to discover the female had been shot and he was charged with the crime. He went to trial and was found guilty of involuntary manslaughter, even though he repeatedly declared his innocence. He spent approximately one year in jail. He must have done a lot of thinking while incarcerated and decided to change his life when he was a free man again. Upon his release, the first person he went to see was Cindy. He apologized for all the years he had been unfaithful and asked her to forgive him for all his wrongdoings. He also asked Cindy to remarry him and promised her that things would be different.

At first Cindy was hesitant, but then she remembered her prayers for Hobert to change. She decided to give him another chance to prove his true love to her and he did, over and over again. He spent the remainder of his life trying to make up for all the bad things he had done. He borrowed money and opened a car dealership, Cindy's Used Cars, and a small grocery store, Cindy's Market. He also had a game room for children and young adults, Cindy's Game room. Cindy and her children helped run the businesses and they became financially successful for the first time in their married life. Things were going very good for Hobert and Cindy. He bought Cindy a beautiful home, and she decorated it the way she had always dreamed.

In 1983 Cindy became ill and suffered from severe pains in her chest. She also had difficulty breathing. She went to her physician in Athens who treated her for pneumonia. For months Cindy continued to see her regular physician who treated her with penicillin shots in his office. Her health condition did not change. She still had pains and difficulty breathing. Hobert and the children convinced her to seek the advice of another physician. She made an appointment with another physician who referred her to an ear, nose and throat specialist. The ear, nose and throat specialist performed surgery on her sinuses. He stated that a blockage caused by an earlier injury to her nose during one of her many fights with Hobert was why she was having breathing problems. After several weeks, the doctor removed the packing in her sinuses. She still had difficulty breathing and one month later, while working in her flower garden, Cindy coughed up a huge blood clot. She also got sick at her stomach and thought it was due to the surgery to her nose, but she later found out it wasn't. She went to the emergency room and was checked by Dr. Holiday. He did not know what was wrong with Cindy and admitted her into the Athens Community hospital. Dr. Holiday ordered several diagnostic tests for Cindy. He was a kind and very caring physician. He prayed with Cindy before the tests were performed and prayed with the entire family on many future visits.

After several unsuccessful results, one final test was performed. The surgeon had to cut an opening in Cindy's throat and insert a tube into her lungs to take a closer look. They discovered a small tumor at the end of a gland in her left lung. The medical term for this was Aden Carcinoma. This is a malignant tumor originating in the epithelial cells of glandular tissue and forming glandular structures. This type of cancer is inoperable. The only treatment at that time was radiation.

When the results of these medical tests were revealed, it was devastating to Hobert. Their youngest daughter watched her father through the kitchen window, arriving home from the hospital and parking his truck. She watched him as he sat in his truck. This was the first time she had ever seen her father cry. He propped his arms over the steering wheel and laid his head on his arms and cried for a very long time. She instantly knew that Cindy's test results were bad and ran into her mother's bedroom. She knelt down beside her mother's bed and began to pray. She asked God to help her because she knew she must be strong for her mom and dad. She knew in her heart, after watching her dad cry, that the results of the medical tests were very serious.

Cindy was a fighter and endured many painful radiation treatments. Chemotherapy was not an option. This type of cancer spreads through the lymph glands to other organs in the body. Cindy developed a tumor on her brain and had to endure more radiation treatments.

In March of 1988, as Cindy was recuperating from her radiation treatments, Hobert came home and complained about pains in his left arm. Cindy told him he should go see a doctor and made him an appointment with one in Etowah, but he later canceled it because the pain went away and he was feeling better. Hobert knew that something was wrong with his heart and had his friend loan him some of his nitroglycerin pills.

On Mother's Day, Hobert died from a massive heart attack. Cindy blamed herself for Hobert's death. She had been praying for Hobert's salvation. She thought she was going to die first and she wanted him to join her in heaven. She believed her prayers were answered because her belief was that if one person in your household is saved, the entire family would be saved. She didn't want to believe that her prayers caused his death.

Cindy fought her battle against her devastating cancer for almost five years. On the evening of June 30, 1988, at 11:15 p.m. she began having trouble breathing and was choking on blood. Her youngest daughter ran to her bedroom to help. Cindy was sitting on the edge of her bed with a strange look on her face and suddenly fell to the floor on the same spot where her daughter had knelt and prayed years earlier. Her daughter immediately dialed 911. There was a gurgling sound. Cindy was hemorrhaging and drowning in her own blood. The tumor had burst and filled her lungs with blood. The ambulance and paramedics arrived and transported Cindy to the hospital, but it was too late. All of Cindy's siblings rushed to the hospital. The doctor at the hospital pronounced Cindy dead at 12:01 a.m. on July 1, 1988. Cindy was only 50 years old.

CHAPTER 28

E liza's second child, Beulah Lee, was 16 years old when Eliza was tragically killed. She knew something had happened to her mother the night of her death. She was awakened by a strong wind that came through the house in Englewood, where she and her husband, Randy, were living. Beulah sat up in bed and started shaking and crying. It was the wind of Eliza's spirit coming to say good-bye to her.

Beulah only completed the sixth grade and knew very little about the world she lived in. The only life experience Beulah received was in Tin Can Holler. Seig gave her a lecture when she begged him to sign for her to marry Randy. Seig told her, "If you make a mistake, so be it. When you make your bed, you must lie in it." She always remembered what he said.

Beulah was crazy about Randy. He was tall, slender-built with light brown hair and hazel eyes. Beulah thought he was the most handsome man in the world. Beulah met Randy at the Strand Theatre in Athens. Seig had given Beulah and Barbara money to go to the theatre one night, and they had walked to it from Tin Can Holler. Randy sat behind them and played with Beulah's ponytail. He flirted with Beulah even after she asked him to leave her alone. He kept flipping her ponytail until she finally turned around to look at him. They started talking and Randy offered to drive Beulah and Barbara home. Beulah agreed to let him take her home after Barbara insisted. Barbara didn't want to walk home and loved the idea of riding in Randy's car. From that moment on, Randy would come by the house to see Beulah every day. Beulah would sneak out of the house to be with him. A week later Randy proposed to Beulah in the front seat of his car.

Beulah regrettably disregarded Eliza's warnings and advice, but she believed that life with Randy would be better than the life she had in Tin Can Holler. Even though she was very young, Beulah did her best to make the marriage work, because she loved Randy. Randy was 18 years old when he married Beulah. He was a high school dropout and could not accept the responsibility of taking care of Beulah, and he took all his frustrations out on her. He drank too much and developed a violent temper and mistreated her horribly. The beatings and mental and verbal abuse she endured for years from Randy broke her spirit. He attempted to choke her to death on several occasions. Beulah always had black eyes and bruises from his beatings.

She was miserable and very unhappy. She cried all the time and wanted to run away but had no place to go. She was still a child herself, and she didn't know what to do. She was so naive and inexperienced in taking care of herself. What she expected from Randy was what she had always read in the fairy tale books, but what she didn't realize before she married him came as a shock and a big disappointment, because he was not her knight in shining armor or a man. He turned out to be her worst nightmare. Beulah's marriage and life with Randy went from bad to worse as the years went by. Randy would take Beulah for a ride in his car, stop it and reach across her and open her door. He would take his foot and physically kick her out onto the street. She wouldn't know where she was and would start walking. She spent many nights sleeping in unlocked cars in used car lots and would go days without food. After several days, Randy would come looking for her. One time when this happened, Beulah was on the Athens by-pass heading toward Sweetwater when a nice, well-groomed man in a pickup truck, who looked to be in his late thirties or early forties, stopped and asked her if she needed a ride. Beulah told him, "Lord, yes I do." As this man was driving he questioned Beulah about her life and why she was walking all alone. Beulah told him that her husband had kicked her out of his car with no money or food and she was walking back home. When the nice man realized where Beulah lived he took her all the way home because it was too far for her to walk. She thanked him for giving her a ride. Several years later she would see this man again but under completely different circumstances.

Beulah never knew what made Randy angry, but she realized that he enjoyed inflicting her with pain. He also enjoyed locking her outside. One night she broke the window pane at the back door to get inside and cut her wrist severely. She almost bled to death before he took her to the hospital. If Beulah cooked something he didn't like, he would throw the food all over the kitchen and sling more on the ceiling. Beulah would always clean up the messes he made.

Randy did not have a permanent job. Sometimes he would work for his brother-in-law cutting down trees and selling them to Bowater's, a local paper-mill company. Less than a year into their marriage, he also began to seek the attention of many, many other women. Beulah became aware of his cheating when a man came to their house in Englewood one night and accused Randy of seeing his wife. This man was furious and wanted to kill Randy. Randy and this man had a confrontation in the front yard, and Randy was warned to stay away from his wife. Beulah never found out who this man was but hoped Randy would not see this man's wife anymore.

When Randy did not have money to buy gas he would make Beulah stand as a lookout while he siphoned gas from cars and trucks parked in people's yards. Randy would look for old, abandoned houses searching for copper and steel or old car parts … anything he could get a few bucks for at the junk yard. One day, Randy needed money for cigarettes and beer. He made Beulah go with him for a ride. He came upon a little red country church and parked his car in front of the building. Randy made Beulah go into the church and steal two electric floor heaters. Beulah told him she did not want to do that because it wasn't right. She knew he would beat her if she didn't do as he told her, so she stole two heaters for him. The next day Randy took the heaters to Seaton's junk yard in Athens and sold them. Randy got less than $10 for both heaters, but it was enough money to buy his beer and cigarettes. Beulah lived with this guilt her entire life.

Randy would leave on Friday nights, and Beulah wouldn't see him until Monday morning. He would take all his money and leave Beulah without any food in the house. Beulah began to lose weight and became very undernourished because Randy was not taking care of her. He did not care that Beulah was starving to death. During the summer months when the neighbors' gardens were in full bloom, Beulah would sneak to their gardens in search of tomatoes and cucumbers. She would put as many as she could hold in her blouse and would run back home. She would also walk the country roads in search of apple trees or anything she could find to eat. She would always carry a glass jar in case she found any blackberry bushes and would need something to put them in.

Whenever Beulah would question Randy about his whereabouts, he would become angry and tell her it was none of her business. Beulah would find evidence in his car that he had been with other women. She would find soda cans and coffee cups with lipstick on them. She also found match covers with women's names and telephone numbers on them. When she would confront Randy about what she found in his car, he wouldn't deny being with other women. He told her she could like it or lump it and there wasn't a thing she could do about it. He enjoyed flaunting these other women and would laugh in Beulah's face. This activity became a Friday night ritual, and he was not the least bit ashamed for anyone to know about his infidelity.

Late in 1959, Randy took Beulah to live on a dairy farm in Sweetwater, Tennessee, owned by Charles and Laura Powell. The Powells, both in their late thirties or early forties, were highly respected and well-known within the Sweetwater community. They were friendly with all the public government officials and law enforcement officers. They had no children of their own, but adopted children, mostly boys to work on their dairy farm. The Powells provided free housing on their farm for Beulah and Randy in exchange for work and a small weekly salary.

There were four houses on the farm used as housing for the workers. These houses were one- and two-bedrooms with small kitchens and small living rooms. Only two of the houses had indoor plumbing. They all had open front porches. The first house Randy and Beulah lived in had no indoor plumbing. Beulah would carry water in 5-gallon milk cans and heat it on the stove to bathe in. Each house had its own outhouse. There was a shower in the barn that Randy would use.

Charles was a very strict man who expected all his workers to do their assigned jobs. He would not hesitate to order lazy workers off his property. Otherwise, Charles was a kind person with a big heart. He always wore a black hat similar to a cowboy hat, workboots and denim overalls. He was about 5 feet 10 inches and weighed around 175 pounds; he was a stocky man. He also owned an auto salvage yard in Sweetwater, and that is where he spent his days while his workers tended to the dairy farm.

Laura was a big-boned woman around about 5 feet 10 inches. She had a very fair complexion with short, light-colored hair. She was strict and very aggressive. She demanded loyalty from her employees who lived on the dairy farm. Laura was also employed part-time by the hospital in Sweetwater where she worked as a nurse.

On the dairy farm, Charles relied on Randy to be the supervisor. Randy would oversee the milking of the cows, the mowing of the grain and the storing of the feed in the silos. He made sure that all the farm animals were fed twice a day. The diary farm was huge, and the barn could hold 200 cows that had to be hand-milked. Beulah would work in the milk processing/straining area. She cleaned and kept the entire area sterilized. Twice a day she would scrub the floors and the milk buckets. This was very hard work and a big responsibility for a 16-year-old girl. At the end of each day Charles would talk to Randy to make sure that all the work on the farm had been done as he instructed.

While Randy and Beulah were living on the dairy farm, Randy continued his infidelity habits even with some of the other women that lived on the dairy farm with their husbands. He had no scruples or conscience. The only things Randy cared about were his liquor, cigarettes, money and women. Beulah became pregnant in November 1959. When it came time for Beulah to deliver the baby, Randy drove Beulah to Tin Can Holler and dropped her off at Hobert and Cindy's house. Cindy and Edna Robinson, Howard's wife, took Beulah to the old Foree hospital in downtown Athens.

On July 9, 1960, Beulah, at the age of 16, gave birth to her first son, Nathan. When Nathan was a couple of months old, Randy disappeared and deserted them both. He left them alone on the diary farm. Beulah nursed Nathan and gave him cow's milk. She, too, lived on cow's milk as she had no money or food. A couple of days after Randy left the dairy farm, Laura approached Beulah and discouraged her from keeping Nathan. Everything Laura said to Beulah was negative. There were no words of happiness or joy, nor did she offer to assist Beulah in any way. Beulah was scared and all alone and did not know what to do. Laura convinced Beulah that she wasn't capable of caring for little Nathan and had no money since Randy disappeared. She said, "Beulah, you are sitting here all alone, broke, no food and you can't sit here and watch your baby starve to death. You need to give Nathan to me and let me adopt him and you can come see him anytime you want to."

Laura wanted Nathan and convinced Beulah to give him to her. This broke Beulah's heart … she cried and cried and waited for Randy to return to her and Nathan, but he didn't. She looked for him but didn't know where he was. A week later, she stopped looking for Randy and went to Laura. As she stood holding Nathan with tears flowing down her face, she handed Nathan to Laura and agreed to let her adopt him, because Beulah did not want him to starve to death. Beulah immediately called Cindy and Hobert and told them what happened. They arrived the next day and took her to their home.

Five months later, in December of 1960, Randy knocked on Cindy's front door looking for Beulah. Beulah was angry and yelled at Randy for leaving her and Nathan. Beulah informed Randy that she had to let Laura adopt Nathan. Randy showed no remorse or regrets.

He never even said he was sorry. The only person he cared about was himself. He told Beulah he wanted to get back together and wanted to start over. He promised her things would be better. He refused to tell her where he had been or what he had been doing while he was away. Beulah was hesitant and had many doubts, but she also felt she had overstayed her welcome with Cindy and Hobert. They did not discourage Beulah from going back with Randy, so she left with him.

Randy took Beulah and returned to Charles and Laura's diary farm, to the same house they were living in before. Randy was always a good worker while on the dairy farm, so Charles and Laura were happy to see them return. One month later, Beulah became pregnant for a second time. Randy's promise did not last long. He started drinking and leaving on weekends again. He would tell Beulah that he was going out of town to see his mother and would be back when she saw him. When Beulah went into labor, Charles and Randy drove Beulah to the hospital. Beulah, at the age of 17, gave birth to Gary on October 9, 1961, in the old Foree hospital in Athens.

During the next year, Billy, at the age of 16, came to the dairy farm to live with Randy and Beulah. While he was there he fed and milked the cows and plowed the fields. He did whatever needed to be done to help Charles and Laura. Randy did not want Billy there, but Beulah was overjoyed that her brother had come to stay with them. Randy stayed mad all the time as though he had a chip on his shoulder toward Billy. Randy wouldn't talk to Beulah or Billy, and when they attempted to talk to him he would only grunt and groan. He gave them both the cold shoulder. While Billy was there, Randy knew he couldn't mistreat Beulah, but he continued his drinking and leaving for the weekend.

Randy would get mad when Beulah would cook for Billy; Randy would throw the food out the backdoor to the dogs. He would yell, "Nobody's going to eat this food but the dogs." He grabbed all of Billy's clothes and drove down the road throwing them out of his car window. Beulah and Billy ran after him picking up the clothes. Randy saw them and turned his car around and came back toward them. He stopped his car, jumped out with a 22 automatic rifle and started shooting at them. He yelled, "I should kill both of you!" Beulah and Billy were standing out in the open with no place to hide. Billy told Beulah to stand still, because if Randy wanted to shoot them, he would. Beulah and Billy froze in their tracks and could feel the wind from the bullets passing them. Billy yelled at Randy, "Put that gun down and fight me like a man!" Randy jumped back into his car and took off. Billy yelled at him, "I'll be waiting on you at the barn tonight!" That night at milking time, Charles showed up and informed them both that there would not be any fighting at the barn or anywhere on his property. Billy ignored Randy and helped with the milking. He collected his wages from Charles, gathered his clothes and left the farm that evening.

One year and three months later, on January 12, 1963, when Gary was 15 months old and Beulah was 18 years old, she gave birth to her third son Eddie by herself, with Gary lying by her side. Randy was standing by the bed watching. Beulah told Randy to get Laura to cut the cord. Laura came and cut the cord and assisted Beulah in passing the afterbirth. Gary never woke up during this entire delivery. When Gary woke up the next morning Beulah showed him his baby brother, Eddie. Gary loved his baby brother. He would pat him on the legs and hug and kiss him.

Soon after Beulah delivered Eddie, Charles and Laura brought a big yellow school bus and parked it on their property across a creek from their main house right in the middle of the cow pasture. Charles put a roof on it and hooked electric to it. They put an antique cooking stove and small refrigerator in it. Charles and Laura made Randy, Beulah, Gary and Eddie move into the bus, so another family could move into the house they had once lived in. Randy continued working on the farm and continued leaving on the weekends and leaving Beulah alone with her two young sons while he ran around with other women spending his weekly wages on them.

One of the farm workers who knew how badly Randy was treating Beulah brought milk to her and the children when he would see Randy leaving as usual on Saturday morning. He would tell Beulah, "Here's a jug of milk for you and the boys so you won't go hungry." It was difficult living in a bus with a newborn and a 15-month-old. The only means of heating the bus during the winter was from the cook stove. Beulah would leave the burners on low continuously, so Gary and Eddie would not get cold.

One day Randy found an old wringer-washing machine with missing wringers and brought it to the bus for Beulah to wash his clothes. She would let his clothes soak all night, then wash them the next morning. She had to wring them out by hand and carry them to the nearby creek to rinse them. She'd hang them up on a line she strung up between two trees near the bus. Beulah would spend her days sitting on the floor of the bus playing with her two sons. Randy never cared for or played with either of his sons. The only attention they received was from Beulah. She was growing much attached to her wonderful little boys. She missed Nathan and saw him playing on the farm and it broke her heart, because she wanted to grab him and hug him. But she knew it would confuse him if she did, so she observed him from afar looking out the bus windows every day.

One of the other women who lived on the dairy farm gave Beulah an old blue stroller that she no longer needed. Beulah would put Gary and Eddie in it and push them up and down the road so she could get a closer look at Nathan as he played with his adopted brothers on the farm. One day, Nathan ran up to Beulah to see Gary and Eddie. He rubbed Eddie on the head and turned and ran off to play, not knowing that these two little boys were his brothers. Beulah cried all the way back to the bus that day.

In late November 1963, Beulah was pregnant again. As soon as Randy realized this he left the farm and left Beulah alone with Gary and Eddie. The nightmare started all over again. Beulah waited and waited for Randy to return. Charles and Laura had become accustomed to Randy disappearing and never questioned Beulah regarding his whereabouts. Laura knew that Beulah was alone and approached her several times to question how she was going to care for the children all by herself at such a young age. Beulah was devastated and had become attached to Gary and Eddie. Laura knew this, but she was persistent in her attempts to convince Beulah to give her Gary and Eddie. She told Beulah, "You have two little boys and another child on the way, how are you going to handle this, and what if Randy never comes back?"

Laura's constant questioning and negative attitude toward Beulah in her current situation eventually broke Beulah's defense shield she had placed around herself and her children. Beulah's children were all she had in the world, and Laura wanted to take them away. She convinced Beulah, again, that she knew of people that could take both of her sons and give them a good home. Beulah asked her if she was sure they were good people. She told Beulah the Clark family of Sweetwater, Tennessee, was desperately seeking children and would give her two sons a good home and everything they needed. She told Beulah she would never have to worry about the well-being of her sons if she would only let the Clarks adopt them.

Beulah did not give her an answer for several days. She knew the Clarks owned a store in Sweetwater and were financially secure. Beulah did a lot of soul-searching and decided to let the boys go. She wanted her little boys to have the life she knew she could never provide. She wanted them to have so much more than growing up living in a school bus, which was all that their father was capable of doing. Beulah knew that Randy had no interest in providing a good home for her or the children. Beulah put the children's best interest, well-being and safety before her own desire to keep her children close to her and with her. She convinced herself it would be much better for her sons to grow up with a mother and a dad in a loving environment than with her and their biological dad who was an abuser and an alcoholic adulteress. She also feared that Randy would someday abuse his children just as he had always abused her. She convinced herself that she was doing the right thing by letting the Clarks adopt Gary and Eddie. The only stipulation Beulah gave to Laura was that her sons stay together, because they were brothers and they loved each other. Beulah made it abundantly clear to Laura, who assured Beulah they would remain together.

One week later, Laura brought Mrs. Clark to meet her, Gary and Eddie. Beulah again made each of these women promise that they would never separate her two sons, and they both assured her they wouldn't. Mrs. Clark told Beulah she had only wanted one son, but if that was the only way Beulah would agree to letting them adopt, they would take both of her sons.

A couple of days after Beulah gave Gary and Eddie to Laura for the Clarks to adopt, Laura and Charles told Beulah she would have to find another place to live since Randy had not returned. Beulah did not know what to do, so she started walking down the road by the dairy farm. She remembered seeing a woman who lived alone in a big, two-story house that was once occupied by soldiers during the Civil War. Beulah decided to stop and talk to her if she was home. Beulah saw the woman sitting on her back porch peeling tomatoes and asked her if she could talk. The woman told Beulah yes and to come up on the porch and have a seat. The woman's name was Sadie. She was in her early forties. Sadie had long dark hair that she kept pinned on top of her head. She stood about 5 feet 5 inches and was an average-sized woman.

Beulah sat on the porch and told Sadie her life story and everything about Randy and her babies and that she was pregnant again. She told Sadie she was homeless and needed to find a place to live, but she had no money. Beulah also told Sadie she would help her around her farm to earn her keep just as she had done at the dairy farm. Sadie listened to Beulah's sad story and said, "You poor girl." Sadie told Beulah that she got lonely around her big house and could definitely use her help. Beulah walked back to the dairy farm and gathered what clothes she had out of the bus. She informed Charles and Laura that she would be living with the lady down the road from them, who lived in the big Civil War house. Beulah quickly returned to Sadie's home.

For the next year, Beulah lived with Sadie and was treated with much kindness. Beulah soon learned that Sadie was a very unique person compared to the other people she had come in contact with. Sadie was very compassionate and caring. Beulah had never experienced this type of kindness before. Sadie showed Beulah her food pantry and all the shelves of canned food she had prepared. The room had row after row of shelves from the floor to the ceiling. Sadie told Beulah that she had plenty of food and assured her that she and her unborn baby would not go hungry. Beulah felt like a little girl being there with Sadie.

Sadie kept Beulah busy all day with chores around the house and farm. Beulah would clean the house, feed the cow, pigs, chickens and turkeys, and assist Sadie in canning tomatoes, corn, green beans, pickles, okra, squash, cabbage, beets, peaches, apples and blackberries. Sadie taught Beulah how to churn clabbered milk to make butter. Sadie did not own an automobile, so a man, possibly her brother, would take her to town once a month to purchase dried goods such as flour, corn meal, sugar, coffee and chicken feed in 25-pound burlap sacks. Sadie did not have a television; all she had was a radio, but this was the best life Beulah had known since leaving Tin Can Holler. She was relieved that there was plenty of food for herself and her unborn child, because she did not have the money, or transportation, to receive prenatal care.

Life with Sadie was wonderful. Sadie kept her busy during the day, with little time to think about her life and all the misery she had been through. But, at night when Beulah would lie in her featherbed in the long hallway of the big house, all the memories of her sons, Nathan, Gary and Eddie, would come rushing at her like a locomotive. Beulah would have panic attacks, because in her mind all she could hear were the voices of Nathan, Gary and Eddie calling, "Mommy, Mommy." She would answer their cries by telling the voices in her head that she hoped one day they would understand she really did love them and the love she had for them was the reason she had to let them go. She would cry herself to sleep every night with a blanket over her head trying to block out their cries. Beulah continued to hear their little voices for many years.

During Beulah's nine months of pregnancy, while Sadie was working in her garden, Beulah was visited by Laura again. This was the first time they had seen each other since Laura and Charles informed her that she would have to find another place to live. Laura came by to ask Beulah if she had decided what to do with her unborn child. Beulah told her she had not given it any thought other than keeping the baby. Beulah was now 20 years old. Laura began lecturing Beulah about all the responsibilities in caring for a baby. Once again, she was negative and discouraged Beulah from keeping her child. Laura said, "Beulah, you don't have any money, no job and you are still all alone. How long do you think you can stay here with Sadie with a newborn baby? This is a hard life. Is this the way you want to raise a baby? What will you do if Sadie makes you leave? Where will you and the baby go? How will you take care of a newborn baby?" She told Beulah she needed to think very hard about this. Beulah told Laura that she would think about it. Laura said she would give Beulah a week to think about it and would come back. That night, Beulah sat down with Sadie and told her what Laura said. Beulah asked Sadie if she had any idea or advice she could give her. Sadie told Beulah that this was her life and her baby, and that decision would have to be her own. She could not and would not advise Beulah on what she should do regarding her baby.

After many long days and sleepless nights of thinking about her baby, Beulah got the urge to walk to town. She found herself on the railroad tracks in Sweetwater when she realized her labor was beginning. She walked across the highway and up the hill to the Sweetwater hospital and entered the emergency room. As soon as Beulah informed the emergency room staff that she was in labor they admitted her to the delivery room section of the hospital. An hour later she gave birth to her fourth son, Michael, who weighed almost 11 pounds. It was August 3, 1964. She had a very difficult delivery because Michael weighed so much. The doctor told Beulah that her son was a big baby boy with the biggest blue eyes he had ever seen on a newborn. Beulah was anxious to see her new son, Michael. When the nurses checked and cleaned Michael they placed him in Beulah's arms.

Beulah had only been holding Michael for a few minutes when Laura walked into Beulah's room; Laura worked at the hospital part-time. She told Beulah that she heard about her delivering a big baby boy and wanted to see him. She had heard from all the nurses that he had big blue eyes and she wanted to see them too. She immediately started asking Beulah what she was going to do with Michael. Beulah told her she had been thinking but had not come to a decision. Laura told Beulah she must hurry up and decide, because she had a couple who was excited and wanted to take Michael that very day! That didn't leave Beulah very much time to get a plan together, so she could keep Michael. Laura gave Beulah the impression that time was of the essence and she needed an answer immediately. Laura's pressure on Beulah weakened her defenses, and she agreed but told Laura she wanted to meet the couple first. Laura told Beulah she could have the couple at the hospital in less than 30 minutes, and she did.

When Laura brought the couple into Beulah's room, Laura introduced them. They were Mr. and Mrs. Ingram. The man immediately recognized Beulah. He was the nice man who gave Beulah a ride to Sweetwater from the Athens by-pass years earlier, when Randy had kicked her out of his car. He asked Beulah if she remembered him picking her up. As soon as she remembered who he was, Beulah told them she was glad her son would be with them, because he had been very nice to her several years back. She told him she knew he would be a great father and role model for her son, since his biological father did not want or care about him.

Laura left the room and came back a short time later with the adoption papers, while Beulah got acquainted with the Ingrams. The nurse came into the room and carried Michael back to the nursery. Mr. Ingram looked at Beulah and promised her that he would take very good care of her son. Beulah thanked him, and the Ingrams left. Laura got the adoption papers in order and had Beulah sign them in numerous locations. Just as before, with all the other adoptions, Beulah was not given time to read the adoption papers and Laura never explained anything to her.

The next morning Beulah was released from the hospital and Laura drove her to Sadie's house and dropped her off. Beulah greeted Sadie, who immediately noticed that Beulah was no longer pregnant and didn't have her baby. Sadie told Beulah she had been worried to death and didn't know what had happened to her. Beulah told Sadie everything that happened and about Laura's visit to the hospital. Sadie told Beulah that was a terrible thing Laura did. Beulah stayed with Sadie for a couple more weeks. When she was feeling better she walked up the road to Laura and Charles's dairy farm to use their telephone. Beulah called Cindy and told her everything that had happened and that she was living with a woman down the road from the dairy farm. Cindy told Beulah that she and Hobert had started an upholstery business and they could use her help if she wanted to come live with them. Beulah said yes because she wanted to get away from Sweetwater. Hobert came the next morning to pick her up.

About eight months after Beulah moved in with Cindy and Hobert in Chattanooga, Randy showed up looking for Beulah. Randy made Beulah the same promises and said things would be better. Hobert offered Randy a job in his upholstery business and when Randy agreed, Hobert said he could stay with them until he could find their own place to live. Beulah helped Cindy and Hobert by watching their five children while they worked in their upholstery shop, which was on the ground floor of the building. Their apartment was above their shop.

Occasionally, Beulah would walk around the sidewalk of the building just to get some fresh air. On one of her daily walks, Beulah was standing on the corner waiting for the light to change when a pink Cadillac slowly approached her. The man in the backseat rolled down his tinted window and waved at her. To Beulah's surprise it was Elvis Presley! Beulah waved back when she saw who it was. Beulah was so excited that she ran back to the upholstery shop to tell Cindy she just saw Elvis!

In July of 1965 Beulah, at the age of twenty-two, became pregnant again. She gave birth to Sandra Lee on April 4, 1966, at Erlanger Hospital in Chattanooga. After Sandra was born, Randy rented an apartment in the back of an elderly man's home. It was a nice, clean apartment. Every other weekend Randy started leaving for the weekend again. Beulah and Sandra would sit on the front porch with the landlord. They became friends because most of the time Beulah and Sandra were there alone. Beulah told the landlord all about her life with Randy. He told Beulah she deserved a better husband and Sandra deserved to have a good daddy. He advised Beulah to take Sandra and get away from Randy.

Randy never took Beulah and Sandra anywhere. The only time they left the apartment was when Cindy needed Beulah to watch her children. Late one Friday afternoon, Randy cleaned up and left the apartment. Later that afternoon Beulah, Sandra and the landlord were sitting on his front porch watching cars go by, when she spotted Randy's car coming down the road. As she looked closer, she noticed a blond-haired woman sitting right next to Randy. Randy had his arm around this woman. Beulah jumped up and handed Sandra to the landlord and asked him to watch her. Beulah took off running and caught up with the car at the next red light. She pulled the car door open and reached inside, grabbing the woman by the hair on her head and tried to jerk her out of the car. Randy was yelling at Beulah to let the woman go, and he attempted to hit Beulah and knock her loose from the hold she had on his female companion. The red light turned green, but all the traffic at the intersection came to a halt because everyone was watching the three of them. Randy started moving the car forward and told Beulah if she didn't let go he would drag her butt down the road. Beulah let go and jumped away from the car. The traffic stopped completely for Beulah to get out of the street. Many of the cars honked their horns at Randy when they noticed what he had done to Beulah.

By this time, the landlord was carrying Sandra toward Beulah on the sidewalk. He told Beulah he had never seen anybody do what she just did and survive. He made Beulah promise never to do that again, because if she had gotten killed who would take care of Sandra. That night, around 1:00 a.m. Beulah heard Randy coming into the apartment. She was waiting on him with a hunting knife in her hand. When he came through the door she lunged at him and stuck the knife to his stomach. She told him she wanted to kill him, but he wasn't worth her going to prison over. Randy called Beulah a crazy bitch and went to bed.

Three months later, in July 1966, Beulah was pregnant for the sixth time. Randy decided he did not want to work for Hobert anymore and took Sandra and Beulah to live in Benton, Tennessee, where he got a job working on another dairy farm. Beulah agreed because Billy and his wife, Linda, and Uncle Defoyst Mowery and his wife, Wilma, also lived in Benton. Beulah thought she and Sandra would be safe living near relatives. The owner of the dairy farm said they could live there rent-free with a small salary in exchange for work. This old house was in bad shape, but it was much better than the school bus they lived in at the Powells' dairy farm in Sweetwater.

The house was located next to the barn, and in the summertime the flies swarmed by the hundreds, but it had electricity, running water and inside plumbing. Beulah and Sandra stayed inside the house most of the time to avoid the flies and gnats. There was no air conditioning, and it was like an oven inside the house. One night, Beulah fixed black-eyed peas and cornbread for Randy. The flies were swarming inside the house so bad, Randy ate a few flies before he realized it, and he made Beulah stand in front of him with a paper fan to keep the flies off his food. This made Randy so angry that he slung the rest of his food all over the floor and stormed out the door. It wasn't long after this incident that Randy decided to take off again. He left Beulah and Sandra alone at the dairy farm in Benton.

Beulah was upset and went to see her brother, Billy, who let her and Sandra stay with him. Uncle Defoyst and Aunt Wilma also lived nearby and helped Beulah and invited her and Sandra into their home. Beulah kept hoping that Randy would come back, but after a couple of weeks she knew she wouldn't see him again for a long time.

One day, while Beulah and Sandra were visiting with Wilma, Wilma told Beulah that she had a good friend who lived in Chattanooga who was desperately seeking a baby to adopt. Wilma said she had talked to her friend and told her about Beulah's problems. Wilma's friend told her she would gladly take Beulah and Sandra into her home, provide medical care and a safe environment for them if Beulah would let the woman and her husband adopt Beulah's expected baby. They did not care if it was a boy or a girl. Beulah wanted to meet this couple before she made any decisions, so Wilma drove them to Chattanooga to meet her friends, Mr. and Mrs. Anderson. They lived in an upscale neighborhood and had a beautiful home. The Andersons welcomed Beulah and Sandra into their home and treated them with love and kindness. Mrs. Anderson was an average-sized woman, about 5 feet 7 inches, with a fair complexion and light short hair. She was a very attractive, sophisticated woman who spoke softly. Mr. Anderson was a slender-built man, around 5 feet 9 inches, with dark hair. He was average looking and very well groomed. He was a quiet, serious kind of guy. They were probably in their early thirties. Mr. Anderson had a full-time job and went to work every day. Mrs. Anderson did not work and stayed home with Beulah and Sandra. They had tried for years to have a baby of their own. They loved children and desperately wanted a child. Mrs. Anderson and Beulah became friends. The Andersons provided Beulah and Sandra with all the necessities they needed and made them feel welcome and very comfortable in their home.

Once a month, Mrs. Anderson would take Beulah to her doctor. This was the first time that Beulah had received any prenatal care. They made all the arrangements with their attorney for the legal adoption procedure, and Beulah signed the paperwork in his office. This was the only time anyone had ever explained the adoption procedure to Beulah and asked her if she understood what she was signing.

The night Beulah went into labor it was pouring rain. Beulah awoke Mrs. Anderson, who drove them to Erlanger Hospital in Chattanooga. Mr. Anderson stayed at home with Sandra. Beulah gave birth to Scarlet on April 30, 1967, at the age of 23. Beulah stayed in the hospital for three days and was released. Mrs. Anderson took Beulah and Scarlet back to her home to care for them. They were very excited over the birth of Scarlet. Scarlet had big blue eyes and blond hair just like Sandra. Mrs. Anderson immediately bonded with Scarlet and loved her with all her heart. Beulah knew that Scarlet would be loved and would grow up in a loving home. Mrs. Anderson told Beulah she could hold Scarlet, but Beulah knew if she held Scarlet in her arms she would not want to give her away.

Five days after Beulah had returned to the Anderson home, Randy pulled into their driveway. Beulah was shocked to see him. She went outside and asked him how he knew where she was. He told her, "I've got my ways." Randy never asked Beulah about the baby that was just born. He wasn't interested in even knowing whether it was a girl or a boy. Beulah asked Randy why he came there. He said he wanted Beulah and Sandra to go with him to Okeechobee, Florida. He said he had gotten a job on a large dairy farm and they would furnish them with a house and a paycheck. He said everything was furnished in the house and the only thing he would have to buy was food. Beulah asked him why he was telling her all that. Randy told Beulah that she and Sandra could no longer stay with the Andersons and asked Beulah where she thought she would go. He told Beulah he wanted her and Sandra to come with him and that it would be better. Beulah told him it better be, because she was sick and tired of living this way and now they had a daughter to take care of. He promised Beulah, again, that things would be better and told her to go back into the house and get their stuff and tell whoever … thanks, so they could get on the road.

Randy did not meet nor have any desire to meet the couple who had adopted his daughter, Scarlet. Beulah went back into the house and told Mrs. Anderson that she was leaving with Randy. Mrs. Anderson was very kind and promised Beulah that she would take very good care of Scarlet and for her not to worry. She hugged Beulah and Sandra good-bye and watched them get into the car and leave with Randy.

On the trip to Okeechobee, Randy refused to buy diapers for Sandra, who at the time was only 13 months old. Randy told Beulah she needed to get Sandra off the diapers and the next store he found he was going to buy her training panties. He did not want to spend his money on diapers for his own daughter. By the time they reached Okeechobee, Beulah almost had Sandra potty trained. She would sit little Sandra, who was very tiny, on the toilets at the rest areas or would let her squat down by the car.

The trip to Okeechobee took two days. Randy rented a nasty, bug-infested room for them to sleep in. The room was infested with cockroaches, and Beulah sat up all night watching Sandra to make sure no bugs crawled on her. Beulah stuffed toilet paper in Sandra's little ears just in case she too fell asleep. Beulah was surprised when they arrived at the dairy farm the next day, because it was exactly the way Randy had said it was. They moved into a large white block house with a big front yard for Sandra to play in. The house was very clean and well taken care of. While Beulah was standing and looking at all this she said to herself, "Please Lord, let everything be all right this time."

For a little while, things were going okay. Beulah had started to relax and Sandra was happy being with Mommy and Daddy. On days that Randy didn't have to work, he would ride Beulah and Sandra around in his car to show them the area. Randy took them to a pier to see the ocean for the first time. Beulah was thrilled because she had never seen this much blue water in her life. Randy was also giving Beulah and Sandra more of his attention and time, and Beulah thought everything was fine.

Randy seemed to be happy, and Beulah thought everything would be okay. This happiness only lasted from May 1967 until March of 1968 when once again, Beulah was pregnant. Randy's good behavior and attitude started changing after Beulah announced her pregnancy to him. Several days later Randy came rushing into the house and told Beulah that he had just received an urgent call at the dairy farm from his sister. He told Beulah they needed to leave immediately and ordered her to get Sandra because they were leaving. He told Beulah not to bother packing, because they wouldn't be gone long and one change of clothes was all they would need.

During this trip, Randy drove nonstop. He drove all day and all night and arrived in Athens the next day around noon. Randy left Beulah and Sandra in Billy's front yard and said he would be back later that night to pick them up, but he never showed up. Sandra had bonded with Randy and cried for him after he disappeared. This upset Beulah because she felt the same pain that Sandra felt. Beulah and Sandra stayed with Billy and Linda. Linda was also pregnant with their second child.

Beulah went into labor on October 22, 1968, and gave birth to another daughter she named Teresa, at the age of 24. Teresa was born at the Foree Hospital in Athens, Tennessee. When Beulah was released from the hospital, she and Teresa returned to Billy's home. Beulah knew they were cramped for space in Billy's small home that he rented. She helped Linda with the housework and took care of the children, but Beulah knew this could only be a temporary situation.

There had been no calls or visits from Randy since he dropped them off. Beulah had no idea where he was unless he returned to Okeechobee without her and Sandra. He knew Beulah was pregnant, but he wasn't the least bit concerned. As the weeks went by, Linda could tell that Beulah was worried about how she could raise both her little girls alone. Billy made good money, but he and Linda were having their own children and had many expenses. Because Billy was employed, they did not qualify for food stamps or state assistance.

One day Linda asked Beulah to sit down, because she needed to speak to her about a very important matter. Linda told Beulah that she had an older sister and brother-in-law who knew of her situation and would love to adopt Teresa and raise her as their own child. Beulah told Linda no, that she couldn't do it because she had already lost five children. Linda told Beulah she couldn't tell her what to do, but she should think it over and to try to put the child's needs before her own desire to keep her. Linda had a lot of sympathy for Beulah, but she was concerned about how Beulah was going to take care of herself and two little girls with Randy out of the picture.

Linda knew that Beulah would like her sister and brother-in-law if she only knew them, so one day she invited them to her house to meet Beulah. Linda was right. Her sister and her brother-in-law talked to Beulah for a very long time. They told Beulah that if she would let them have Teresa they would take very good care of her. They told Beulah they had a daughter and a son and had lost another son at birth. Beulah could tell that they loved their children very much and were good parents. As they continued to talk to Beulah about her situation and how they could help her, as much as Beulah hated herself, she decided the best thing for her to do for Teresa was to let them adopt her and raise her in a loving home.

Beulah continued to stay with Billy and Linda and help take care of their daughter while Linda was in the hospital. Linda went into labor weeks before her due date. To everyone's surprise Linda was carrying twins and delivered them prematurely. Billy and Linda were not equipped to care for twins, so Beulah stayed to help care for them.

Several months later, as the twins got bigger and much stronger, Beulah decided it was time for her to find a job so she and Sandra could get a place of their own. Beulah's sister, Barbara Jean, helped her to get a job at Robett, Inc., in Riceville, Tennessee. Barbara would come by and pick Beulah up and take her to work. This was the first job Beulah ever had. She worked as an inspector for men's clothing. Beulah saved her money and when she had enough to get her own house or apartment she looked in the newspaper to see what was available in the Athens area.

Beulah found a house at 515 Hillside Lane. She got a childhood friend from Tin Can Holler to drive her to the house so she could look at it. As they were going up the hill to the house, Beulah saw a man working in his yard. This man and Beulah exchanged glances and smiles at each other. At that moment, Beulah had no idea that this man would become a very important person in her future.

Beulah loved the house and felt safe because the landlord owned a bigger house directly in front of her. It was only a one-bedroom, but it was affordable and she liked the location. The only furniture in the house was a bed. The landlord gave her a couple of forks, glasses, plates and a cooking pan. It was early spring in 1969, and Beulah still had not seen or heard from Randy.

Beulah continued to work and do the best she could for Sandra. One afternoon, when Beulah got home from work, the man who lived in the first house on the hill began knocking at her door. He introduced himself as Elvon Daily. He told Beulah that he knew her father, Seig, and remembered her when she was a child in Tin Can Holler. Elvon offered Beulah and Sandra a big bowl of poached rabbit that he had cooked. Beulah accepted it, and she and Sandra feasted that night. Beulah, at the time, did not know that Elvon was the father of the man she exchanged glances with. After that night, whenever Beulah would be outside, Elvon would holler at her and would talk to her across the fence. Beulah enjoyed these friendly conversations because she did not have a radio or a television and nobody to talk to but Sandra.

Several weeks went by, and unknown to Beulah, Elvon was telling his son all about her and Sandra. Late one afternoon, Elvon called Beulah and invited her to come to his house. Beulah got Sandra and walked over. He introduced Beulah to his son, Ray. At that moment, Beulah realized that Ray was the man she exchanged glances with on the day she moved into her house.

Beulah had never been with another man besides Randy, and she was very shy around Ray. After that day, Ray started coming to the fence to talk to Beulah and would always give Sandra candy. Ray and Beulah continued to talk across the fence for several weeks, and then Beulah invited him to sit on her porch. Beulah felt that she should be honest with Ray and let him know that she was married. Ray told Beulah he knew all about her life with Randy because her girlfriend from Tin Can Holler told him everything. Ray told Beulah that he was currently in a relationship and didn't know where it was going. He said he didn't see any harm in the two of them talking.

Beulah was now 25 years old and was getting her life in order and felt very comfortable about her friendship with her neighbor, Ray Daily. Ray was a 34-year-old bachelor who shared his home with his dad, Elvon. He was 5 feet 9 inches and weighed about 165 pounds. He was slender and kept himself in good shape. Beulah thought he was very handsome and enjoyed his company immensely. Sandra also liked him, because he would play with her in the yard. Ray was very sweet and shy in an innocent way that Beulah found very attractive. He was also a down-to-earth gentle man. She had never met anyone like Ray before.

Everything was going along fine until one afternoon when Beulah noticed a nice car coming up the hill. She had never seen this car before and wondered who it was. A couple of seconds later the car pulled into her driveway and Randy opened the car door and stepped out. Beulah screamed, "Why in God's name are you here?" Randy replied, "I've been looking for you and Sandra!" Beulah told him she didn't need him in her life anymore … she wanted him out of her life. He told Beulah that she was his wife and Sandra was his daughter and he had a right to be there. Beulah told him no, he did not, because he had walked out on them and she couldn't believe he had the nerve to show up again after she had to give another baby away. So, there they stood arguing in the front yard, creating a scene.

Beulah's landlord came out of his home that was directly in front of her house and told them to stop all the yelling and quiet down. The landlord did not want his children hearing them argue. Randy followed Beulah into the house. She asked him where he had been all this time. He said he had been running around, working here and there. Beulah told Randy that she was working, she and Sandra were happy and she was trying to make it on her own. He told Beulah he wanted to stay with her for a couple of weeks to see if they could patch things up. He claimed he wanted to make up for leaving her and Sandra. Beulah told him she would prefer that he leave and get out of her house, but she didn't want to cause a scene in front of her landlord and in front of Sandra.

Beulah said okay but for only a couple of weeks. She didn't trust him for a minute and knew he was just blowing smoke. He started taking Beulah and Sandra for rides in his car when Beulah got home from work each day. One Friday night, Randy took them to the drive-in movies. When they arrived home and pulled into the driveway, Beulah told Randy that somebody must been in her house, because the lights were turned on and she always turned the lights off. Beulah jumped out of the car and ran to open the front door to her house. In front of Beulah stood a woman she had never seen before ripping Randy's clothes.

This unknown woman was much bigger than Beulah with strawberry blond hair. She stood about 5 feet 5 inches and probably weighed 150 pounds. This woman also had on Beulah's necklace, which she grabbed off her neck and asked her what in God's name was she doing in her house. She told Beulah that she was Randy's wife! Beulah told her no, she wasn't, that she was his wife and Sandra was his daughter. Beulah and this woman had a nasty confrontation in the living room, because this woman was hysterical. Beulah told her she could prove she was his wife. This woman also said she could prove she was Randy's wife. Beulah told her she married Randy in 1959 at the age of 15. Beulah ordered Randy and this woman out of her house and not to come back or she would call the police.

Beulah found out later that this woman had taken a taxi from downtown Athens, after getting off a bus from Nashville, Tennessee. She took a taxi to the top of the hill and knocked on Elvon Daily's door asking where Beulah lived. Elvon told this woman where Beulah lived, because he thought it was one of her sisters coming to visit her. As soon as Ray heard about what happened at Beulah's house, he went to see Beulah to make sure she and Sandra were okay. Ray told Beulah that she needed to get rid of that garbage once and for all and not to have anything else to do with Randy. He told Beulah that Randy did not love her; because a man who loves a woman does not do all the horrible things Randy had done. Ray also told Beulah that he broke it off with his girlfriend and would like to start courting her. He reassured her that they would go very slow, because he knew how badly she had been hurt by Randy.

A few days later, Beulah's landlord came to see her and told her that he did not want anymore fussing and fighting and people coming on his property. He hated to evict her, but it would be better if she found another place to live.

Beulah talked to Ray and told him about her dilemma. She immediately started looking for another house or apartment and found one in town. She moved into a one-bedroom furnished apartment with the landlord living upstairs. Her landlord, who was known as Mae Brown, was an older woman who lived alone and was set in her ways. She did not want anyone coming around unless they rented from her. When she found out that Ray was visiting Beulah, she would walk right into Beulah's apartment and start talking. This constant interference irritated Ray and Beulah, because they could not have any time together.

This courtship with Ray was a new experience for Beulah. Ray lifted her spirits and made her feel like a schoolgirl again. He was so attentive to Beulah that she didn't know how to act around him. She was shy and giggled a lot. Ray treated Beulah with a kindness that she had never experienced from a man. After two weeks, Beulah moved out of Mae Brown's apartment. She found another one-bedroom partly furnished apartment for her and Sandra on Depot Hill in Athens. Beulah needed a car, so she borrowed money from the Security Finance Company and bought her first car. The relationship with Ray continued to blossom even though Ray had a lot of male friends he enjoyed spending time with. They were sports fanatics and hung out together in their homes. Beulah accepted the friendship he had with his buddies and never complained. Everything was wonderful in her relationship with Ray.

Randy wouldn't leave Beulah alone, even after she made it perfectly clear that she no longer loved him. He knocked on her door late one night holding a little boy and asked her to watch his son for him! Beulah's blood began to boil and her blood pressure rose. She called him a lowdown dirty dog....and said, "How dare you … how dare you … bring another woman's baby here and want me to watch it … how crazy do you think I am?" "You left me, and I had to give away my babies and you think I will watch your son you fathered by another woman while we are still married?" She screamed at him and ordered him to leave. She threatened to call the police because he had committed bigamy by marrying that other woman from Nashville, Tennessee, years earlier. He had married another woman and fathered two sons by her while married to Beulah. He took his son and left in a hurry.

Beulah's romance with Ray continued. She fell madly in love with him and gave birth to their first daughter on September 15, 1972, at the age of 28. She named their daughter Tracey Lee. Tracey was five days old when Beulah went to court to finalize her divorce from Randy. Ray went to court with Beulah and held Tracey as they stood in front of the judge. On their way out of the courthouse Ray turned to Beulah and said, "Thank God that man is out of your life!" Beulah felt as though the weight of the world had been lifted off her shoulders and acknowledged what Ray had said with a big smile.

When Randy realized that Beulah was going to divorce him, he sent his mother to Beulah's apartment to try and change her mind. Beulah told her, "Randy is like an old record you play over and over. He has been playing the same tune since 1959, and now the record is broken" and she wanted him and anyone associated with him out of her life forever! Beulah ordered her to get out of her apartment and never come back again.

As Randy's mother left her apartment, Beulah wondered how many other women he may have married or co-habitated with and how many other children he may have fathered. He had deserted her so many times, he probably did the same thing to many other women. Beulah wondered how many other women Randy had victimized and regretted that it had taken her 13 years to remove the spell he had over her. She was grateful to Ray for his love, understanding and encouragement. He opened her eyes, showed her true love and gave her the courage to end her relationship with Randy permanently.

On May 9, 1974, Beulah gave birth to Ray's first son, Jason Ray. Beulah was now 30 years old. As soon as Ray heard the news from work, he raced to the hospital to meet his son and to check on Beulah. Ray was ecstatic and very proud. Beulah and Ray never consummated their relationship in marriage. Ray asked Beulah to marry him and promised to be a father to all three of her children, including Sandra. Beulah loved Ray with all her heart, but she had been scarred so badly by Randy that she was afraid to take a chance. She continued her relationship with Ray and their friendship strengthened as the years went by. She knew that Ray would always be her best friend.

Ray was a wonderful dad to all the children and always treated Beulah with the utmost respect. Beulah allowed him to see his children anytime he wanted. Ray helped Beulah financially and always spent every holiday with her and the children. He also made sure that the children had plenty of toys for Christmas. He wanted to lavish Beulah with gifts, but she would not allow it, not even flowers. She told Ray that having him in her life was the best gift of all and that he was the most wonderful man she ever knew. Beulah felt that she was the luckiest woman in the world to have a man who loved her like Ray did, but deep in her soul she thought she was not worthy of him because of her past and growing up in Tin Can Holler.

Ray knew about her past, but he never looked down upon her or criticized her for any of her past actions. He tried to reassure Beulah that what happened in her past was not her fault. He repeatedly told her that if anyone should be blamed, it was Randy. Beulah always said Ray was a kind man with a heart as big as Texas. As the children grew, Ray helped them move into a larger apartment and was always there for them if they needed him. All Beulah had to do was call him and he would come.

In 1989 Beulah's daughter, Sandra, at the age of 23, moved to Calhoun, Georgia. A year later, Beulah's daughter, Tracey Lee, moved to Calhoun to live and work with her older sister. In 1991 Beulah took Jason, who was 17, and moved to Calhoun to be near her daughters. Whenever she and her children visited in the Athens area, they would always call Ray. They knew he had a serious medical condition, but they did not know it was as serious as it was. On September 6, 1997, Ray passed away. When Beulah received the call that Ray had died, a little part of her died with him. She regretted that she never married Ray and moved the children into his home as he had asked her to do so many times. By the time Beulah and the children found out that Ray had passed away, they had missed his funeral.

Nine years after Ray's death, Beulah and the children were told by his sister that he was asking for them before he died. He wanted to see and talk to them one last time. Ray continues to contact Beulah through her dreams. He comes to her when she is sleeping and lies with her in his arms. He tells her that he loves her and that everything will be okay. Beulah never understood the meaning of her dreams until she found out that he was asking for her and the children on his deathbed.

Beulah's fears from her past kept her from enjoying her life. She was an overly-protective mother with Sandra, Tracey and Jason and worried about them constantly. She did not want them to go to school because they would be out of her reach and her protection. Most children cry when they start to school, but Beulah was the one crying.

Through the years, Beulah has also carried the memories and the pain of losing her other six beautiful children. Every time Beulah had to give up one of her children, a piece of her heart died. Today she has severe heart problems and it's because of all the times it has been broken.

One Sunday morning, during the late 1970s, Beulah took Sandra, Tracie and Jason to Mr. Sips, a convenient store, in Athens. As she stood at the counter to be helped, Beulah heard someone come in behind her, because of the bell on the door. She thought one of her children had followed her inside the store, so she turned to look. As she looked around, a young man walked up next to her. She suddenly became weak and started shaking. As she looked at this young man she knew immediately that it was her son, Eddie. She breathed hard and found the courage to speak to him. She asked him if he was Eddie from Sweetwater. He replied, "Yes, how did you know?" Beulah told him she had been in his parents' store before, and they had shown her a picture of him. Of course, that was not true, but she had to tell him something so not to cause any suspicions on his part. That's all the words that were exchanged between the two of them, and Eddie purchased a pack of cigarettes and walked out of the store. Beulah stared at him until he got out of sight.

When Beulah returned to her car, Sandra was sitting in the front seat next to her. She asked Sandra if she saw Eddie coming out of the store and Sandra acknowledged that she had. Beulah told Sandra that Eddie was her big brother. Sandra asked, "He is my big brother?" Beulah said, "Yes, and I had to give him away." She told Sandra she couldn't help it. At that moment Sandra started crying and kept repeating, "I've got a big brother." Sandra cried all the way home. Beulah thought about this encounter for months and how happy she was to see Eddie. Eddie had grown into a very well-mannered, handsome young man, and she could tell that he had a proper upbringing. She was so overjoyed to see that he looked healthy as he stood next to her wearing his toboggan cap.

As this story was being written, Beulah's fourth son, Michael, found Beulah through her sister, Rozetta. Michael placed an ad in one of the local newspapers in the Sweetwater area searching for his siblings. Both of Michael's adopted parents had passed away, and Michael was yearning to find his biological family. The ad was seen by Cindy's youngest daughter. She called Rozetta in Florida and read the ad to her over the telephone. The next day Rozetta called Michael on the telephone. They talked for a very long time. Rozetta promised Michael that she would come see him on her next visit to Tennessee, which was planned for February 2006. Rozetta told Michael that she was writing a book about their family tragedy and was very excited that Michael could be reunited with his biological family. In February 2006, as promised, Rozetta traveled to Sweetwater to personally meet Michael for the very first time. It was a moment they will never forget. Since their first meeting, Michael has become a very important part of her life. Michael met his older brother Nathan years earlier and took Rozetta to meet him too.

Several days later, Rozetta traveled to Resaca, Georgia, to find her sister Beulah to tell her the wonderful news about her sons, Michael and Nathan. Beulah was excited and nervous at the same time. On August 3, 2006, as a birthday surprise to Michael, Rozetta took him to Resaca, Georgia, to meet his mother. It was a magnificent reunion of mother and son with a river of tears that flowed from every eye in the house. Beulah held Michael in a bear hug for a very long time and cried on his shoulder. Michael, too, cried with his mother. It was tears of pure joy that they finally found each other after 42 years of separation.

Michael told the family that his adopted parents said they paid over $10,000 to adopt him. He also recalled the first time he met Randy. Randy looked at Michael and stated, "If you have a problem with the way you were adopted, you can turn around and go back out that door!" Beulah was shocked and angry because she was never given any money. She never sold any of her babies and never received any money from anyone! Money was never mentioned. The entire family was upset and wanted to know who got all that money. Laura had brought the adoption papers to Beulah's hospital room on the day Michael was born. There was no attorney involved, so the only person who could have taken the money was Laura! Beulah felt terrible that Michael may have believed all his life that she sold him for money. Laura always told Beulah she would handle everything on the adoptions of her four boys.

We will never know how much money was exchanged or given to Laura for all four of Beulah's sons. Beulah always remembered Laura approaching her and convincing her that she wasn't capable or financially able to provide for her children. Laura always knew couples who wanted Beulah's children. How did Laura find these couples? Was she searching for someone to pay her for finding them a baby? Did she use the money to persuade Randy to sign off on the adoptions? Was there a connection between Randy and Laura? We do not have the answers to these questions and may never find out the truth. Beulah, after finding out this information, cried and cried. She felt that she had purposely been used as a baby-making machine for the profit of others. Michael and Beulah write to each other weekly. The lines of communication will never be broken again.

As of the publishing of this book, Beulah lives with her daughter, Tracey Lee, and her grandson in Georgia. She remains a recluse and never comes out of her home unless she has to. Her daughter, Sandra, and her son, Jason, visit with her weekly, trying to encourage her to forget the past and to start living again. Beulah built a protective barrier around herself and refuses to talk to anyone other than her siblings and her children. She doesn't want to have anything to do with the outside world. She wants other women who read her story and who are victims in similar situations not to let any man do to them what she allowed Randy to do to her.

Beulah's favorite song is "I Just Called to Say I Love You" because that is what she wanted to say to her six children whom she had to give away. She fought with herself for years because she wanted to call and check on her children, but she believed it would be best not to interfere. She did not want to upset the families who adopted her children. She hopes all her children will read this book and understand how difficult it was to give them up and that she always carried them in her heart. She said the good Lord was watching over her children, because their biological father was only concerned about himself, not the well-being or safety of his own children. Beulah had only her children's best interest at heart even though it broke her heart.

Due to her circumstances, she knew she was doing the right thing for her children. Today, Nathan is 46, Gary is 45, Eddie is 43, Michael is 42, Scarlet is 39 and Teresa is 38 years old. Beulah hopes that each of them is living a happy life filled with love, peace and happiness. Now that the truth is known, she hopes her children will forgive her. Rozetta promised Beulah she would do everything possible to find all her children. Rozetta has made contact with all of her children except Gary and Eddie. Their whereabouts are unknown.

CHAPTER 29

Eliza's third child and only son, Billy, was 13 years old when she died. Billy was a very confused young man after Eliza's death. He had been a difficult child and hated authority, because Seig was not a good role model for him. Life in Tin Can Holler was all Billy had ever known, and he felt comfortable there. He knew everybody and everybody knew him. He thought he was tough and could take care of himself, but he knew this time was going to be different. This time he knew his life would never be the same and there would be no family to come back to. None of Eliza's family members came forward to offer any help or to take any of her children, even on a temporary basis, so Billy did not know what was going to happen to him.

In the past, when Seig was sent to jail or prison he always returned and got the family back together when he was released. Billy knew that Seig would not be coming home for a very long time and there would be no returning to the life as he had always known it, carefree and running wild in Tin Can Holler doing as he pleased. He felt alone, angry and afraid. Billy knew he would be taken away to a place he did not want to go. This became a reality three months after Eliza's death.

Cindy had been informed by the Department of Public Welfare that the Holston Methodist Home had been notified about the children by Reverend Gordon Sterchi from the Keith Memorial United Methodist Church on the request of Harry Evans, who was an active member of that church. The orphanage that had taken the children before would be sending their former case worker, Miss Flenniken, to pick up Billy and all his little sisters. They would be returning to Greeneville, Tennessee, to be placed into the foster care system again.   Billy did not want to go and told everybody he wasn't going back to that place.

Billy was staying with friends in Tin Can Holler when Clifford Charles, who lived across the street from the Mowerys in Tin Can Holler, told him one day that Uncle Harry wanted to see him. Billy rushed to see Uncle Harry. He told Uncle Harry he did not want to be sent away and begged him to stay with him. Uncle Harry felt sorry for Billy and told him he could stay with him in his home in Athens. Billy knew that Uncle Harry had always been a family friend and had looked out for the Mowery family from a distance all his life, but did not know why. He did not know if Uncle Harry would help him, but he was desperate and did not want to be sent away. Uncle Harry was very involved in the local community in Athens and everyone knew him, including the local authorities, so when Billy moved into Uncle Harry's house, no one questioned him. The local authorities did not threaten to come get Billy. Billy thought that was strange since Uncle Harry wasn't a family member, but he did not care what anybody thought or said as long as they left him alone. He only wanted to do his own thing.

Uncle Harry gave Billy one of the bedrooms on the second floor of his huge two-story house. He had his own television set and a radio/stereo. Billy was thrilled because he had never had a room to call his very own. Uncle Harry got him back into the Forest Hills School and gave Billy spending money every day. Billy was comfortable and secure living with Uncle Harry but still had the urge to escape at night and hang out with his Tin Can Holler buddies. He would sneak out of his second-floor bedroom by climbing out his bedroom window onto the roof and jumping down to the ground. He would return in the middle of the night or early morning by climbing back up the same way he climbed down without waking Uncle Harry.

Everything was fine between Uncle Harry and Billy, but Uncle Harry had a live-in housekeeper/cook/butler by the name of Mr. Edgemon, who did not like Billy. Mr. Edgemon did everything for Uncle Harry; he cooked and cleaned, did the laundry, washed the cars and mowed the grass. He did all the grocery shopping and ran errands whenever Uncle Harry needed something. Uncle Harry didn't do anything except come home and sit in one of his many rocking chairs on his front porch. He would sit there every night admiring the view of downtown Athens.

Mr. Edgemon was a man in his late fifties or early sixties who stood about 6 feet 2 inches and weighed about 250 pounds. He was balding with light brown thin hair. He had worked for Uncle Harry for 25 or 30 years and was set in his ways. He was Uncle Harry's servant but made it very clear to Uncle Harry that he was not going to be a servant for Billy. He was a grumpy old man and did not have patience for Billy's silly antics. Billy would come home from school and would immediately go to the kitchen where Mr. Edgemon usually stayed. This annoyed Mr. Edgemon. Billy would aggravate him by turning the TV channel to watch the "Three Stooges," and Mr. Edgemon would turn the channel back to the program he was watching. Mr. Edgemon complained about Billy to Uncle Harry all the time to no avail.

Eventually, Mr. Edgemon couldn't stand it any longer. He wanted to get rid of Billy for good. He threw chicken bones under the dining room table one night and told Uncle Harry that Billy threw them there. Billy became outraged that Mr. Edgemon had falsely accused him. Billy and Mr. Edgemon had a verbal confrontation in the kitchen in front of Uncle Harry. Mr. Edgemon gave Uncle Harry an ultimatum, "It's me or that kid. If you don't get rid of him, I will quit." Uncle Harry did not want Mr. Edgemon to leave his employment, and he knew that Billy did not want to go back to the Holston Home in Greeneville, Tennessee.

Unbeknownst to Billy, Uncle Harry went to the Department of Public Welfare and talked to them about other placement alternatives for Billy. Several days later, a man from that office came to visit Billy and Uncle Harry. This man convinced Billy that he would like the TPS in Nashville and if he didn't choose to go there he would immediately be sent to Greeneville. Billy decided he would rather go to the TPS and told this man okay. Two days later two police officers in a police car showed up at Uncle Harry's home. They told Billy it was time for him to leave for his trip to Nashville and they were going to personally drive him there. Billy wasn't eager to leave, but he said good-bye to Uncle Harry and went with the two police officers.

The trip to Nashville went fine. Billy thought it was cool riding in a police car since he had never been in one before, which he thought was a good thing. The two police officers sat in the front seat and Billy sat alone in the back seat. They talked to Billy and had long conversations with him. The police officers stopped at a little town and took Billy into a restaurant and bought him lunch. They bought Billy a hamburger, french fries and a coke.

When they arrived at the TPS in Nashville, Billy's first impression was fear. There were kids everywhere, staring at him getting out of the police car. He was afraid he couldn't blend in with all those kids, but he soon found out it was easy. The Tennessee Preparatory School was not a reformatory or a treatment center. It was a place that provided a home and education to children who did not have the opportunity to have these things in their own family environment. The school had no fences, and the children were not locked in. The property consisted of 365 acres of land and some 50 permanent buildings, but there were no security guards or police officers. It helped neglected, abused and underprivileged children. The TPS was a co-ed school with girls on one end of the campus and the boys on the other. They accepted children of all ages and housed the children in separate dorms according to their ages. The coaches would tell the boys they could look all they wanted, wish all they wanted, and think all they wanted, but to keep their hands off! Billy's house parents were Mr. and Mrs. Hearn, who had three children of their own. Their quarters were on the first floor, and their children's rooms were next to theirs. Billy's room was on the second floor. He shared a large room with 30 other boys. The beds were lined up around the wall. On one side of the room were large windows with Venetian blinds.

They had their own elementary school and high school with excellent teachers. The high school had a large trophy display case in the hallway. Billy has several trophies in the display case that he won in track-and-field competitions. He could outrun and out-jump the seniors, but it didn't count because he wasn't a senior. He won his trophies in the 100-yard dash, 440-relay and the running broad-jump when he competed with other schools. The large football field, baseball field and track were located directly behind the high school. Billy wasn't old enough to play any of the sports, but his friend, Larry Wayne Nathans, played football, baseball and basketball. He was good in all three of these sports. Many of kids at TPS were so good, they received college scholarships.

Billy had a math teacher he really liked. He was an older man who would tap the children lightly on their heads with a stick if they were not paying attention to him. He didn't care what the children did as long as they paid attention while they were in his class. The school had one of the best academic curricula in Tennessee, a superb athletic program, an excellent vocational program, and many student clubs and organizations. The children competed in all the surrounding local school competitions.

They had their own hospital and a separate building where the children were assigned work details when they were not in class. There was structure and discipline. The children knew what they were supposed to do from the time they awoke in the morning until they went to bed at night. This was something Billy had never known. They had their own church building, and on Saturday nights they would pull down a large screen in the church and entertain the children with a movie and popcorn. The TPS also had its own large cafeteria. All the children gathered there for their meals. Each dorm had to take turns working in the cafeteria. The children would assist with the cooking, serving and cleanup duties. They rotated the dorms weekly so all the children participated during the month. Directly behind the kitchen were the railroad tracks.

The children who saved their money would be allowed to go shopping for clothes and shoes in downtown Nashville. Their work detail assignments also paid them small wages. This taught the children how to earn money and how to save their money for the things they wanted. One of the work buildings at the TPS was set up with a printing press. The children would print professional stationery and envelopes for companies around Nashville. This provided additional revenue for the school to operate. The state of Tennessee subsidized the TPS, but additional funding was needed in order to provide the children with the best care and education possible, so they could compete for scholarships just as all the other public school children did.

Billy's work assignment was to assist the driver who delivered the stationery to the various offices around Nashville. The driver, who was an older man employed by the TPS, would sit in his panel truck smoking his pipe, while Billy delivered the boxes of stationery. Billy knew people on a first-name basis at the Capitol building. The driver would back his panel truck up to the loading dock at the back of the Capitol building. Billy would unload all the boxes and separate them according to what floor they were to be delivered to. He loaded them onto a two-wheel dolly and took the freight elevator to each floor. He walked down a long hallway to each office and someone signed for the deliveries. He also delivered to all the state buildings, including the Cordell Hull and Clover Bottom buildings. They would also make stops for deliveries at the Central State Mental Hospital which was located southeast of the city. Billy liked this job because he was given a lot of freedom going into the office buildings. He met many nice people and was liked by everyone who met him.

The biggest boys on campus would mow the grass during the spring, summer and fall. The campus grounds were huge; 365 acres is a lot of grass to mow, but the school owned about 100 push mowers with revolving blades to cut the grass. They would line the boys up at one end of the football field, each with a push mower. They would start walking down the football field, one behind the other. When the last one crossed the line they would be finished. They would use this same procedure all over the campus.

The TPS had an employee, an older man, who operated a farm and cannery on Berry Hill. Part of the Civil War was fought at this location. This employed farmer would plant the vegetables, and the boys would help pick and can them after harvest time. They would pick the corn, tomatoes, green beans and eggplant, and take them to the cannery for processing. The farmer was a nice man in his forties and was very good to the boys. One time when the boys were picking the corn and tossing them into the wagon, Billy accidentally hit him in the head with an ear of corn. Billy thought, "Oh God, I'm in trouble now!" Billy thought the farmer was going to get really mad at him, but the farmer said, "Ah, that's all right, son ... no harm was done ... accidents do happen." Billy told him that he reminded him of his dad because he had the same stature and wore a baseball cap just like Seig had.

At the cannery big pots were used to boil the tomatoes. After they were blanched, the tomatoes were placed in a trough in front of a big table. Billy and the other boys would sit for hours peeling skins off the tomatoes and placing them on a conveyor belt. They had a building where they stored all the processed canned food. The canned food provided many meals for all the children. The girls, who were not allowed in the cannery because of all the machinery, were assigned to the laundry room. Everyone had a job to do. The TPS was a highly organized, self-sufficient operating campus.

Young Billy was adjusting to his new lifestyle at the TPS, but he continually got into trouble. He would get spanked for smoking cigarettes. They had a ball bat that was sanded down to half an inch thick with holes drilled into it that they used to spank the oldest children. Sometimes, instead of spankings, the children would have to clean all the Venetian blinds in their room. The house mother, called the "Matron," would inspect their work with white gloves, and if she saw any speck of dust, they would have to start all over again.

Billy would save his wages, as would all the other children, but he wouldn't buy clothes. Instead, as he delivered the stationery in all the office buildings, he had access to the cigarette vending machines. Other children at the TPS who smoked, and knew Billy was getting cigarettes, would give him their money to purchase cigarettes for them, too. He would return with pockets full of different packs of cigarettes. Most of the girl smokers preferred the York brand because they were longer. The girls would break them in half and get two smokes out of them. All the children who smoked would hang out together. They would have a difficult time pronouncing Billy's last name, so they nicknamed him "Maverick." During dinnertime they would gobble down their food as fast as they could. Before they were allowed to leave the cafeteria, they were required to clean their trays and show them to the "Matron" who had cafeteria duty. This person was usually one of the house parents. Once the Matron acknowledged them by nodding her head, they could leave the cafeteria. They would run as fast as they could to the back of one of the big buildings. They would huddle at one end, usually in the corner, and smoke their cigarettes. Billy would buy cigarettes without filters, so they could let the entire cigarette burn out. They knew not to flip any cigarette butts on the ground. By the time the "Matron" came outside all the smoke would be gone and the kids would be on the basketball court.

Occasionally, the "Matron" would ring a very loud buzzer. Whenever she rang that buzzer, all the kids would line up in a single row on the sidewalk in front of their dorms to be inspected. She would sniff and smell each child as she walked down the sidewalk. If she smelled anything suspicious on any of them she would grab them by their shirt and pull them out of the line. They were made to stand there until she walked all the way to the end of the line. She could always pick out the smokers. She would determine their punishment. They knew it was either a spanking or cleaning the Venetian blinds. Sometimes she would walk into the boys' rooms at night to make sure they were behaving after the lights were turned off. She was strict with all the boys when it came to personal hygiene. She made sure they all brushed their teeth and took showers at the same time. Everything was done according to her regimented schedule. Whenever she heard the boys laughing and carousing in the big shower room, she would walk in with her big paddle and swat them on their behinds. They could hear her shoes clicking on the hallway floor as she paced down to the showers to see what all the commotion was about. The paddle would hurt like the devil when it landed on a naked fanny!

Billy quickly made a lot of new friends at the TPS, especially with the young ladies, because he was very handsome. The girls were goo-goo eyed over him, and he loved the attention he was receiving. He got a little too friendly with one girl, Anna Mae, and that upset her boyfriend. Anna Mae was very pretty and had long black hair. When this other young man saw his girlfriend walking with Billy and holding his arm, he became very angry and approached Billy. Billy was friends with Anna Mae and was escorting her to her dorm by way of the sidewalk. The boys were only allowed a certain distance from the girls' dorm before they had to stop. Billy and Anna Mae had stopped and were standing together talking when her boyfriend approached the two of them. He was much bigger, taller and older than Billy. He was in the oldest age group and lived in a different dorm. He approached Billy and tried to hit him. Billy, who is left-handed, swung at him from the left. Billy tried to hit him in the face, but he wasn't tall enough to reach him. Billy accidentally hit his windpipe, and the boy started having trouble breathing. He doubled over to catch his breath. From that moment on, this young man never bothered or approached Billy again. Katie was another young lady who admired Billy. When a new girl was admitted to the TPS she would ask the other girls, "What are we going to do to keep her away from Billy?"

As time passed, Billy talked to all the boys in his dorm to find out why they were at the TPS. Most of them came from broken homes, and some of them were court-ordered there. A small percentage of them were sent there by their parents, because they could not handle them at home. They were sent to the TPS to keep them out of trouble or to teach them a lesson because of their unacceptable behavior. Not all the children came from poor or low-income families, though. One young man, about Billy's age, was sent there by his parents. His name was Roy. He stayed in the same dorm as Billy and shared the same bedroom. Billy liked Roy and befriended him because he was a nice guy. All the boys thought he may have come from a wealthy family, because he had nicer shoes, shirts and Levi jeans. He was about the same size as Billy and would trade clothes with Billy sometimes. Billy and the other boys knew there was something wrong with Roy because he would go into rages of anger and throw fits, but nobody talked about it. The staff realized that his placement at the TPS was a mistake and they could not handle Roy's special needs. Roy was removed from the TPS. All the boys who shared a room with Roy wanted to know where he went. They were told that he was sent to a hospital where he could be properly diagnosed and treated. It wasn't long after he left that they received information that Roy had hanged himself in his hospital room. Sadness fell all across the campus. Everyone felt very bad about what had happened to their friend, Roy. The girls cried, and the boys consoled them.

Billy's birthday, December 8th, was just another day. He was now 14 years old. There was no birthday cake or birthday cards from anyone. Christmas also came and went, and Billy had no visitors and no letters from loved ones inquiring about him. Most of the children spent the holidays with their families, but those like Billy had to stay. There was a huge Christmas tree and presents for all the children. This year was special because a big truck loaded with boxes of gifts arrived from Elvis Presley! Elvis gave each child a special pink guitar with his signature on it! Billy also got a shirt and miscellaneous toiletries. Even though he had a good Christmas, Billy was overcome with sadness and depression. He eventually stopped asking if he had any letters, because he knew that no one was going to write. He thought about his little sisters, Barbara, Shelia, Marcella and Rozetta, and how much he missed them. He hoped they were okay. He also wondered how his big sisters, Beulah and Cindy, were doing. Other than his desire to continue smoking, Billy adjusted very well to his regimented schedule. He continued to make new friends and for the first time in his life, he was doing very well in school.

It was now the summer of 1960, and the children who did not have families to visit attended a two-week summer camp program before harvest time at the farm began. The children who had family members who took them for the summer either received bus tickets or a family member came to the TPS and picked them up. Billy had never been to a summer camp before and wondered what all the excitement was about. By this time, he and the other children were tired of school and wanted to have some fun. There was a lot of anticipation from the children as they awaited their turns to participate in the summer camp program. It finally came time for Billy's turn to go to camp. Summer camp was great, and Billy had a lot of fun swimming and canoeing. All the kids were transported in buses to Buffalo Mountain. It was similar to a Boy Scout camp with little buildings that had canvas roofs on them. They had a large dining hall with a full staff of cooks.

The children did not have to work at the camp. They were given lots of privileges as long as they obeyed the rules. The children could participate in many activities such as swimming, canoeing, archery, horseback riding, rope and river activities, music, storytelling, hiking, crafts, nature activities, as well as Bible studies and worship. There were counselors, lifeguards, and adventure leaders. Billy became friends with one of the counselors who needed his help building a treehouse in the top of a huge oak tree that was at least 100 feet or more off the ground. The counselor got ropes and climbed up the tree. He figured out how to build the floor and came up with a plan.

Billy helped the counselor with the boards and other supplies he needed. He would tie the supplies to a rope and hoist them up to the counselor. When the counselor got the floor built, he started constructing the sides of the treehouse and then the roof. Once the floor was finished, Billy was allowed to climb up and help him with the walls. The floor and walls had cracks in them, so Billy was given a 5-gallon bucket to take to the river and scoop up mud. Billy and the counselor used the river mud to fill in the cracks on the boards to make it airtight so the wind couldn't blow in. When it was completed it was a nice, big, pretty treehouse. All the kids were amazed how they built it. Billy was granted two extra weeks at the camp because he contributed so much of his time to helping the counselor build the treehouse. Billy was ecstatic and tickled to death that he was being allowed to stay two more weeks.

One afternoon, he and some of the other boys were allowed to walk down the country road to the little country store several miles from camp. On the way, the boys passed a nudist camp with a 10-foot-high wooden fence. They tried unsuccessfully to get a look inside, but they couldn't see anything. Some of the bigger boys tried to lift the smaller ones up so they could see over the top, but they kept slipping off balance and gave up. When they got to the country store, Billy had some money to buy gum or candy, but instead he bought himself a big cigar.

Later that afternoon, Billy got one of the canoes and paddled to the middle of the lake to smoke his cigar. Unbeknownst to him, all the counselors were standing on the bank watching him. He sat there in the canoe puffing his cigar. When he was finished, he paddled back to the dock and was greeted by the counselors. They told him that the smoke from the cigar looked like a steamboat! They told him he would have to leave and that he knew smoking was not allowed at the camp. Billy apologized, but they canceled the two extra weeks he was promised and returned him to the TPS.

The summer months went by quickly for Billy. He had to do a lot more of the work around the campus because many of the boys went home to their families for the summer. Soon, all the other children returned to the TPS, as did the teachers, since school was back in session. One of Billy's special friends was a young man from the Kentucky border of Tennessee. His name was William. They talked a lot about how they missed their friends and families and how they were fed up with all the stupid rules and regulations at the TPS.

Billy began asking people and looking in books to find out which way the trains would go or what highway to take to get to Chattanooga. He knew the way from Chattanooga to Athens, but not from Nashville to Chattanooga. As soon as he got the answer, which was in late October, Billy and William decided to run away from the TPS. They did not think about the distance they would have to travel, nor did they think about what they would need to take with them. In the middle of the day, with no food or extra clothing, they made their big escape. All they took were the clothes they were wearing, which was a shirt, Levi jeans, a jacket and their Brogan shoes.

The railroad tracks ran directly behind the kitchen, so they decided to start walking down the tracks. They walked for hours and hours. As night crept down upon them, they both became frightened because they were in unknown territory. They did not know where they were. They ventured off the railroad tracks and started walking through a big field. They crossed a main highway and ran toward street lights that they saw in the distance. They were both hungry and wanted to go to sleep. They continued to walk through a neighborhood wondering what they were going to do and where they were going to sleep for the night. They noticed a house that had a door at the foundation where the owner stored the lawnmower underneath the house. Billy and William went over to the house, opened the door very quietly and crawled beneath the house. As they lay there huddled together they could hear the family above them walking through the house.

At sunrise the next morning, opening the door very carefully and closing it behind them, they left in a hurry. The people who lived in the house never knew they were there. They ran down to the main road and started walking. It soon dawned on them that they were visible to all the passersby. They were fearful that they would be found and returned to the TPS. They high-tailed it back to the railroad tracks. They would walk and rest, walk and rest. When they came near any farmhouses, William would go to the front door and knock, while Billy hid in bushes or stayed on the railroad tracks. William would tell great stories to get sympathy from the people who opened their doors. He would tell the people that while he was in Nashville his aunt died and he needed to get back home for her funeral, but he had no money for food. The people were very nice and would invite him into their homes. If it was dinner time they would invite him to eat with them. He would talk to the people and pass the time with them while Billy was waiting for him to return with food for him.

Billy was too ashamed and embarrassed to ask anybody for food or money, but William wasn't, so Billy let him do it. Unfortunately, most of the time when William came back to the railroad tracks he returned empty handed because he had just eaten a meal and couldn't ask for anymore. Billy would go hungry for days until William finally started asking for any type of canned food he could have. They would open jars of canned green beans or peaches or whatever they were given and chow down like two starving maniacs. When it rained, they would look for old abandoned barns for shelter.

Billy and William walked for months, stopping along the way for William to ask for food whenever they saw a farmhouse. They almost froze to death several times, seeking shelter in old barns under hay or in abandoned farmhouses. Many times it was miles and miles between the farmhouses or they were so far from the railroad tracks they could not see them. They lived along the railroad tracks until springtime! When they were lucky, they found gardens along the way and picked small ears of corn and ate it raw off the cob. They would fill all their pockets full of corn so they would have something to eat later. They were constantly looking for water to fill their mason jars. One time they drank water from a cow trough that was full of leeches because they were dying of thirst. There were many times they went for days on end without food. When they were desperate, they would look for anything that resembled a country store and would leave the tracks to search for food. They came across one country store that was operated by an old man who treated William with a lot of kindness while Billy stayed outside and waited for him. The old man gave them several pieces of bologna and a loaf of bread. They sat in front of the country store and ate all of it, even the entire loaf of bread.

They were afraid they would starve to death if they continued to walk the railroad tracks and decided to take a chance and walk along the road since they knew they had to be a long way from Nashville by now. It wasn't long until a couple, heading for Chattanooga, offered them a ride. They graciously accepted and were glad to be sitting inside an automobile. Their appearance was frightful. Their hair had grown out and was hanging in their faces. Their clothes were filthy dirty and they smelled terrible. The old couple that picked them up must have wondered why they looked and smelled so bad, but they never questioned Billy and William. As soon as they got in Chattanooga, the couple dropped them off at the first city bus stop they came to. Billy and William thanked them for the ride and got out of their car.

As they sat down on the bench at the city bus stop Billy took off his shoes. His feet were hurting because he had not taken his shoes off since they left the TPS in October 1960. It was now the spring of 1961 and Billy was now 15 years old. It took them over five months to walk 135 miles and they still had 60 more miles to Athens! Once Billy took his Brogans off, his feet began to swell. He kept pushing and pushing to get his feet back into his shoes. He finally had to take the shoestrings completely out to make room for his swollen feet.

Billy and William looked so terrible, they wanted to get out of town as soon as possible and looked for the railroad tracks again. They walked the railroad tracks until they reached the town of Charleston. When Billy saw the huge Bowater's paper factory on the river he knew where he was. When he smelled the horrible stench from the paper factory, he knew they were getting closer to Athens and Tin Can Holler. They crossed the river and came into the city of Riceville by the train depot. They were exhausted and very hungry as they looked for food along the way. They both spotted an orange lying on the rocks by the railroad tracks that the conductor from the last train threw out, and raced toward it each hoping he could grab it first. Billy and William both made a dive for it. William pulled out his pocket knife. He and Billy started scuffling over the orange. William didn't cut Billy with his knife, but he accidentally cut himself between his index finger and thumb. At that point he handed Billy the orange so he could cut it in half. They each took half and gobbled down what little juice was left inside it. They continued walking until they got to the railroad depot in Athens. They got off the tracks and found their way to Tin Can Holler.

Billy finally made it home to Tin Can Holler and was overjoyed! He went to Cindy's house and was told she didn't live there anymore. He walked all around Tin Can Holler and couldn't find any of his old friends. He walked up Howard Street to Hobert's parents, Hugh and Myrtle Lunsford. They were both in their 80s but remembered Billy. They invited Billy and William into their home and explained to them that Cindy and Hobert were living and working in Chattanooga. Billy wished that he had known that while they were in Chattanooga days before. Billy could smell the pot of beans and cornbread that were cooking on the stove. Billy told Hugh that he and his friend, William, had not eaten in days and were very hungry. Hugh told them they could have all they wanted.

Billy asked Hugh if he knew where his sister, Beulah, was living. Hugh told Billy they had not seen Beulah in a very long time and did not know where she and her husband, Randy, were. When they finished eating Billy and William sat for a while talking with Hugh. When it started to get dark outside, Billy knew that he and William should leave. They thanked Hugh and Myrtle for the food they had given them and left. Billy remembered an old barn that used to be next to Tin Can Holler, so he and William started looking for it. They found it and stayed there during the night. The next day they walked to Highway 30 and got on the bypass that went toward Knoxville.

Billy and William stopped at Konn's Grocery Store. Billy remembered that Mr. Konn was a nice man and used to tease him by telling him that he sold TV dinners in color. Billy told William to go inside and talk to him, because he felt sure that Mr. Konn would give him some food. William came out with a bag full of food, including several moon pies, just as Billy predicted. They sat behind the building out of sight and gorged on the food from the big brown paper bag. They rolled down the paper bag and carried the remainder of the food with them. Billy couldn't find any family members or friends to stay with in with Tin Can Holler, so William told Billy he could go home with him. Billy didn't know what else to do, so he and William got on Highway 11 and walked to Niota, Tennessee, and hitchhiked to Knoxville.

Once they got into Knoxville, William took the lead, because he knew where he was going. They continued walking for days and if they were lucky they hitched rides in the back of pickup trucks. After a couple of weeks they finally made it to William's home.

William's family was worse off than Billy imagined. They were the poorest people he had ever seen. They were living on government military rations that were given to them. They had cans of dried powered eggs and dried milk. William told Billy that his family made charcoal and showed him the tents they used to burn the wood that made the charcoal. Everybody in this area was dirt poor. The old houses were thatched and patched and had roofs that looked like they would blow away in the wind. This place was much worse than Tin Can Holler. There was a woman who lived in the nearby town and who helped the poor families. She would let Billy and William come to her house and watch TV. She was a nice woman who had a big heart for those who were less fortunate. She loved doing nice things for the poor families and their children. She caught a baby possum and put it in a pin in the back of her house where she fed it corn for months. When the possum grew to be a very large size, she told William that he could take the possum home for his family. She said it would be the best possum they had ever eaten, because all she fed it was corn. William grabbed it by the tail and carried it home.

The next day William picked up the possum by the tail and brought it into the house and into the bedroom where he and Billy had been sleeping. He was also carrying a long 3-foot metal pipe in his other hand. Billy watched in horror as William laid the possum down and placed the pipe across its neck and then stood on the ends of the metal pipe … one foot on each side of it, as he tried to choke the possum to death by breaking its neck. William thought he had killed it and stepped off the pipe. Just as the pressure was released from the possum, it jumped up and hissed at William and Billy. William tried again to kill the possum with the pipe but couldn't. Billy watched as William grabbed a hammer and hit the possum numerous times in the head until it was dead. William's grandmother cooked the possum for the entire family to eat. She reminded Billy of Little Abner's mom from the cartoons he watched as a small boy. She wore a toboggan cap all the time, even to bed, and she wore several men's shirts, one on top of the other to keep warm. She would sit smoking a corncob pipe.

Billy wasn't happy there, but he didn't know what else to do and he didn't have any other place to go, so he hung out with William all day doing nothing until one day the local police showed up at William's house looking for Billy. Uncle Harry had been notified that Billy ran away from the TPS with William and was concerned. Uncle Harry purchased a bus ticket for Billy to return to Athens. Billy returned to Uncle Harry's home and stayed with him for several days. The local authorities again transported Billy back to the TPS in Nashville. By this time summer had already passed and school was back in session again. Billy turned 16 in December, and the holidays passed with no visitors, phone calls or letters. He never got into trouble again, and he never attempted to run away. Billy did as he was told and resumed his regimented schedule. As summer 1962 approached, Billy was yearning to leave. He started writing letters to Cindy asking her to please let him come visit her for the summer. He contacted Judge Jack Johnson in Athens in hopes that he would grant him permission.

Judge Johnson contacted Cindy and they agreed to let Billy come home for the summer. Billy was given a bus ticket to Athens. He hadn't been this happy in years. He jumped up and down when he got off the bus in downtown Athens! He stayed with Cindy and Hobert until they left Tin Can Holler again and moved out of state. He found out that Beulah and her husband, Randy, were working on a dairy farm in Sweetwater, and he went to stay with them. Billy hated Randy because of the way he treated Beulah, and Randy hated Billy. When Randy tried to shoot him, Billy decided it was time for him to leave.

Billy had saved enough money while working on the dairy farm to purchase a '56 Buick, so he packed his belongings and left. Billy returned to the only place he had ever known, Tin Can Holler. He lived out of his car beside the church that was behind Edna Grady's house in Tin Can Holler. Nobody bothered him, and he didn't bother anybody. He couldn't and wouldn't ask anybody for help … he was too proud to do that. Edna Grady knew that Billy was living in his car, so she would bring him a mason jar of coffee and a sausage biscuit every morning. While he lived out of his car for eight or nine months, he would hang out with his friends who would steal gas for Billy so they could ride around in his car.

His friends would sleep in the car with Billy when he would refuse to stay with them at their homes. They didn't want Billy to be alone. Many cold nights they slept in the car and almost froze to death. Hobert's sister got married and rented a two-story house.

She and her husband occupied only the upstairs. One day Billy approached them and offered his '56 Buick in exchange for allowing him live in the downstairs apartment. They took his offer and let him move into the apartment beneath them.

Billy was now 17 years old. He started looking for work and found a job with three roofing guys from Tin Can Holler, who paid him for toting their shingles from the ground to the roof. He was paid $6 a day … they each gave him $2 of their own wages. This was the first real job Billy ever had, carrying 25 to 30 square shingles.

He saved his money and lived on sodas and moon pies. Billy liked to go to the movies. He loved the western movies. One Saturday, while he was standing in line to get his ticket at the theatre, his friends, Carlos and Junior, showed up with several girls by their side. Carlos introduced Billy to a young lady by the name of Linda Brown, who lived in Etowah. Linda was tall and thin and had long brown hair and big brown eyes. Billy thought she was attractive. They each said hello, and Billy got his ticket and went inside the theatre. He told his friends that he would see them later because he wanted to watch the new movie that had just been released.

The next Saturday afternoon he went to the movies again. A short time later someone tapped him on the shoulder. He turned to see who it was and it was Linda Brown, the young lady he had been introduced to the week before. She asked him if she could sit with him and he said, "yes." They sat together during the movies and walked out together. Linda didn't have a ride home to Etowah, which was a 15-minute trip, so Billy got a taxi cab driver he knew by the nickname "Local," who always smoked a cigar, to take her home.

Linda came to see Billy every weekend. One Saturday afternoon Linda showed up with her brother, Robert, and his fiancée, Barbara. Linda told Billy that Robert and Barbara were going to Ringgold, Georgia, to get married and invited him to ride along with them. At the courthouse, waiting their turn with the county court clerk to get their marriage license, Robert and Barbara turned to Billy and Linda and said, "You two should get married too!" Billy said, "I don't have any money." Barbara said she had money. Billy asked the notary public how much it cost to get married and he said only $10 and he wouldn't charge for the ceremony. Billy and Linda decided to get married alongside their friends, Robert and Barbara, on December 12, 1964, in Ringgold, Georgia.

Billy and Linda lived apart for several months after they got married because their marriage was spontaneous and not planned. Linda continued to live at home with her parents and did not tell them that she had gotten married. Billy would not bring Linda into his basement apartment because he was ashamed of it. The only thing in the apartment was an old mattress that was thrown on the floor. A couple of months later, while at work with the roofing guys, Clifford Charles told Billy that Uncle Harry wanted to see him. Clifford did a lot of work for Harry Evans and saw him on a regular basis. He would relay messages to Billy from Uncle Harry.

Billy went to see Uncle Harry at his mansion in Athens. Uncle Harry was very happy to see him and gave him a big hug. He told Billy that he had heard he had gotten married and asked where Billy and his bride were living. Billy explained the situation to Uncle Harry and he was very sympathetic. He took Billy to his back yard and showed him the two little houses he had on the left side of his property. He handed Billy some keys and said, "Here, this is yours," as he pointed to the little house. He let Billy and Linda move into the little house. The little house was much better than the apartment Billy had been living in, but it was small. It had a small living room, a small bedroom, small kitchen and small bathroom, but it was perfect for the two of them.

Uncle Harry bought an air-conditioner for them and a sewing machine for Linda. They had well water, but Uncle Harry even paid their electric bill. They were living in the little house when their first child, Angie, was born. One day when Uncle Harry came to visit he noticed that Linda was trying to rock Angie in a straight-back chair. He didn't like that and told Billy to follow him to the front of his house. He pointed to one of the many rocking chairs he had on his big front porch and told Billy he could have one for Linda to rock the baby. Billy carried the rocking chair to the little house for Linda. Linda was excited and thanked Uncle Harry for giving it to them.

During the two years Billy and Linda lived there, Uncle Harry would have Billy drive him around in his big black car. Billy drove him all over town. He liked spending time with Billy. Uncle Harry was elderly and had a lot of health problems. He was a diabetic and had to take insulin shots, but he couldn't or wouldn't give himself the shots. He would walk every day to the clinic near his home to have a nurse give him the shot. He had a big boil on his back and he'd get Billy to squeeze out the pus and put medicine on it, because he couldn't reach it to do it himself. He couldn't control his bladder, nor his bowels. Many times he would yell at Billy, "Pull over, pull over now" and he would squat down beside the car and relieve himself no matter where they were. He would always carry a handkerchief in his suite pocket to wipe himself and throw the handkerchief on the ground before he got back into the car. There were many times when Billy would have to pull over for Uncle Harry in the middle of town. Uncle Harry didn't think twice about squatting next to the sidewalk in front of people if he had to go. Billy never discussed Uncle Harry's medical problems with him, but he knew he had some serious medical issues every time he had to pull over and Uncle Harry jumped out of the front seat of the car no matter where they were.

Uncle Harry would also ask Billy if he needed any money and would hand him his wallet. He'd bend over stretching to reach his wallet in the back pocket of his slacks. Uncle Harry had a habit of sticking out his tongue to one side of his mouth and would bite down on it with his teeth. He'd tell Billy, "Just take what you need son." His wallet would be full of money … 10-, 20-, 50- and even 100-dollar bills. Billy would take a 20-dollar bill and hand Uncle Harry back his wallet. He never took more than a 20 because he was grateful to Uncle Harry for letting him live on his property in one of his little houses. Billy and Linda lived in the little house for two or more years, and as their family grew they had to move into a bigger house.

They never forgot Uncle Harry's kindness and generosity, but always wondered why he was nice to them. Billy continued to work in the roofing business for many years. He also drove a dump truck for several years for P. D. Wade. Years later, Billy's friend, Clyde Waters, bought a Peterbilt truck and offered Billy a job as a backup driver. Billy and Clyde traveled cross country for weeks at a time, and he made a lot of money during those years. When Billy got tired of being on the road and decided to stay at home, he went back into the roofing business. Linda always worked as a waitress and still works today. Billy and Linda had been married 42 years and had five children, eight grandchildren and one great-grandchild when he was diagnosed with lung cancer and leukemia in April 2007. He received many heavy doses of chemotherapy to shrink the tumor in his lung. Weekly trips to the hospital to receive pints of blood were required, because the leukemia was destroying his blood cells very rapidly. His body got weaker and weaker as he desperately tried to fight these two very devastating diseases. He lost most of his gorgeous black hair. The small amount of hair that remained, turned white overnight. He refused to shave his head. He believed his hair would soon grow back. He suffered immensely, but was a real trooper and never complained. On Sunday afternoon, July 29, 2007, while at home watching TV, Billy began to have horrible and excruciating abdominal pains. He thought he needed to go to the bathroom. He tried to walk, but the pain grew even worse. Before Linda left for work she wanted to take him to the emergency room, but he refused.

He told her, "Oh, I'll be alright....you go on to work. I keep getting the urge to go the bathroom, but I can't go...I don't know what's wrong with me." Linda begged and begged him to go to the hospital, but he refused. He thought the pain would eventually go away, but it didn't, it got worse.

While Linda was at work Billy tried everything to relieve his abdominal pain. He drank a bottle of Pepto-Bismol and gave himself two enemas, because he kept feeling the urge to go to the bathroom, but couldn't. Linda worked late that night and came home to find Billy moaning and groaning in ways she had never seen him before. She helped him to the bathroom several times, but he still couldn't go. In the early hours of the morning Billy woke Linda up yelling, "Linda, take me to the hospital now! I would rather be dead than to have these pains....I can't stand this anymore!" On the way to the hospital, Linda called their eldest daughter Angie and informed her of Billy's condition. She told Angie to call her siblings and to also call his sister Rozetta, whom he had grown very close to. Rozetta was in North Carolina speaking at a fundraiser, but when she received the call about her brother's condition, she immediately rushed back to Athens to be by his side.

Linda rushed Billy to the emergency room at the hospital in Athens. They immediately began to administer morphine to ease his pain. Within a couple of hours he became catatonic. The family wanted to know what was wrong with him, because he couldn't talk, his eyes were frozen wide open and his mouth was slightly open with no movement in his entire body except for his breathing. He was not responding to anyone. The doctor ordered x-rays and then called the entire family into his emergency room to give them the bad news. The staff doctor informed the family members, who were gathered around his bed, that he had an intestinal blockage and there was nothing he could do for Billy. He explained that the heavy doses of chemo had destroyed a section of Billy's intestines and the acid in his intestines was now leaking into his abdominal cavity and his other organs. His body was basically killing itself. The doctor made arrangements to move Billy to a private room so they could be with him during his final hours of life. At that moment, no one knew, not even the doctor, how much longer Billy would be alive. One by one the family members began to cry and some had to leave the emergency room. The emergency room staff hugged Billy's children and his sister Rozetta as Linda held Billy's hand telling him how much she loved him while kissing his forehead. She asked the doctor if Billy could understand what she was saying and he said, "Yes, he can."

Linda overhead the doctor advising the nurse, "Give him more morphine to ease him out." She knew at that moment there was no turning back....she was losing her lifelong sweetheart and this would be her last goodbye.

Billy was sixty-one years old when he took his last breath at 6:05 p.m. on July 30, 2007 with his wife Linda and his sister Rozetta holding his hands. All of his children and grandchildren, and Cindy's children, crowded around his bedside to tell him goodbye. Billy's funeral was beautiful, but very sad. His childhood friend, Jerry Stephens from Tin Can Holler, preached the sermon with tears flowing down his face and onto the pulpit. He spoke fondly of his younger days with Billy in Tin Can Holler and how he loved Billy like a brother. There was not a dry eye in the entire room. All of Billy's friends from Tin Can Holler came to pay their respects and offer comfort to his wife and children and his sister Rozetta. His grandson Ray, who was named after him, and his entire high school football team were his pallbearers. They came dressed in their football team jerseys! Billy loved watching those boys play ball and they had the honor of carrying him to his final resting place.

CHAPTER 30

Eliza's four youngest children, Barbara Jean, 11, Shelia Ann, 9, Rozetta, 7, and Marcella, 5, were cared for after her death by her dear friends, Bryant and Estelle Gennoe in Tin Can Holler. When no family members came forward and offered to care for the girls, even on a temporary basis, Bryant and Estelle Gennoe took them into their home and cared for them until Miss Flenniken came to get them. Estelle and Bryant Gennoe were very good to them and loved them as though they were their own children. They comforted them when they cried and told them everything was going to be okay. When Estelle was informed that the children would be leaving, she cooked a huge dinner with all their favorite foods, and Bryant, on his way home from work, stopped at the bakery and bought them a pie for dessert.

Miss Flenniken, their former case worker from the Holston Methodist Home for Children, whom they liked very much, picked them up in her nice, big comfortable car that they always loved to ride in. Miss Flenniken had a special place in her heart for the Mowery children, because she had worked with them before and knew their family history. When it was time for them to gather their things and leave, Estelle and Bryant and all their children hugged them goodbye. Everyone was crying, but Estelle cried the hardest. She was heart-broken to see them leave. She was like their second mother, and she wondered if she would ever see them again.

Miss Flenniken, who was always very sweet, explained to them during their two-hour trip to Greeneville that they were going back to the Holston Methodist Home. She knew they were upset and very scared. She told Shelia, Rozetta and Marcella that they would be going to a foster home together and Barbara would be staying in the girls' group home, which was on the campus grounds. When they first arrived on campus they noticed that it looked different from the first time they were there. There was a new entrance and new cottages, and they all laughed when they saw the big ugly bus. They were greeted by Mr. Hutchins, a tall handsome young man in his middle twenties who was about 5 feet 11 inches tall and weighed about 170 pounds. He had black hair and pretty green eyes. He smiled at the children and spoke with a very kind and caring voice. The children did not recognize him or any other staff workers in the office, but they were all very kind to them. Mr. Hutchins, who was a minister and social worker, took them into his office and talked to them for a very long time. He asked them a lot of questions to determine if they might require any special needs or counseling. All their test results came back normal except for Rozetta's. She had an unexplained speech impairment, which was not noted in her file from the first time she was at the Holston Home. Now, for some strange reason, all she could do was babble and no one could understand a word she said. He requested a speech therapist for her. He could not determine if this would be permanent, but knew that she needed professional help immediately to correct her speech problem. (It took over a year of intense therapy for her to overcome her speaking impairment).

Mr. Hutchins was very surprised that there were no serious psychological problems with the Mowery sisters due to their childhood trauma and losing both parents at the same time. He thought he made a mistake and called a colleague of his in Greeneville to redo the testing. The colleague's results came back the same as Mr. Hutchins's, except for Rozetta's. He spent more time with Rozetta than with her sisters. He noted his test results in her file by stating, "Rozetta is different from her three siblings; she stands alone." He absolutely agreed that she needed a speech therapist immediately and no further comments or suggestions were made.

After comparing notes and evaluations of the Mowery sisters, their conclusion was someone had loved them and bonded with them and made them very strong little children. After observing the girls, they knew who that person was. It was their mother Eliza. Her love stayed with them. It comforted them and kept them strong. She taught them to love each other. This was very evident in their big sister Barbara, who constantly looked after them.

After they completed their initial interview and testing, Miss Flenniken led them downstairs. The room in the basement was very large, with tables and shelves of clothing. One of the staff workers assisted Miss. Flenniken in deciding what size each child needed. They were given new panties, socks, petticoats, dresses, slacks, shorts and blouses. They each got a new pair of shoes and were allowed to take one toy. They each got a big bag full of clothes and shoes. They were excited about all the new clothes, even though they weren't brand new; they were much better than the clothes they were wearing. Miss Flenniken told them she had another stop to make, so they all climbed back into her car with their big bag of clothes. She took them to the local health department for updated immunization shots. The girls were terrified. They started screaming and tried to run away from the nurses. They were scared to death! Barbara tried to comfort Shelia, Rozetta and Marcella by huddling her sisters tightly together. One by one they were taken into a separate room to see a doctor. Besides the shots that were required, they were in good physical health. When they were ready to leave, one of the nurses gave each of them a lollipop. They loved the candy and settled down for the ride to their foster home. Barbara insisted on going with them so she could see where Miss Flenniken was taking them. Barbara was very protective of her little sisters and acted like a mother hen.

Miss Flenniken took them to the Holmes family in Greeneville. They were an older couple, probably in their mid to late fifties. Mrs. Holmes was a full-time homemaker, and Mr. Holmes was a janitor for the Highlands Elementary School, where they would be attending. Mr. Holmes was a tall, thin man about 6 feet, with gray hair. Mrs. Holmes was a stocky built woman about 5 feet 5 inches, with dark brown shoulder-length hair that she kept dyed, but her gray roots were showing. She also had a big mole on the tip of her nose that grossed the children out. Miss Flenniken introduced them to Mr. and Mrs. Holmes, and they talked for a while. A short time later, Miss Flenniken said she had to take Barbara back to the campus and get her settled into her cottage. The three girls hugged their big sister and Miss Flenniken good-bye.

There was much communication between the Holston Home and the Department of Public Welfare concerning what would be best for the Mowery sisters. It was uncertain what decisions could actually be made for them until Seig's prison sentence was determined by the court. That could be months away since he had filed for a retrial. They contacted Uncle Harry because they knew he had a great deal of influence on Seig and would be the person who could possibly convince him to give up his parental rights so his daughters could be adopted. The following letters were written regarding this subject:

(1)
Attn: Miss Mary B. Flenniken, Caseworker
RE: Mowery Children
Dear Mr. Matthews:
I am pleased that the girls have adjusted with less difficulty than was anticipated. Billy Ray is now at the Tennessee Preparatory School in Nashville.

The two younger girls might have more advantages if they were placed for adoption. I do feel that this is not the time to approach Mr. Mowery to get his consent. I received a letter from him recently in which he seemed sure that he would be released at any time soon. He lacked two years and eight months from his previous sentence and surely will receive some time for his wife's death. This case will be heard in February, 1960. After the hearing, if he knows he will be in the penitentiary for a long time, he might be more able to release the children for adoption. I do feel that Mr. Harry Evans has a great deal of influence and would be a good person to work through in helping him see that this is a better plan for the children.

If the children are to be placed for adoption, would your planning include our securing the guardianship of the children with you making the adoption placements?

Sincerely yours,
Ruth Garrett
ATHENS MENTAL HEALTH CENTER

(2)
Dear Miss Flenniken:
RE: Mowery Children

Thank you for referring these four children to us. It has been very enjoyable working with them. I was somewhat apprehensive about trying to see four persons from the same family lest I should get all of my impressions confused. That difficulty has not developed, and the contacts have been very pleasing ones.

I have written you a separate letter concerning each child so that if you have "case files" on your children, the separate reports may facilitate your dealing with them.

As a general statement concerning these four children as a group I suppose my strongest impression is that I am really surprised that there are no greater problems present in their adjustment. What we know of their history certainly leads one to believe that these children would be experiencing very great emotional difficulty. I was struck with the general impression that the degree of emotional and intellectual disturbances in these children relates fairly directly to their age, the youngest child being less disturbed and the oldest and the middle children being at an intermediate point on a rough scale of psychological disorder. This observation may reflect the ages at which the children have been subjected to the undesirable events and the ages at which they were given greater opportunities of group and boarding-home life. In a similar way I felt that the suitability of these children for adoptive placement varies with their age-the youngest child again being more amenable to this approach than the older ones.

These written reports may meet the needs in regard to these children. Should this not be the case, as always we want you to feel free to come back and talk with us about them. If it is your wish to do that, please let us know and we will arrange some time of mutual convenience.

Sincerely yours,
Ruth Garrett
ATHENS MENTAL HEALTH CENTER

(3)
Attn: Miss Mary B. Flenniken, Caseworker
RE: Mowery Children
Dear Mr. Matthews:

I have delayed letting you know about Mr. Mowery's trial since I was trying to find out exactly how long he would be in the penitentiary. To date I am still very uncertain.

He was tried in Criminal Court and was given a sentence of from two to ten years in the State Penitentiary. There seemed to be some question as to whether he would have to serve all of the years left on the other felony charge before starting the two to ten years for this charge. Mr. Mowery immediately filed for a new trial and the decision on this is to come up next week. I have never been able to determine whether he will have to serve approximately two years or whether it will be many years, I do intend to talk with the Judge when he is back in this County next week.

While Mr. Mowery was here I did go to the jail and talk to him about plans for the children. At that time he was real sure that he could get a new trial and not get any time at all. He was under the impression that if he pulled the right strings he wouldn't have to serve more than a year and a half. If this were true he would not want to release the children. I was able to get him to say that if he did receive a long term it would be better for the children to have a family and two parents of their own.

The Sheriff assured me that he would probably be here until a decision was made in March, but they took him back to Petros. As soon as I am able to find out about the length of time he will probably have to serve I do plan to see him here or write to him in Petros to make plans for the children.

Cinderella and her husband are up North and Beulah and her husband are living in Monroe County and neither of them came to the hearing. I am very pleased to know that the children are getting along quite well. Hopefully I will be able to give you some more definite information in the near future.

Sincerely yours,
Ruth Garrett
ATHENS MENTAL HEALTH CENTER

After Seig received his prison sentence, Ruth Garrett from the Department of Public Welfare spoke to him about releasing his parental rights to the Holston Home so his youngest daughters, Shelia, Rozetta and Marcella, could be adopted. Seig refused to give up his parental rights and guardianship. He said he would never agree to that and would never sign anything … and he never did.

CHAPTER 31

Barbara, 11 years old, was placed in Cottage 1 on campus because she was very independent and headstrong. Foster care would not have been a good choice for her. She was placed with other girls her own age. There was a married couple who lived in the cottage with the girls. They were the house parents who instructed the girls on their daily activities and oversaw and supervised disciplinary actions when necessary. They were a nice couple who treated all the girls fairly. There was no favoritism, and Barbara got along with most of the girls in the cottage.

Barbara had a friendly, outgoing personality like her mother and made friends very easily. All the other girls looked up to her and nicknamed her "bones." She adjusted very well to her new surroundings and would write letters to Sheila, Rozetta and Marcella every week. In her letters, she always told them she wished they had a big house, so they could all be together and when she left the Holston Home she would come back and get them. Miss Flenniken thought it was very important for Barbara to continue seeing her younger siblings, so Sunday afternoon visits were arranged every couple of months. Sometimes she was allowed to call them on the telephone between visits.

Barbara did very well living on the campus until one of the girls would mouth off to her and then she would get mad and kick their butt. She got into trouble many times for fighting with some of the other girls in her cottage and would be sent to Mr. Hutchins' office. He was firm and very direct with Barbara. He told her that type of behavior would not be tolerated on campus. It was strictly forbidden. Children were not allowed to hit another child or do bodily harm to one another. He told Barbara that the Holston Methodist Home was a Christian-based organization and there were many other ways to solve disagreements. He warned her never to do that again. Barbara, while seated in front of Mr. Hutchins' desk, would cross her arms on her chest, huffing and pouting. He also reminded her that she had house parents and they were the ones in charge of her cottage, not her. He advised her to stop being bossy with the other girls.

Barbara was very argumentative and always wanted to tell him her side of the story. Mr. Hutchins was a kind man and let her talk. Being a counselor he knew she needed to be heard, and she was, by everyone in the office, because she talked very loudly. It only took a few times of disobeying the rules until Barbara learned her lesson. But, as she grew older, it wasn't the girls that concerned Mr. Hutchins anymore but the boys Barbara would sneak off campus to meet. She was very popular and played on the volleyball team at Greeneville High School. She could have done better scholastically, but she goofed off a lot. She liked the attention she got when she flirted with the boys during class and after school while waiting for the Holston Home bus to arrive.

When she got older she was moved to a different location. The older teenage girls lived together in a house they called the group home. It was a big two-story brick house that was off the main campus area but still on the Holston Home property. She thought this was great. She would make plans to sneak out on Friday or Saturday nights to meet her boyfriend but would always get caught sneaking back in through her bedroom window. She would tell the other girls to cover for her, and they would until it was time for bed checks. The last time she sneaked out to meet her boyfriend in the barn on campus, Mr. Hutchins caught them. She got punished and was not allowed to leave campus with the other children when they went to town or to the movies.

One weekend, Barbara convinced a group of girls to run away with her. Mr. Hutchins did not panic because he was experienced in this type of behavior in children. He notified the police department to be on the lookout for them and to call him if they were seen in town. He knew the girls did not have enough money to last for very long and didn't have any place to stay. He knew when they got hungry and tired of sleeping on the streets they would call or come back. He also knew a group of girls would be safer than one.

After a couple of days walking around town together they were seen by a police officer and a call was made to Mr. Hutchins. He and another counselor drove to their location and pulled up next to them as they were walking down the road. All the girls were happy to see him and jumped into the car, except Barbara. She yelled at them and told them to leave her alone because she wasn't going back. Mr. Hutchins tried to talk to her, but she kept yelling at him to go away. Mr. Hutchins told the other counselor, who was driving the car, to return to the campus. Later that afternoon Barbara walked back to the group home.

The older Barbara got, the more she became restless being at the Holston Home during the summer months. She started pestering Mr. Hutchins to allow her visits with Beulah, Billy and Cindy. No one ever came to visit her, but Beulah would write to her sometimes. She wrote to Beulah and asked her to talk to Billy and Cindy about coming for a visit. Miss Flenniken talked to Cindy on the telephone and made arrangements for Barbara to go to Athens for a family visit. Her younger sisters were not told about her visits and were not included in the plans.

During Barbara's second home visit, Billy introduced her to a friend of his from Tin Can Holler named Carlos. Carlos worked with Billy in the roofing business, and they had been friends for several years. Barbara liked Carlos, but he was not good for Barbara. He smoked marijuana and encouraged her to smoke it, too. Barbara and Carlos became inseparable, and Barbara thought she was in love. When Billy returned Barbara to the Holston Home she went to see Mr. Hutchins and told him she wanted to get married to her boyfriend, Carlos, from Athens. Mr. Hutchins advised her that she needed to finish school, but Barbara did not listen. She was 18 years old and would have been a senior, but she wanted to leave anyway. Mr. Hutchins couldn't force her to stay even though marriage was not in her best interest. She got the rest of her belongings and left the Holston Home. She was so excited, she did not go see her younger sisters to tell them good-bye but did return a year later to show them her baby boy, Matthew.

Barbara's marriage to Carlos was not good. He was a heavy drinker and smoked marijuana daily. He was a good looking guy who was in good physical shape, probably because of the work he did as a roofer. He was almost 6 feet tall with black hair and brown eyes. He was a tough looking character with dark skin. He may have been part Mexican or Indian. Barbara's happiness did not last long. She left Carlos many times and tried to take care of Matthew alone, but Carlos would always find them and convince her to come back. He would slap Barbara around when she made him mad, and she did that a lot. After years of his abuse, when her son Matthew was five years old she left Carlos and refused to go back. She worked in a factory in Athens and found an apartment to move into. She saved up enough money to get a divorce and free herself from Carlos.

Several months later, while in Bill's Bar & Deli in Sweetwater with her girlfriends, she met a guy named Joseph. He was friendly, a big stocky man about six feet tall. He was a Vietnam vet who had served with the Green Beret Special Forces and received a Purple Heart. Barbara liked Joseph, and they were married a few months later. Life with Joseph was good; much better than the life she had with Carlos, but Barbara would not stop smoking marijuana cigarettes. Her addiction to marijuana, which was introduced to her at a young age by her first husband Carlos, would follow her all the way to her grave.

Joseph was a long-distance truck driver and away from home more than he was at home, and that bothered Barbara. She and Joseph had one daughter they named Jessica. Barbara was very proud of her little girl. Because of Joseph's work, they moved many times between Tennessee, Georgia and Alabama. While living in Georgia, Joseph was involved in an accidental shooting of his best friend and had to serve 20 months in prison for involuntary manslaughter. Barbara had to get a job and support her family. She struggled until Joseph was released and came home. She had made a lot of friends while he was away in prison and knew exactly who she could get her marijuana from. She eventually got busted along with 41 other people in Resaca, Georgia, and went to prison for two years. Joseph took Jessica to his mother's in Alabama, and Michael went to live with his dad, Carlos, in Athens, Tennessee.

When Barbara got out of prison they got the family back together. Barbara's son, Matthew, was now uncontrollable and getting into trouble constantly. He too began smoking marijuana. He brought marijuana into the house while Barbara and Joseph were still on probation, and they got busted for it. They both had to go back to prison to serve 10 more months, and Barbara was court ordered into drug rehab. She completed the course successfully, but she eventually went back to smoking marijuana. Matthew left the state and when he returned he was placed in juvenile detention. Jessica was passed around to different family members until her parents were released.

When they got the family back together for a second time, they moved to Cleveland, Tennessee, to start over. Matthew went to live with his dad again. Barbara wanted a new lease on life and decided to have gastric bypass surgery to help her lose weight. She always battled with her weight and hated being fat. She lost the weight, and she looked marvelous, but she wasn't happy being with Joseph anymore. She started working in a restaurant and became good friends with the couple who owned it. She decided to leave Joseph and Jessica and pursue her own happiness elsewhere for a while. She rented a mobile home from the couple who owned the restaurant. She started partying a lot. She would go to the local bars and night clubs. She would ask the band members if she could sing….they always said, "Yes," and she would sing all night if they would let her. Barbara could sing like an angel and wrote many of her own songs like her mother, Eliza, had. The audiences loved her singing! Barbara was a spiritual person, but somewhere along the way she took the wrong path in life and it was her downfall.

Barbara was a beautiful, friendly person who could talk to strangers and make new friends instantly, but she couldn't stay away from the marijuana cigarettes. Even though it wasn't noticeable, Barbara said she stayed nervous all the time and claimed the marijuana cigarettes kept her calm. When she was going through menopause she said the marijuana helped keep the hot flashes away. The police never asked her why she smoked it, and the judge didn't want to hear any excuses either. She was arrested for possession again and had to go to jail in Cleveland, Tennessee. When she got released, she called Joseph, because she had no other place to go. He took her back and reconciled their differences. They all moved back to Georgia. Matthew also came back to live with them.

Being stuck at home all the time made Barbara restless, so she decided to take the Commercial Driver's License class and received her license in 1995. She had always wanted to go with Joseph cross country and help him drive his 18-wheeler. Her CD handle was "Big Mama." Matthew's drug habit escalated from marijuana to cocaine, and he started burglarizing homes, stealing cars and robbing stores to support his habit. He was eventually caught and went to prison for 15 years.

Barbara continued to work with Joseph until she injured her shoulder on the job in 1999 and had to stop working. She couldn't climb into the big trucks anymore. She had a lot of problems with the trucking company and filed a lawsuit against them, because they wouldn't pay for her medical expenses. She eventually won her lawsuit, but they were slow in paying her. She and Joseph had just bought a mobile home, and she was getting very stressed. She feared losing the first home she had ever owned. She got involved with selling drugs again to make money, and her daughter, Jessica, got addicted to drugs. Jessica would get violent and she and Barbara would have terrible arguments and fights.

On the night of April 21, 2004, Barbara and Jessica had their last confrontation. Jessica yelled horrible things to Barbara and told her she was a terrible mother. Barbara got so upset that she had to get away from Jennifer. She stormed out of her house and jumped into her 1995 Intrepid that had only one headlight and slick tires. Joseph yelled for her to take the other car, but she was too upset and left in a hurry. Barbara, who was an excellent driver, was killed instantly when the car she was driving was struck head-on by a Mohawk Carpet truck on a two-lane road in Resaca, Georgia, less than an hour later. She was 55 years old.

As a child, Barbara had a lot of hopes and dreams. It is unknown whether she ever got any of the things she had always hoped for in her life, because she was so addicted to marijuana. It controlled and consumed her entire life. The only short moments of stardom she probably ever had were the few times she sang on stage in the local nightclubs. Joseph was devastated; he and Barbara had been married for 28 years. Matthew was still in prison when his mother was killed, and Jessica was too distraught to attend the funeral. Every day, Jessica lives with the pain and the blame of causing her mother's death, but Barbara was in charge of her own destiny.

CHAPTER 32

Shelia, Rozetta and Marcella were placed into the home Mr. and Mrs. Holmes in Greeneville, Tennessee. The girls were told to call them Mama Holmes and Daddy Holmes. Soon after their big sister, Barbara, and Miss Flenniken left that day, Mama Holmes made all three girls follow her into the kitchen. She put a chair in front of the kitchen sink and made them stand in the chair holding their heads down in the sink. She started scrubbing their hair and digging into their scalp with her fingernails. She deliberately let the shampoo get into their eyes and made them cry. She spanked Rozetta for not wanting to let go of her doll. Rozetta was so scared, she started hyperventilating and couldn't get her breath. Mama Holmes spanked her again because she said she was doing it on purpose. She was a cruel, mean woman.

Mama Holmes made them take their baths together and slapped them because they didn't get themselves clean. She almost ripped off their ears, because they didn't clean behind them and made them all use the same towel. Their bedroom had two beds. Shelia got to sleep alone in the small bed that was on the right side of the room, while Rozetta and Marcella slept together in the big bed on the left side of the room. By the time they got into bed they were exhausted and horrified.

The next morning, when Mama Holmes woke them up and discovered that Marcella, who was a bed-wetter, had soiled the sheets and mattress, she went into a rage and spanked Marcella until her bottom was red as blood. Marcella, who was 5 years old, got spanked a lot for wetting the bed. Mama Holmes eventually put plastic on the mattress. She told Marcella she was doing it on purpose and to stop. Marcella got a deformed nipple because Mama Holmes pinched her so hard.

Later that same day, Mama Holmes got Toni perms for the girls and made them sit through the torture of her tightening the curlers. If Mama Holmes wanted them to know that she was mean, she did a very good job, because they were terrified of her. Rozetta got spanked for using too much toilet paper, so she stopped using toilet paper and her bottom got blistered. Mama Holmes found out and made her sit in a tub of ice cold water for a long time. The girls had to use the toilet at the same time before they were allowed to flush it. They were not allowed to flush the toilet until they asked Mama Holmes first.

The girls were enrolled at Highlands Elementary School and had to walk to school every day because the Holmeses did not own a car. They had to walk everywhere they went. The Holmeses were too old to be foster parents. They had none of the patience, love or kindness that the girls needed so desperately. They were unloving people. Apparently they needed the extra money they made for having the girls in their home and that's the only reason they were foster parents.

The girls were not allowed to play in the house. No matter what the weather, Mama Holmes made them play outdoors. They spent hours of each day sitting on the front steps by the sidewalk watching cars and people going by, and singing the "Lord's Prayer" that their mother had taught them. A lot of friendly people spoke to them or smiled and waved at them. They would smile and wave back at the strangers. When it rained, they had to stay on the back porch. Mama Holmes was very particular about her house and had strict rules. If they misbehaved she would get the hickory stick she broke from a tree in her yard and whip them across their legs until welts came up. During those days, girls were not allowed to wear pants to school and they would be seen with red marks all over their legs. Nobody ever said anything or even asked them how those red marks got there!

Mama Holmes had no patience for Rozetta's hyperactivity. She would spank her and make her sit on the sofa and fiddle her thumbs. Rozetta's nerves caused her to break out in rashes, and she would throw up a lot because she would get upset stomachs all the time. She also sucked her thumb and chewed off her fingernails. She would get spanked every time she was caught with her thumb in her mouth and Mama Holmes would rub hot peppers on her thumbs that burned her mouth and lips. Rozetta's caseworker took her to a doctor who gave her yellow salve, which smelled like rotten eggs, to rub on her skin. The salve would make Rozetta gag. She was also forced to drink lots of Pepto-Bismol for her stomach problems.

The Pet Milk Company was next to the Holmeses' home on Loretta Street in Greeneville. The male employees who worked there could see the girls playing and would hand them ice cream bars through the windows. The girls told the men that they were foster kids and lived across the street with a mean woman. The girls never knew their names, but they never forgot the kindness shown to them by these strangers on the other side of the windows.

There were apartments above the Pet Milk Company where a lady lived with her teenage daughter who had a mental and physical disorder. This lady, too, befriended Shelia, Rozetta and Marcella. She would invite the girls into her apartment and would give them cookies. Her daughter could not speak and had a difficult time walking. The girls would help her with her daughter. The lady would sit her daughter in the window, so she could look outside and see them playing. Shelia, Rozetta and Marcella would wave at her as she sat at the window in her second floor apartment. She couldn't wave back, but they could see her smiling.

The Holmeses had a dirt basement and a coal burning furnace. Shelia, 9 years old, and Rozetta, 7 years old, had to shovel coal into the hopper. One day, by accident, Shelia hit Rozetta in the face with her shovel. Rozetta screamed and cried as blood poured down her face. Shelia started crying, too, because she did not mean to hurt her sister. The corner of the shovel hit Rozetta above her right eye cutting the skin all the way to the bone. The skin was laid open, and this frightened Shelia more than Rozetta because Rozetta couldn't see her injury. Mama Holmes gave Rozetta a towel to hold on her face and made them walk downtown to the doctor's office alone. Shelia thought her sister was going to bleed to death before they finally made it to the doctor's office. Rozetta required about 10 stitches above her eye.

Mama Holmes had an old fashioned wringer washing machine in their basement and made Shelia and Rozetta do the laundry. One day as Rozetta was putting the clothes through the wringer from one washtub to the other; her little hand got caught between the rollers. Shelia quickly turned the machine off and yelled for Mama Holmes to help get Rozetta's hand loose. No compassion or love was ever shown to the girls ... they only had each other. From that day forward, Shelia never let Rozetta put the clothes through the wringer; she let her catch them on the other side and helped pull them through.

Christmas time was the best. Each United Methodist Church in the Holston Conference would sponsor children for the holidays. The ladies of the church would ask the children to make a list of five things they wanted for Christmas; then the ladies would buy the gifts and wrap them. They knew the ages, sizes and gender of the children and bought clothes, toys, and necessities such as gloves and scarves, raincoats and umbrellas, belts and sometimes boxes of chocolate-covered cherries for them. The girls would get hair accessories such as bows, barrettes and hairbands. The ladies of the church made sure each child had a good Christmas. The fond memories of those Christmas days were never forgotten by Shelia, Rozetta and Marcella. Their favorite gifts were new roller skates and a transistor radio. They spent weeks teaching themselves how to skate on the concrete slab in the backyard where a trailer once sat. They would sit on the concrete steps in the front yard for hours listening to and singing the songs they heard on the radio. As they got older they each wrote thank you letters to those wonderful ladies after Christmas was over.

Mama Holmes did not want the girls to talk on the telephone. They were not allowed to make any calls to their friends and were made to hang up on their friends if they called their house. The telephone was the only way their older sister, Barbara, could contact them, but Mama Holmes would not allow them to talk to her either. She would take the telephone away and hang up on Barbara. This would upset Barbara. She did not know that the letters she was writing to her sisters were being opened by Miss Flenniken and were not mailed. The attempts to keep Barbara from her sisters frustrated her and made her very angry. Miss Flenniken apparently thought Barbara's influence on her little sisters would not be good. This is a letter Barbara wrote to Shelia stating that when she left the Holston Home she would get a home for them, but this letter was never mailed:

Dear Shelia,

Please don't let anyone read this note. Tear it up when you are through reading it. The reason I haven't called you this week and maybe never call again is that Mrs. Holmes gets mad every time I call. She made Marcella hang up on me twice. Miss Flenniken got mad and told me I'm not to tell you all what to do just because I wanted you to take that second book.

I love you all very much and someday I hope to make a home for you all. Tell Marcella and Rosita I said hello and I love them with all my heart as I do you. The reason I am writing you is I thought you might be wondering why I haven't called you. Now tear this up, and remember not to say a word about this to no one. I hope you will do this! And also remember I love you all very much.

Love,

Barbara Mowery

PS: I love you all. Hugs and Kisses. Tear it up now!

When Shelia began to go through puberty, no one explained it to her. When she started having her period she was terrified and started screaming. Mama Holmes called their new caseworker, who was a young woman straight out of college. She was a sweet woman, but she didn't know how to explain it to Shelia either and gave her a book to read. Shelia, Rozetta and Marcella sat together on the front steps to the house and read the book and looked at all the pictures. This was their introduction to their sexuality and the difference between boys and girls. The girls giggled when they saw the pictures in the book of the male productive organ. At first, Mama Holmes did not buy sanitary pads for Shelia. She took old sheets and ripped them into strips and made them for her. She showed her how to pin them into her panties with a safety pin. This was not good enough for Shelia, and she messed her underwear and clothes. Mama Holmes got upset with Shelia because she had to start buying sanitary pads.

The Holmeses had one son who was married to a woman who drove a weird looking little foreign car. The doors opened the opposite way. They had two children. The Holmeses' son was a nice young man and was kind to the girls. He was good in math and had a natural talent for drawing. He would help Rozetta with her homework and school projects. He and his wife were very good to Shelia and sometimes took her to their apartment to spend weekends. Shelia would help with the house cleaning and babysitting.

Daddy Holmes would walk the girls to church every Sunday morning. He took them to a church that was far away from their house. They always took a shortcut and walked along the railroad tracks. Mama Holmes never went. She stayed home and cooked Sunday dinner. The only good thing she did was cook. She was an excellent cook and made all kinds of delicious desserts. It was during these walks to church, after Shelia started maturing, that Daddy Holmes started putting his arm around her and fondling her breasts. She was afraid to tell Mama Holmes because she knew that Daddy Holmes would spank her with his belt, something that already happened a lot. Shelia was terrified and didn't know what to do. There was no one for her to talk to except her sisters.

CHAPTER 33

In November 1962, when Shelia was 12 years old, the Holmeses did not want her anymore and she was taken away. She had been there three years. They told the caseworker at the Holston Home that she was a troublemaker. Shelia was not a troublemaker; she did not like the way she and her little sisters were being treated, but no one believed her. She was taken away and placed in another foster home in Kingsport, Tennessee, the Jones family.

The Joneses lived in a two-story house on a farm in the country. They had two children: a 17-year-old daughter and a 12-year-old son. Shelia tried to get along with the family but felt they only used her for house cleaning and all their dirty work, while getting paid for her living there. They did not have a bedroom for Shelia, so they put a small bed in the loft for her to sleep on. Shelia knew this family had no love for her. The Joneses allowed their 17-year-old daughter to boss her around and tell her what to clean and scrub while the daughter did no chores at all. Shelia felt like she was their slave.

Shelia worried about her little sisters and was not allowed to call them. She wished she could have stayed with the Holmeses where she could protect them. Whenever she was alone in the loft she would cry because she felt lonely and missed her sisters, Rozetta and Marcella. She wondered when she would see them again.

Ten months after Shelia arrived at the Joneses' foster home she was removed, because of a fight she had with their son. The caseworker came and got Shelia and took her to another foster home. She was taken to the Lillard family in Jonesborough, Tennessee. They owned a small dairy farm in the country. Mr. Lillard was employed with Eastman Kodak Company in Kingsport, and Mrs. Lillard was a housewife who took care of their dairy barn. They were a younger couple in their early thirties. They had a 5-year-old daughter and a 13-year-old son.

Shelia was told she would be sharing the daughter's bedroom and sleeping in the same bed with her. As she looked around at this new foster home, Shelia wondered what they would be making her do, and she soon found out. She feared that she would be used as a slave again. Her responsibility was to watch the children while Mrs. Lillard milked the cows and to go into the field and run them to the barn every morning and evening.

Every other Saturday morning in the summertime, Mrs. Lillard made Shelia clean the windows in the house and mow the grass. She also had to clean the house and wash dishes. During autumn, they made Shelia pick up tobacco leaves in the field that were left behind by the picker. They also taught her how to tie tobacco. Every week or so Mrs. Lillard would laugh and make Shelia bathe and clean Mrs. Lillard's elderly mother-in-law's feet and give her a pedicure, because Mrs. Lillard refused to do it. Shelia knew at that point that she was being used and made fun of. Mrs. Lillard would slap Shelia across the face whenever she complained about anything.

Shelia felt no love from these people. Whenever Shelia would ask Mr. Lillard to help her with her homework, Mrs. Lillard would get hateful with Shelia and tell her to go to her room and do it herself. She did not want her husband helping Shelia. Shelia felt that Mrs. Lillard was jealous and did not want her husband around her. Feeling no love from these people drove Shelia to rebel against Mrs. Lillard and all the chores she forced her to do.

One Saturday morning, Shelia and Mrs. Lillard got into an argument because Shelia told her, "I am sick and tired of doing all this cleaning and being treated like a slave!" Mrs. Lillard walked up to Shelia and slapped her so hard that she felt as though she was going around in a circle. Mrs. Lillard ordered Shelia to go to her room and wait until Mr. Lillard got home. When he got home, Mrs. Lillard told him what happened. He got a paddle and went into Shelia's room and confronted her. He attempted to spank Shelia. When he started swinging the paddle at Shelia, she started defending herself and fell on the floor. He ordered Shelia to get up and out of his house. She had no place to go so she went to the barn and hid in the hayloft. Thirty minutes later Mr. Lillard came to the barn and yelled, "Get down ...out of there ... are you going to act like a cow in here?" He told Shelia to get back into her room.

The next day, they called a caseworker at the Holston Home. By this time Shelia was 15 years old and had spent two years with this family. Two days later a caseworker from the Holston Home came to the house. Shelia told her she desperately needed to talk to her in private. Shelia cried and told her caseworker the entire story about what had happened with Mr. and Mrs. Lillard and that she was not happy living there. She was honest in expressing how Mrs. Lillard treated her and how she felt no love from them. Shelia begged the caseworker to get her out of there or she would run away. Shelia stated she did not want to go into another foster home because she felt like she was just being used by people and was very unhappy. Since Barbara had left the Holston Home campus, it was decided that the best place for Shelia was the teenage cottage for girls her own age where she would be treated the same as all the other children.

Shelia was placed on campus with other teenage girls her own age. She loved it there and made many new friends. All the girls had chores to do every day, and everyone was treated exactly the same. Six months later, after Shelia turned 16 years old, a new boy arrived on campus that everybody called Eddie. They made eye contact on the bus trips to school and eventually started talking to each other. They soon became sweethearts. Shelia was a year older than Eddie. They were seen on campus together and at school. Eddie would rush from his classes to walk Shelia to hers. Everyone would see them walking together hand in hand down the halls of Greeneville High School.

When Shelia turned 17 years old she was moved to the group home for older girls, but she continued her courtship with Eddie. One Saturday morning in early spring of 1967 it was Shelia's turn to clean the Holston Home office. While cleaning the front office building, a young woman in her early thirties walked into the office for an appointment she had with Mr. Hutchins. She spoke to Shelia and asked her if there were any snacks in the kitchen that she could have, because she was hungry. Shelia went to the kitchen and brought her a snack. She thanked Shelia and went into Mr. Hutchins' office.

After a few moments, Mr. Hutchins called Shelia into his office and introduced her to the woman she had just spoken to. He told Shelia her name was Darlene. He asked Shelia if she would like to start spending the summer and holidays with Darlene at her home in Oak Ridge. He knew that Shelia had no relatives she could visit during the summer months or spend the holidays with, so he thought this was a nice invitation from Darlene.

Darlene, a Methodist member and a single woman, came to the Holston Home to find a child, preferably a young teenage girl, she could help. She liked Shelia from the moment she met her and could see the sadness in her eyes. Darlene's heart went out to Shelia. Shelia was excited that Darlene wanted to be her friend and would free her from having to stay on campus all summer alone. Shelia now had something in her life to look forward to. When school adjourned for summer vacation, Mr. Hutchins made arrangements for Shelia to ride the bus to Oak Ridge and meet Darlene.

During that summer vacation, the two of them bonded together. For the first time since Eliza was killed, Shelia realized what a mother-daughter relationship felt like, because Darlene treated her like a daughter. She took Shelia shopping and treated her very well. She helped Shelia get a summer job working as a nurse's aide at a local nursing home in Oak Ridge, but the biggest event that occurred while Shelia spent the summer with Darlene was a weekend Christian retreat in North Carolina. During the youth fellowship all the other young people seemed to be very happy, singing, shouting and lifting up their hands to God.

Shelia had never been around fellowship like that before and all of a sudden she started crying. The youth counselor came over to her and asked her why she was crying. Shelia said she didn't know. The youth counselor told her she needed Jesus in her heart to be saved, and then she would be happy. She led Shelia in the sinner's prayer. Shelia felt the love of Jesus come into her life. This was the moment that changed Shelia's life. When she needed love the most in her tender years after her mother died and didn't get it from any of the foster homes, she now knew that Jesus loved her and always had.

When summer ended, Shelia returned to the campus and continued her teenage romance with Eddie, then spent the Christmas holidays with Darlene. The following summer, Shelia returned to Oak Ridge again to visit with Darlene. Eddie spent the summer with his sister in the Johnson City area but missed Shelia. Shelia talked about Eddie all the time. Darlene informed Shelia that it was forbidden for her to see Eddie while visiting with her.

While Darlene was at work one day, Eddie showed up at her house. Shelia asked Darlene if it would be okay to go out with Eddie and Darlene told Shelia "no." Shelia and Eddie made plans that night to go to the drive-in movies anyway, and Shelia sneaked out of the house to meet him, disregarding the rules. Darlene was very upset. The next day Shelia and Eddie took the bus back to Greeneville and called for someone from the Holston Home to come pick them up. They both walked into Mr. Hutchins office to tell him about Darlene getting upset with them and why. Mr. Hutchins already knew what happened, because she called him immediately to report what they had done.

Mr. Hutchins pointed to an empty office and told Shelia and Eddie to go in it and decide what they wanted to do. By being forced into a decision, Shelia and Eddie decided the only thing left for them to do was to leave the Holston Home and get married. Shelia had never been given the freedom to make decisions of her own before, and she made a big mistake. She had no knowledge of what and how this decision was going to ruin her life. Eddie contacted his older sister to come pick them up the following weekend, and they left the Holston Home together.

The next month, Shelia and Eddie got married. She was 18 and Eddie was 17. Sometime in August, Shelia realized she was pregnant. When Eddie found this out, he panicked. He didn't know what they were going to do since they were still living with his sister and brother-in-law. Eddie's buddy convinced him to enlist into the Marine Corps. A few months later Eddie was gone and Shelia was stranded, but Eddie's sister and brother-in-law were very good to her.

Eddie completed boot camp and was transferred to South Carolina. Shelia stayed with Eddie's sister until their son Beau was born on May 4, 1969. Beau was less than a month old when Eddie brought them to live on the military base with him. Eddie was a cook on the base for two years, and all their necessities were provided to them by the military base. Shelia was so shy that she stayed at home most of the time and never met any other military wives, except the ones that Eddie would invite to their home with their husbands. He started drinking a lot with his military buddies and his personality changed. He introduced Shelia to drinking beer. He was not the same sweet young man she had met years earlier at the Holston Home. He became wild and verbally abusive to Shelia.

One night when they and another couple were drinking together, Eddie wanted Shelia to participate in wife-swapping with the other couple. Shelia got very angry. She could not believe that Eddie wanted her to do such a thing. She was a virgin when she met Eddie and had never been with another man and could not understand how Eddie, who said he loved her, would want her to participate in such a degrading and disgusting ordeal. She told the other couple to leave and told Eddie that he couldn't possibly love her if he wanted her to have sex with someone else.

From that point on, Eddie and Shelia's relationship went from bad to worse. After he completed his two-year commitment with the Marine Corps they moved back to Johnson City and rented an apartment. The verbal abuse, drinking and the arguments continued. Shelia separated from Eddie several times and wanted out of the marriage. She eventually took Beau and moved to her hometown of Athens, Tennessee, to start her life over. She got an apartment and worked in a sewing factory. Eddie filed for divorce. During their five-year marriage they were only together for about three years.

Shelia's loneliness led her to drinking. While working at a local restaurant in Athens she met another man, who would become her second husband. One night when they were drinking together he asked Shelia to marry him. Her insecurity and low self-esteem made her say yes to him even though she did not love him and barely knew him. This marriage ended in failure and unhappiness for both of them in less than two years.

Beau was getting older and out of Shelia's control. She knew he needed more discipline and decided the best thing for him would be to live with his dad in Johnson City, so she took him to live with Eddie. While in the area, she met her third husband, Joe. Soon after they met, Shelia moved in with him. They both had been through bad marriages and were not ready to get married again, so they lived together for two years. During that time period, Shelia and Joe drank and went to the local bars a lot. As Shelia's desire for alcohol increased, she became an alcoholic. Every time she would get upset about anything she would start drinking.

After two years of living together and upon Shelia's persistence, they decided to get married. Shelia was 28 years old, and Joe was 29. A year later she gave birth to their daughter.

Joe was a country boy who grew up farming. He bought some property and built a home for his family in Jonesborough, Tennessee. Shelia soon became a country girl at heart. She did not know a thing about country living, so Joe taught her. A very important part of his love of nature was his yearly garden. He taught Shelia how to grow crops and how to can the food they harvested from the garden. They picked wild berries, and he taught her how to make homemade jelly and jams.

Shelia worked at meager jobs but was not happy. She decided to go to beauty school and got her state license in 1979. They both continued to drink, which led to many arguments. Shelia would get upset and leave the house to go to the bars alone. Several times she wrecked her car and was charged with DUI's. The judge eventually sentenced her to 45 days in jail. Shelia's happiness was slowly fading, and she began to pray for guidance.

She remembered when she was 17 years old and accepted Jesus Christ as her savior. As she reflected upon her life, she knew that the hand of God had been protecting her. She turned to God for answers. She asked God to show her if there was more to life than what she was experiencing, because she didn't like the person she had become. She was tired of the drinking and asked God to take the desire for alcohol away and to show her what she needed to do to turn her life around. She told God if this was all there was to living, she would rather be dead.

On weekends, Shelia would have yard sales by the busy highway in front of their home. During one of her yard sales, a woman approached Shelia and started talking to her. The woman told Shelia that God had sent her and she had a message to give her. She invited Shelia to a revival in Jonesborough and she went, because she had been praying and asking God what he wanted her to do with the rest of her life. During this weekly revival she rededicated her life to Jesus. She was filled with so much joy that the people around her said she was glowing with the glory of God. Her desire for alcohol also left her. Joe refused to go to the revival with her and resented that she was seeking God in her life.

In 2003, Shelia's wild past and years of drinking caught up with her. She went for years not knowing she had high blood pressure. Shelia suffered from major heart problems at the age of 53 and was rushed to the hospital emergency room in Johnson City. The heart specialist told her that she could not go home because she needed triple by-pass surgery immediately and scheduled it for the next morning. She made it through the surgery and felt that God had taken care of her and gave her a second chance at life. She must now take heart medication and high blood pressure medicine for the rest of her life. She and Joe have been married 28 years and her life now is much calmer. She spends her days at home watching her religious programs on TV or enjoying her weekly yard sales as she looks forward to visits from her daughter and granddaughter.

CHAPTER 34

After Shelia was removed from the Holmes foster home, life for Rozetta and Marcella got worse. They missed their big sister and now were isolated from both Shelia and Barbara since they were not allowed to talk on the telephone because of Mama Holmes. They were scared all the time. Rozetta continued to be taken to the doctor many times for skin rashes, nose bleeds and upset stomachs. The doctor did not know what was wrong with her. It would be years later before she realized what was causing all her health issues. Nothing they ever did was good enough for Mama Holmes. They couldn't sit right, stand right, or walk right in her eyes. She would constantly fuss and yell at them.

Rozetta and Marcella were much older now and felt like prisoners. They knew they were being mistreated and were not loved by Mr. and Mrs. Holmes. They desperately wanted to talk to their caseworker, but Mama Holmes would not allow them to talk to her on the telephone, and whenever she came for a visit they were ordered to stay outside. The caseworker only heard what Mama Holmes wanted to tell her.

Rozetta, who was now in the 7th grade at Greeneville Jr. High School, desperately needed to get to the Holston Home to talk with Mr. Hutchins. He had always been a kind, understanding counselor and caseworker, and Rozetta knew if she could talk to him he would do something for her and Marcella.

One day after school Rozetta didn't get on her regular bus but stood with the kids who lived on campus at the Holston Home. She knew most of them and told them why she needed to ride their bus. As soon as the bus pulled onto the campus the bus driver let Rozetta off at the office building where Mr. Hutchins was located. Rozetta went into the building and asked to see him. She told the receptionist it was very important. Mr. Hutchins came out of his office to greet Rozetta and was surprised to see her. As Rozetta started crying he took her into his office, so he could find out why she was upset. Rozetta told him how unhappy she and her sister Marcella were and how they hated living with the Holmeses. She told him all the things

165

that Mama Holmes had done to them over the years and that they wanted to live somewhere else. Mr. Hutchins immediately found another foster home for Rozetta and Marcella.

Rozetta and Marcella were taken to the home of Jack and Coleen Shankle in Jonesborough, Tennessee. They were a couple in their late thirties or early forties. They had one son named Lynn. He was their only child. Marcella and Lynn were the same age. This was a good Christian home. Rozetta and Marcella felt loved for the first time since their mother died. They went to church as a family and were treated like family, not just kids who needed a home. Jack would read a daily devotional every morning before breakfast, and no one ate until he said a prayer.

They were enrolled in school and soon made lots of new friends, especially Rozetta. She had a sweet personality and made friends very easily. Her best friend at Jonesborough High School was Diane. All of her friends were allowed to visit, including the boys, and Rozetta was allowed to spend time at Diane's home. She had never gotten to do this before. Rozetta was very popular with her new classmates, and lots of kids came to the Shankle home to just hang out. Jack and Coleen did not mind. They actually enjoyed having the children come to their home. Rozetta loved being at the Shankle home and loved Jack and Coleen. She felt safe and loved with them. Jack and Coleen were the sweetest people in the world.

Rozetta's medical problems disappeared after she was taken out of the Holmes foster care and placed with the Shankle family. Her nerves were the cause of her problems. Life was wonderful until Marcella started arguing and picking on Lynn all the time. Marcella was the complete opposite from Rozetta. Rozetta was easygoing, but Marcella was mean and a troublemaker. Rozetta was an A student, and Marcella was a D and F student. Marcella didn't like Lynn and could not get along with him. This was very troubling for Jack and Coleen. They tried everything to solve the problems between Lynn and Marcella, but it was hopeless. They contacted the Holston Home and told them about the situation, so they could find another home for them.

Rozetta was heartbroken, and so were the Shackles. They wanted to keep Rozetta but felt that she would grow to resent them later on because they could not keep Marcella. They really did not want to separate the sisters. Since Coleen had grown much attached to Rozetta, it was very difficult and sad for her to let her go. She had a long talk with Rozetta and told her how much she loved her and wanted her to understand. Rozetta understood and was angry at her sister for causing the problems.

Sadly, they lived with the Shankle family for only six months. This was the best foster home Rozetta was ever in. Unbeknownst to Rozetta, Coleen always kept in contact with the Holston Home and updated on her whereabouts. Rozetta was sad to tell her best friend Diane good-bye. They stayed in touch with each other until they were adults, and then they lost contact. Rozetta has been searching for Diane for years to no avail. Rozetta was Diane's childhood friend and desperately wants to find her but does not know her whereabouts.

CHAPTER 35

ozetta and Marcella were placed with the Curtis family in Greeneville, Tennessee. They were a couple in their early fifties. They had no children of their own, but they had one adopted daughter, Jodie, who was several years older than Rozetta and Marcella. There were a lot of children in this foster home, and Rozetta and Marcella had to sleep on the couch in the living room that opened up into a bed. Mr. Curtis was an electrician, and Mrs. Curtis stayed home with her two Chihuahua dogs. This foster home was much different from the Shankles'. It was like a miniature boot camp because all the kids had chores to do all the time and lots of rules.

The only thing Mrs. Curtis did was cook some of the meals and walk around to supervise the work that was being done by the children. The children did everything including the yard work. She did a great job keeping the kids organized. She laid out newspapers for the children to step on so they wouldn't scuff the shiny hardwood floors, and the house stayed immaculate all the time. The entire house had to be cleaned every morning before the children went to school. There were too many children and it was too crowded in the house all the time. It was impossible to have any privacy. Mrs. Curtis was a sweet woman, but she slapped Rozetta across the face one night because she wasn't drying the silverware well enough. This upset Rozetta and she never forgot that slap.

Rozetta got enrolled at Greeneville High School and reunited with all the friends she had gone to school with before. She signed up for the home economics class and had a wonderful teacher who taught her how to sew and make her own clothes. She learned how to make two-piece suits, jumpsuits, slacks, skirts and dresses and anything she wanted.

Jodie was always very bubbly and cheerful. She had her own room and got to choose who slept with her and shared her room. She didn't seem to mind having all those kids in the house with her. Marcella did not like this foster home, and she hated the Chihuahuas because they barked at her all the time. One afternoon after school, Marcella was caught kicking one of them so hard it slid all the way across the shiny hardwood floor. Mrs. Curtis was furious with her and grounded her. Marcella didn't have a good time when they took all the kids to the Knoxville Zoo the following weekend. Marcella and Rozetta would discuss how much money they thought the foster parents were making from all the kids they had in their house and if they were doing it for the money.

Mr. Curtis was a nice older man. He worked long days and always came home very tired. He suffered from ulcers and every night he would get up in the middle of the night to take medicine. He suffered terribly and would sit in his chair next to the couch where Rozetta and Marcella slept. They could hear him moaning and groaning in pain during the middle of the night.

The exact reason Marcella was removed from the Curtis foster home is not known, but she was taken away less than a year after arriving and was sent to live with a family in Elizabethton, Tennessee. After Marcella left, Jodie must have realized that Rozetta missed her sister, and Jodie befriended her. Rozetta got to share her bedroom and sleep with her in her nice big bed. They became friends and went places together after Jodie got her driver's license. Mrs. Curtis would give Jodie a grocery list, and Jodie and Rozetta would go shopping and run errands for her. Mr. Curtis also told Rozetta he would teach her how to drive his car if she could get her learner's permit. He was always very calm and patient with all the kids and never raised his voice. He would take everyone to church on Sunday mornings and Sunday nights. It was at this Baptist church when Rozetta became a Christian and gave her life to Jesus and got baptized.

Rozetta was now 15 years old and needed a copy of her birth certificate before she could get her driver's license and social security card. She wanted to get her learner's permit. When she received her birth certificate, she was shocked to find out what her real name was. It was not Rosita, as she had always been told and taught to spell, but Rozetta! She was astounded!

Even though this family treated her well and she got along with everyone, Rozetta did not feel loved. She had learned at a very young age to go by the rules and to do what she was told. She knew that doing as she was told made her life much easier. She always yearned to be loved and to have a family of her own someday, that no one could take away.

During the Spring of 1968, Rozetta was informed that her Uncle Defoyst Mowery and his new wife, Wilma, wanted to meet her and invited her to spend spring break with them and their family. Rozetta had been in foster homes since 1959, and no family members had ever visited or written to her. She didn't know who her Uncle Defoyst was, but she wanted to meet him. She was pleased that somebody cared about her and got very excited to meet them. Defoyst and Wilma came to the Holston Home and met Rozetta. She liked them and got permission to ride the bus from Greeneville to Benton for a visit with her uncle and his family.

She got off the bus right in front of her uncle's house in downtown Benton. Defoyst was a tall, husky and very handsome man in his fifties. Wilma was tall and skinny with shoulder-length black hair. Wilma was 25 years younger than Defoyst, and they had four children. Rozetta was happy to meet them and thought her little cousins were adorable. The children were all over her. She had never been around little children before, so she enjoyed playing with them. She had a good time and was sad to leave, because she didn't know when she would get to see them again.

Sometime between spring and summer, after Rozetta returned to her foster home with the Curtis family, her Uncle Defoyst called the Holston Home to inquire how he could get her out of the orphanage to come live with him and his family. He and Wilma had discussed it and decided they wanted Rozetta to come live with them. Mr. Hutchins informed them that it would be Rozetta's choice, not theirs. Rozetta was asked and she told Mr. Hutchins, "yes." When school adjourned for the summer, Rozetta said good-bye to her foster brother and sisters, Mr. and Mrs. Curtis and Jodie. Defoyst and Wilma came to pick her up and took her to their home. Rozetta did not realize before she made the decision to leave the custody of the Holston Methodist Home that she was giving up a free four-year college degree; going to college was something she had always wanted to do. She studied very hard to keep her grades above average.

Defoyst and Wilma did everything they could to make Rozetta feel welcome. Defoyst added another room to the back of their little house, so she could have her own bedroom. He had the walls paneled and put down red carpet. There wasn't a door to her room, but at least she had her own room for the first time in her life. Defoyst was a long-distance truck driver and was planning a trip to New York City. He asked Rozetta if she would like to ride with him. Rozetta said, "yes," because she had always wanted to see the Statue of Liberty and all the huge buildings. This trip gave Rozetta the chance to bond with her Uncle Defoyst. He became a father figure for her, and she loved and respected him for what he had done for her.

August 4, 1968, was Rozetta's 16th birthday. Wilma planned a surprise sweet 16 birthday party for her, because she had never had a birthday party. Wilma knew some of the young people in Benton who were close to Rozetta's age and invited them to come to the party so she could make a few friends before starting school in the fall. This was the first time Rozetta felt like a normal teenager. It was at this party that Rozetta met Donald. He was a young man who worked at the local grocery store in Benton, and Wilma had become friends with him on her frequent visits to his store. He was two years older than Rozetta and was tall, dark and handsome. His dad was a full-blooded Cherokee Indian, so he got his good looks from his father. From that day on, Donald became a frequent visitor. When school started in the fall, he introduced Rozetta to everyone at Polk County High School. He was always very sweet and polite.

Rozetta found out very quickly that Defoyst did not make enough money to give her all the things she needed, so she started baby-sitting and saving her money. Wilma had a sewing machine, and to her surprise Rozetta bought material and started sewing. She made all her clothes for the school year. She made wool skirts and vests, dresses and matching skirts with jackets. She even made the blouses she wore with her two-piece suits. Rozetta wanted to look as good as all the other girls in class, and she did. She also worked part-time for a local CPA who taught her accounting procedures and at the Polk County Clerk's Office. She managed to save enough money to buy her high school class ring and to pay for her senior pictures.

Rozetta continued to work part-time and kept her grades above average. She didn't have time to play any competitive sports. At the end of her junior year she became a member of the Polk County High School's National Honor Society. Rozetta loved Polk County High School. Everyone was friendly, and she made a lot of new girlfriends. Her very best friends were Katy and Tanna Jo. She formed a friendship and a bond with these two girls that would last a lifetime. They became the sisters Rozetta had lost.

Rozetta's friendship with Donald quickly turned into courtship, and they were inseparable. Donald asked Rozetta to marry him, and Christmas 1969 he gave her an engagement ring, which she accepted. Donald was Rozetta's first real boyfriend; she never dated anybody else during her junior and senior year. A couple of months before graduation Rozetta called off the engagement. She didn't want to get married. Donald thought she had another boyfriend, but she didn't. Something inside of her was telling her, "No, don't do it." She said a lot of ugly things to Donald that hurt him deeply that she regretted later. Her apology was not accepted ... it was too late to take back the things she said.

Rozetta felt as though she was being pulled in another direction and had to do something more with her life. She wanted to go to college but didn't know how she was going to do it. Before graduation she had already been accepted for a government job with the U.S. Forest Service in Cleveland, Tennessee. Graduation was in May of 1970, and Rozetta graduated with honors. She was the only Mowery child who graduated from high school. She did not realize that her refusal to marry Donald would change her life drastically and put her on a journey she never envisioned. She had to go full circle with her life in order for her to become the person she is today. There were many more lessons for her to learn in a world where she had little experience or knowledge.

Rozetta began her employment at the U.S. Forest Service in June. She did not have a car, but she rode to work with two girls from Benton who were sisters. Wilma began to resent Rozetta and would get upset because she would come home late some evenings. Rozetta was at the mercy of the girls who took her to work, so if they wanted to go shopping or to the movies after work, Rozetta did, too, because she had no other way to get home. Tensions began to build. Defoyst was on the road all the time, and Wilma was left to care for the children by herself. Wilma was in a terrible mood one night and told Rozetta she wanted her to move out. Rozetta believed that Wilma's resentment was due to her breaking off the engagement with Donald, because Wilma really liked Donald and thought he would be perfect for her. Rozetta had lived with her Uncle Defoyst and Wilma for 2-½ years when she walked out the door for the last time.

Rozetta grabbed some of her clothes and threw them in a plastic garbage bag and left the house in a hurry. She walked through the yard to the back of the house towards Highway 411. She crossed the highway and went to the first phone booth she could find. She stood there for a few minutes and wondered who she could call; she didn't know how to get in contact with any of her siblings. She called her girlfriend, Katy. Katy came and picked her up and took her to her house. The next morning Katy took her to work at the U.S. Forest Service.

Rozetta told her girlfriends at work about the argument she had the night before with her Aunt Wilma. They were all older ladies, married with families, and they all adored Rozetta. They told her not to worry about anything; they would find a place for her to live, and they did. By the end of that workday they found Rozetta a cute little efficiency apartment, and Katy helped her move in. Rozetta still didn't have a car, so her friend Katy would take her to work and pick her up. On days that Katy was sick or couldn't go to work, Rozetta would walk to work, which was a couple of miles away. Usually she would be seen by one of the park rangers who would stop and offer her a ride. Everyone at the Forestry Service treated Rozetta with kindness which she never forgot.

There was an older woman in the office named Dana who befriended Rozetta and invited her to spend a lot of time at her home with her and her husband. Dana and her husband had a special place in their heart for Rozetta and treated her like a little sister. They gave her a lot of important advice that she never forgot.

When her job with the U.S. Forest Service was completed, Rozetta found another position at the same bank where Katy was employed. It didn't pay very much, so she found a part-time job at night working in the accounting department at Woolworths. Rozetta saved her money and bought her first car, which was a yellow 1964 Chevrolet. Now she felt more independent.

A few months after Rozetta moved into her own apartment, she received a call from her childhood girlfriend, Judy, from the Holston Home, who was living in Athens. She was surprised to hear from Judy and that she wanted to come for a weekend visit. They spent a lot of time talking about the Holston Home and Mr. Hutchins and how nice he was to all the children. Judy had been through a lot of difficult times since she left the Holston Home. She had married her sweetheart, who was also a Holston Home child, but they were in the process of getting a divorce. He had joined the Marine Corps and spent time in Vietnam. When he came home, he was a completely different person due to drugs and shell-shock.

Neither of them knew that Judy's visit would change Rozetta's life completely. Judy loved to dance, and as she traveled to Rozetta's apartment she noticed the American Legion dance hall. She convinced Rozetta to go out with her on Saturday night. Rozetta had never been in a place like that, but Judy had, because of her marriage to a soldier. She was relentless, and Rozetta finally agreed to go, even though she didn't think they would let her in since she wasn't 21. Rozetta had long, straight dark brown hair and wore only a little makeup. Judy put a wig and makeup on her, so she would look older. Rozetta was terrified, but Judy kept telling her to calm down and follow her and do exactly what she did. Rozetta felt that she looked stupid and was acting it, too, but they both were admitted to the Saturday night dance!

There was a table on the right side of the room where they sat. Judy immediately found a guy to dance with, and Rozetta was left sitting at the table alone. She felt very uncomfortable in the strange surroundings and kept looking around the room and at the people on the dance floor. She kept telling herself she hoped nobody in the place knew her; she was embarrassed to be there with all those older people. She began to laugh at the people who were obviously drunk and trying to square dance. She was sitting there laughing when all of a sudden a man grabbed her by the arm and jerked her up from the table and said, "Come on … you're going to dance with me!"

Rozetta kept telling this strange man that she did not know how to square dance. He told her he would teach her and dragged her by the arm out on the dance floor. Now she knew she looked stupid! When it came time to switch partners Rozetta ran back to her table and sat down. The man who grabbed her was standing in the circle going around and around looking for her! She started laughing again, and he spotted her. He came to her table and sat down. The first thing Rozetta asked him was, "Are you married, because if you are I'm not talking to you." The man started laughing and showed her his hand. He asked her if she saw a wedding band. She said, "No, but that doesn't mean you're not married." He called out to a friend of his and motioned for him to come over to the table. He looked at his friend and said, "Would you PLEASE tell this woman that I am not married, so she will talk to me!" The man reassured Rozetta that he was not married. He introduced himself and said his name was David. She told him what her name was and started asking him all kinds of questions. David told her about his grocery store, the SRS Grocery that was named after his three children: Sally, Robbie and Sammy. He told her he had recently divorced his wife because she was cheating on him with another man. He showed Rozetta the pictures of his children that he carried in his wallet.

Judy and her dance partner finally returned to the table. David suggested they all go to the Waffle House and have breakfast because he was hungry. Rozetta was inexperienced in all this, so she looked at Judy and waited for her response. Judy said, "Okay, let's go!" Rozetta and Judy followed them to the Waffle House in her '64 Chevy. The Waffle House was well-lighted, so Rozetta could finally get a good look at David. He wasn't bad looking but was a lot older than she had hoped he was. He was about 5 feet 10 inches and average built, with very blue eyes. She asked him how old he was, and he told her 38 and then asked her the same question. She told him she was 19. He liked Rozetta, but she wasn't too sure about him. Before they left, David got Rozetta's phone number. He told her he would call her the next day.

The next morning, Judy had to leave and said good-bye to Rozetta. Later that day David called and invited Rozetta to go to the drive-in movies with him to see "Patton." She accepted, and he picked her up in his white convertible Pontiac. Rozetta wasn't interested in the war movie, so she spent most of the time watching David out of the corner of her eye as he ate his big bucket of popcorn. He really loved that popcorn! She didn't know what his intentions might be, so she was a little nervous; she didn't know much about him. He was a gentleman and wasn't the least bit interested in doing anything but sitting there munching on his popcorn and watching the war movie. He had told Rozetta he spent time in the army and was in the Korean War at the age of 16. He said he was in Germany when President Kennedy was shot in Dallas. She told him she was in the sixth grade when that happened. They both laughed because they knew there was a big age difference.

David continued to pursue Rozetta. The next weekend he invited her to go to the river with him and his children. He had a ski boat and they all loved to water ski. She went but told him she was terrified of the water because she couldn't swim. He put a life jacket on her and made her get in the boat with them. He told her to stop being afraid. They all had fun waterskiing while Rozetta sat in the boat and watched. David had his daughter, Sally, and his son, Robbie, with him that day; they were only five and seven years younger than Rozetta. David took the boat to the middle of the river and turned off the motor. He picked Rozetta up and threw her in the water … as she screamed so loud the campers on the riverbank thought he was killing her.

She was horrified and started crying, but she was floating because she was wearing a life jacket. She yelled at him and asked him why he threw her in the water knowing she was afraid of it and didn't know how to swim. He threw Rozetta the water skis and told Robbie to jump into the water and help her put them on. He told her she was not getting back into the boat until she got up on the water skis! She kept yelling, "I don't know how to do this!" Robbie stayed in the water with her and showed her how to position the skis and how to keep her knees together. This 12-year-old kid was showing her what to do. He also told her to keep her arms straight and not to jerk on the rope or she would fall down. Robbie told Rozetta that his dad did the same thing to him and his sister. He swam back to the boat and climbed in.

David yelled to Rozetta and told her what he was going to do next and to just hold on. She did as he instructed her to do and popped right up out of the water and didn't fall. She held on for dear life and must have had a horrified look on her face, because Robbie and Sally sat in the boat laughing so hard they were doubling over. From that day on, Rozetta got better and better at waterskiing, yet she never learned how to swim until many years later.

On September 2, 1972, at the age of 20, Rozetta married David. Her girlfriend, Dana, warned her not to marry him. Dana said Rozetta was making a big mistake because David was too old for her and had children from a previous marriage. She would have only heartache if she married him. Rozetta didn't listen. Shortly after their marriage, David accepted a very good position with a company in Ft. Lauderdale, Florida, to get away from his ex-wife. A couple of years later, after many weekend trips to the Florida Keys, they decided to move to Key Largo. Rozetta and David had three children: Natasha, Nelson and David, Jr., who was nicknamed Bud.

The marriage was rocky from the beginning because David was a control freak. He was hateful and ill-tempered. He complained about everything. His ex-wife was a thorn in his side, and it made him an angry, bitter man. He took all his frustrations out on Rozetta and thought she too would eventually cheat on him. He was also very insecure because of their age difference. She left him twice, but he always threatened her and forced her back.

After the children were born, he threatened to kill her if she ever took the kids and left him. Rozetta lived in misery and in fear. The only joy in her life was her children, which David really didn't want because he already had grown children. He let her know when she got pregnant that the children would be her responsibility, and he would not allow her to return to work. He knew she was very naive and intimidated her to keep her under his control. He controlled every aspect of her life. He would not allow her to have any girlfriends and would take the phone away from her if she ever got calls from anyone. He would sit looking at her and pointing his finger for her to hang up the phone; if she didn't, he would take it away from her and slam the receiver on the cradle. On many occasions he would threaten to pull the cord out of the wall if she didn't hang up on her friends. He would not watch any of the children when she went shopping. He made her take them all with her everywhere she went and would watch the clock until she got home. If he thought she was gone too long, he would question her endlessly and say nasty things to her.

David's brother and his dad came to visit a lot. His dad would tell him to stop being hateful to Rozetta because she was a sweet woman. He would tell his dad that Rozetta knew he didn't mean anything by it … it was just his way. Rozetta would pray for deliverance from him, as she took her children to church every Sunday to the Burton Memorial Methodist Church, where she was an active member. David didn't want her to go to church, because she might make friends in church, and she did. He would take all her money out of her purse so she couldn't pay any offerings. She was very active in the church and taught Sunday school. The children were involved with many youth groups, but he would never go with them.

As David got older, his drinking increased, and his nasty attitude did, too. He became even more verbally abusive to Rozetta and to the children. He was self-employed as a diesel marine mechanic and knew most all the charter boat captains in the Upper Keys. He was one of the best mechanics in the area, and his name became well-known. One day he was introduced to some people who needed his services in the Bahamas. He was also flown to other Caribbean islands to work on boats. He was making more money than he ever had.

Late one night, while David was away on one of his trips, Rozetta was awakened in the middle of the night by a strange man's voice on the telephone. He introduced himself as an attorney who had been hired to represent David. He kept telling Rozetta not to hang up, because David had told him that she would not believe anything he was saying. He had to be very convincing or she would hang up on him. He proceeded to inform Rozetta that David had been arrested by the Bush Task Force on the Bahama Bank for drug smuggling marijuana and was turned over to Federal Marshalls in Miami. He said he was in jail in Miami and Rozetta was to come to the Federal Court House in Miami the next day for the arraignment and bond hearing. Rozetta was in shock and frightened to death, because she didn't know who David had gotten involved with. She was so upset, she couldn't go back to sleep.

David was released on bond, paid by some unknown person. David knew he was going to serve time on this charge, but he made no arrangements or plans for Rozetta and his children. He was sentenced to three years in Maxwell Air force Base Federal Prison in Alabama. Rozetta had refused to sleep with him after he got arrested, and they were not on speaking terms the day he walked out of the house to begin serving his prison sentence. This was the answer to Rozetta's prayers. David would be out of her life now, but what was she going to do? She had three young children and no family to help her. She had not worked in 10 years!

Rozetta went job hunting … with all three children. The mortgage payment was $1,100 a month, and she knew she could not make enough money to pay all the bills. She applied for a job with a large electric company and was hired. She had not forgotten her executive and accounting skills and was soon promoted and transferred to the General Accounting Department. She was making good money but not enough. She worked on weekends cleaning houses; she also cut hair since she was a self-taught barber/beautician and gave perms to her girlfriends . She utilized her sewing talents to sew and mend garments for her co-workers, too.

All of Rozetta's wonderful co-workers knew she was a struggling single mother with three young children. Many of the guys at work told her they would rather give her the money to cut their hair than go to a barber, so she carried her clippers and scissors to work with her. She would use her lunch hour to cut their hair. Some of the guys who didn't need hair cuts would pay her to give them a trim. She utilized every skill she had to support her children and would never ask anyone for help. Many times she would find a huge box of food sitting at her backdoor that had been dropped off by a church member. Reverend Gass was a wonderful person who knew and understood the hardship Rozetta was facing and that she was too proud to ask for help.

This generosity reminded her of her childhood days in Tin Can Holler, and she would cry because she was very grateful to them for their kindness during her time of need. Rozetta got an attorney and filed for divorce. David was furious. He would call the home and yell at her on the telephone. He also wrote letters to the judge begging him to please not grant Rozetta the divorce, stating that she did not know what she was doing! Rozetta got her divorce, and her attorney sent the bill to David in Federal Prison. She had been married to David for more than 15 years.

One day while at work, John, another co-worker, told Rozetta that he heard about her hair-cutting skills and asked her to give him a haircut. Rozetta needed the money and invited him to her home later than evening. John was a couple of years younger than Rozetta. He was a tall, blond, blue-eyed Irish man. He was very handsome with very broad shoulders and was an avid tennis player. While Rozetta was cutting his hair in the middle of her kitchen, John told her he was looking for a place to rent temporarily because he had to get out of his current apartment. He asked her if she would consider renting the back part of her house to him. Rozetta told him she would have to think about it and let him know. She didn't rent to him, but he soon became a frequent visitor to her home.

Rozetta told John her life story and about her marriage to David. He knew she was having financial problems, but he offered no help and she didn't ask for any. He ate many meals at her home, but never offered to take her and the children out to dinner. When Rozetta told her girlfriends at work that she was dating John they were shocked. They thought he was gay because he was in his mid-thirties and had never been married. They told her he hated children and made rude remarks about kids all the time. During her romance with John, Rozetta's son Nelson began having gran-mal seizures while sitting in front of a computer in his kindergarten class. Rozetta rushed to the hospital. Her girlfriend, Kim Harden, took care of her other two children because she would not leave her son alone in the hospital. John did not call to check on Rozetta or her son, and he passed the hospital every day on his way to the tennis court but did not stop. Rozetta was so much in love with John, she failed to notice or take into consideration all the bad flaws in his character. All the red flags were going up and all her girlfriends told her she should not marry him because he was a very selfish, egotistical man who was only interested in himself and what he wanted or needed.

On June 4, 1988, John and Rozetta got married, and John didn't want the kids to be present. He also didn't want to have anything to do with Rozetta's home. He talked her into walking away from her home and moved her and the children into a home he had rented. She tried to convince him that it would be much easier for him to move into her house, so she wouldn't have to uproot her children and switch schools. Realistically it made more sense for one to move in than four to move out, and she told him his name would be added to the deed. He informed Rozetta that he had no intention of moving into her house or maintaining it or investing any of his money into it. He made numerous excuses to convince her to move out and forget about her house. He said his family and friends advised him against having anything to do with her house, even though he never objected to spending time there before they got married. While they were renting a home, John and Rozetta began looking for a home to purchase. Rozetta was heartbroken that she had lost her home. It was owner-financed, and the former owner took the house back.

John found a house. Rozetta told him it was too small for all five of them, but he insisted on getting his way because it was located on a canal in Tavernier, which had ocean access. He said homes on the water had a better resale value and he wanted that house. The house only had two bedrooms and one bath. All three of Rozetta's children had to share the same bedroom. She was upset because her daughter, Natasha, needed her own bedroom. He promised her that he would convert the downstairs storage room into a bedroom for her, but he didn't. Instead, he used that room for all his sporting equipment:

scuba tanks, tennis rackets, golfing gear, fishing rods, coolers, life jackets and a boat motor. Rozetta had a much bigger home and had to sell and give away most of her furniture, because it would not fit into the smaller home, while he kept his furniture. She also had to sell her daughter's piano, which she loved, because there was no room for it.

Soon after they all moved into the new house, John became verbally abusive to Rozetta and the children. He would constantly remind Rozetta and the children that it was his house. The children would get very upset and beg Rozetta to move back to their home in Key Largo. Not once did he tell Rozetta and her children that the house was their new home or made them feel welcome. They all began to feel like unwanted guests. Months later, John became obsessed and angry because he had included Rozetta's name on the deed. He would corner Rozetta and threaten her to sign a paper stating that the house belonged to him. Rozetta would tell him she married him because she loved him and she wanted the marriage to work. Her love for him had nothing to do with the house or his money.

John became angry one night and locked Rozetta out of the house while the children were sleeping and refused to let her back in unless she signed the paper. She started crying hysterically for him to let her in. He finally opened the door but was still angry. He started dwelling on the fact that David would soon be released from prison and would be returning to the Florida Keys. He became frightened because his tennis buddies kept telling him that David was going to be very angry about losing his wife and his home. John convinced himself that David was going to kill him or have someone else do it and purchased a handgun.

During his marriage to Rozetta, John continued living the life of a single person, refusing to wear a wedding band, coming home late at night after hanging out with his tennis buddies at a local bar. He would go to numerous parties and social events without her and would get angry if she couldn't find a babysitter or refused to go if one of her children was sick. His lifestyle did not change during the marriage other than the fact that there were more people living in the house with him, whom he avoided as much as possible and reminded constantly that it was his home.

Rozetta did everything she could to please him. The house was always immaculate; meals were always prepared, even though his dinner had to be reheated for him because he was never home at dinner time. She did all the shopping, laundry and yard work, kept the vehicles washed, and made sure all the garbage was emptied and carried to the street the night before pickup. Rozetta also helped him paint the entire outside of his house including the concrete roof that was two stories high. John was never around when all the housework was being done. He would tell Rozetta and the children that those were their jobs to do since he made the house payments and they were lucky to have a place to live. Rozetta continued to care for her children and their needs just as she always had.

John applied no income toward the upkeep of her children and their expenses. He never purchased any Christmas or birthday gifts for them. He would remind Rozetta and her children that they were neither his children nor his responsibility. He got angry one night and told her he didn't think their marriage would ever work unless she took her kids and dropped them off at the local children's shelter in Tavernier. He would not allow the children to have friends over or birthday parties. He had total domination over Rozetta and her children. Everything had to be his way. He would easily become irate if she even tried to discuss the possibility of changing any of his rules. His anger became very detrimental to the children. He would tease them and make terrible remarks to and about them. He would also call their dad names in front of them. He would get angry if David did not pick the children up every weekend. John would tell the children that David didn't love them or he'd come pick them up. On one occasion he grabbed Bud, who was only 3 years old, by his hair and jerked him up and threw him onto the bed from the bedroom doorway, which was at least six feet from the bed. He did this because he didn't want to hear him cry. He slammed the bedroom door and made him stay in the bedroom alone. Rozetta became furious and yelled at him for doing that.

He would tease Bud because he couldn't tie his shoes. He said all 3 year olds should be able to tie their own shoes. Rozetta taught him how to tie his shoes, and when he started kindergarten he got an award for being the only child in the entire class who could tie their shoes. Bud also witnessed John push Rozetta down. He demonstrated this on another child at daycare the next day in front of the daycare owner and told her that was what John did to his Mommy. John desperately wanted to get rid of the children. He did not have any parenting skills or patience. He would yell at the children anytime they started arguing among themselves. He would bang his fist on the furniture or kick the furniture, knocking the lamps to the floor.

He also refused to allow the children to run the air conditioner in their bedroom; he didn't want to pay for the additional electricity it used. Rozetta would turn it on whenever he wasn't home, so the children would be cool at night. There were continuous arguments because Rozetta enrolled Nelson in little league baseball and would go watch him play ball. John would tell her she didn't need to watch Nelson play ball, because John's parents never watched him play ball. He was jealous because she wouldn't watch him play in his tennis tournaments.

The humiliation continued with the children all the time. Nelson, who was 6 years old, was a bed-wetter. John would say ugly things to embarrass him and accused him of doing it deliberately because he liked to or because he was too lazy to get up and go to the bathroom. Rozetta had flashbacks of her little sister Marcella who got spanked continuously for wetting the bed. This infuriated Rozetta! He would make Nelson drag his wet mattress out on the balcony where everybody could see it. He would constantly question Nelson's intelligence if he forgot to flush the toilet or empty a garbage can. He would yell at Rozetta, "What's wrong with him? Why can't he follow directions and do them correctly?" Rozetta lived in fear of him throwing her and the children out of his house. She tried desperately to please him, but nothing did. Her childhood health issues came back because of the conditions she and her children had to live in.

Rozetta's love for John died, and she was growing weary of constantly trying to please him. The children hated him just as much as he hated them, and they started telling David about him. David reported him to the local children's services and wanted to press charges against him. David came to the house and got into an argument with John. The children's services Director investigated the charges. She spoke to John, and he blamed everything on Rozetta and the children. He said the children needed discipline and that was what he was doing. She quickly informed him that his methods were wrong and that he should take a parenting course and get counseling immediately. He refused to get counseling and said he had no problems. He said Rozetta was too easy on the children and didn't punish them enough. Rozetta took a parenting course and took her children to counseling. The problem was definitely John, but he was never going to accept any blame. He was in complete denial.

Rozetta tried desperately to keep her family together, because she loved her children. She knew she and the children could not live in this type of environment, because everybody was miserable and she was a nervous wreck trying to keep everybody happy. She decided to let the children stay with David until she could save enough money and find an apartment or house to rent. She stayed in the house with John and slept in the children's room. They both had retained attorneys, and Rozetta was advised to stay in the home until the divorce was final. John was happy that the children were gone and became angry when Rozetta refused his advances to sleep with him. She kept the bedroom door locked so he couldn't get in, and it angered him.

One night he came home late and started banging on her bedroom door. He ordered her to open the door and clean something off the floor. When Rozetta opened the door to see what he was complaining about he shoved her against the dresser with his entire body and demanded she give him his VCR she had in the bedroom. When she asked him to please get out of her room, he became angrier and shoved her again. Rozetta ran past him and grabbed the telephone and called the police. When the police came they talked to each of them separately. It was never known what John said to those police officers, but it wasn't the truth. The police officers told Rozetta and John if they had to come back again they would arrest both of them.

The next day, John went to his attorney and told him Rozetta had attacked him and that he was afraid of her. The papers were served on Rozetta at work the next day. John's attorney got a restraining order against her that included an order for her to vacate the premises immediately. Rozetta couldn't believe he would stoop so low and lie to the authorities to get her out of his house, but he did, knowing she had no family and no place to go. As Rozetta was walking back to her office crying, she fainted. As soon as her supervisor, whom everyone called Bubba, saw her fall on the floor, he ran over to help her. When he found out what John's attorney had done, he became angry and went to confront John. John lied again and said he didn't know his attorney was going to do that. He told Bubba Rozetta could stay in his house. He wanted to save face in front of the boss. Rozetta couldn't stay, regardless of what he said, because she had a court order to get out and could have been arrested.

After this incident with Rozetta, Bubba implemented a new policy into the Cooperative by-laws that forbid any kind of actions similar to this one from ever occurring again on company property. Rozetta was allowed to leave work, so she could pack her things and leave John's house.

On her way out of the office, her dear friend, Joette, asked her where she was going to stay. Rozetta told her she didn't know what she was going to do. Joette told her to stop crying and made her wait until she called her daughter, Karen. She smiled at Rozetta and told her Karen wanted her to come and stay with her, and that's exactly what Rozetta did. She and Karen became best of friends, and Karen cried the day Rozetta moved into her own apartment.

The divorce was not final yet, and John was still obsessed with his house. Rozetta refused to sign a quit claim deed because she and her children ended up homeless because of John. She did everything his way and walked away from her home to please him, and now she had nothing. She finally gave in to his demands when she found out he had nude pictures of her that he took one night after she drank too much wine. The thoughts of him showing her pictures to his tennis buddies or strangers at the bars devastated her. She was a mother of three children and never wanted anyone to see those pictures, even though she was married to him when he took them.

She did not have enough money to afford a good attorney, so when she told her attorney about the pictures, his advice was to sign the quit claim deed only if he returned the pictures to her … nothing was ever said about him blackmailing her, which was exactly what he was doing. Her spirit was broken, her heart had been broken, and he had humiliated her in front of her friends and co-workers. The pictures were returned to her, and she signed the quit claim deed. She knew she couldn't fight him because she didn't have enough money, and she felt that he had taken everything from her and would have taken her blood, too, if she had allowed it.

Rozetta had loved and trusted John and let him make decisions for her and her children when he had never had any experience in doing so. He was unqualified and did not act responsibly. Now she and her children were suffering because she allowed it to happen. She had a big enough heart to tolerate this situation out of her love for him, and she tried to get him to love her kids. He never loved any of them because he was too much in love with himself. She made a promise to herself that she would never trust another person to make decisions for her or her children. All her life, she was accustomed to having other people tell her what to do, but NOT anymore. She thanked God that John would soon become a dim memory in her past, but she could never forget what he did to her and her children. She transferred to the Engineering Department, which was in another building, so she wouldn't have to see him while at work.

David still had the children, and Rozetta desperately wanted them back. She only had enough money to rent a one-bedroom apartment, and that wasn't big enough for all her children, so she started cleaning houses again on weekends. One of her regular customers knew she was trying to save enough money to get a bigger place. He was kind to her and told her she could do his ironing if she wanted to and he would pay her the same thing he paid the dry cleaners. She accepted. She spent her nights, after work, in her apartment ironing his clothes to take back to him the following weekend.

David knew how much she loved the children and had always

been a good mother. He started calling her and asking her to come back to him. When Rozetta said no, he became upset and started yelling into the phone. Rozetta decided she was not going to allow another man to mistreat her, and she took control of the situation. She started hanging up on him. She thought, "Gee, that was easy, why didn't I do that before!" David's drinking got worse again, after he realized that Rozetta was not coming back to him. He made the kids miserable, and she knew she must to do something fast.

A little conch house became available for rent that was located directly in front of the electric cooperative where Rozetta worked. She talked to the lady who handled its rental for the owners, who lived up north. The house was old, but Rozetta knew she could fix it up and make it better. She asked the rental agent to tell the owners that she would like to buy the house if they ever decided to sell it. She wanted the first option on it. They agreed, and she moved into the little house. The children were excited to be back with their mother, and she was happier than she had been in years; she also knew she was going to have a hard time. David would constantly tell her that she couldn't take care of the children alone, and he refused to pay her child support. He was trying every way possible to force her to come back to him, and she was determined that no matter what, she would never go back.

The rental home was in need of repair, but Rozetta didn't want to fix it up unless she owned it. She made an offer to purchase the home as an owner-financed mortgage. The owners liked her offer and accepted. She took money out of her 401K as the down payment. This was one of the happiest days of her life. She now owned a home and started remodeling it, one room at a time as she had extra money. She was very grateful to the former owners for allowing her the opportunity to purchase their home.

David's hate, anger and drinking finally caught up with him. He had a heart attack and went to the hospital. He was in the intensive care unit for several days, and Rozetta took the children to visit him. She had sympathy for David when she saw all the tubes connected to him. Regardless of how she felt toward him, she still had compassion for him because he would always be the father of her children. She knew he had a lot of problems and issues that were eating him alive and the heart attack was a wakeup call for him. David was now 57 years old, and she was 39. David kept telling her and the children that he was going to be fine, but Rozetta knew better. She was friends with the physician who was caring for him. She talked to him and asked if David was going to be okay. He told Rozetta that he had advised David to go to the Miami Heart Institute for further testing or to the VA because he would need bypass surgery. The only thing this doctor could do for David was give him nitro-glycerin tablets. She asked him if David would die without that surgery and he said, "Probably."

When David was well enough to leave the hospital, he started making plans to return to his hometown of Cleveland, Tennessee, and he wanted to take the children with him. Rozetta was battling with her own heart now. David had refused to go to the Miami Heart Institute or the VA, and she knew it would just be a matter of time before he had another heart attack. She let the children decide if they wanted to go. Natasha said no, but her sons said yes. She did not want the children in the automobile with him just in case he had an attack, so she told David she would drive them up after he got settled. She knew in her heart that she did not want to leave her boys with David, but they would never forgive her if she refused to let them go and he died. She kept her promise to David. She and Natasha, Nelson and Bud went to Tennessee. David tried to convince Natasha to stay, but she again said no. She knew he would make her be the maid and do all the work, as he had done before when she lived with him in the Florida Keys.

Rozetta cried all the way back to Florida. She did not know how she could live without her two little boys. It was the 4th of July when she took them to Tennessee, and by October the boys were calling her to come get them. They wanted to come home. She talked to David, and he was having a lot of financial problems and agreed it would be best for her to come get the boys. She planned the trip during the Thanksgiving weekend. She and Natasha traveled to Tennessee to pick up her sons. None of them knew that this would be the last time they would see their father alive.

While at work on the morning of January 12, 1993, Rozetta received a call from David's daughter-in-law in Cleveland, Tennessee. She informed Rozetta that David had died from a massive heart attack the night before. As much as she had hated David, she never wanted him to be dead, and she had to prepare herself to tell the children that their father was gone. Natasha was 13, Nelson was 9, and Bud was 5. Natasha and Bud cried, but Nelson got angry. He told Rozetta that his dad had promised him they would do a lot of things together before he came back to Florida.

David's daughter from his first wife, Sally, called to find out if the children were coming to the funeral. Rozetta explained to her that she could not take off work and did not have the money to fly them up. A family friend paid for Natasha's airline ticket, and she flew to Tennessee later that day. Sally called Rozetta again later that day to tell her that her mother offered to pay for Nelson and Bud's airline tickets. Rozetta agreed to allow Nelson to fly to Tennessee but refused to allow Bud because she felt he was too young to see his father dead. She had flashbacks of her own mother's funeral when she was 7 years old and how traumatized she was. It was horrible, and she did not want Bud to go through the same thing. Sally got angry and started cursing Rozetta and even placed blame on her for David's death. Rozetta hung up the telephone. Sally calmed down and called back to apologize. Rozetta took Nelson to the airport, and he flew to Tennessee to attend his father's funeral with the rest of David's family.

Rozetta was looking forward to Natasha and Nelson returning home. She knew they all needed normalcy back in their lives. Nelson would never be the same after the death of his father. He never played ball again. He was a left-handed pitcher and was good. He started misbehaving and getting into trouble at school. One evening he brought home a friend he had met in school whom Rozetta did not know. The next morning, when Rozetta went to the boys' room to wake them up, Nelson and his friend were not there and the bed had not been slept in. She woke Bud and asked him if he knew where his brother was and he said, "no." She noticed that an empty container of Zip Lock bags was lying on the kitchen counter. She had no idea what the boys were up to, but she dialed 911.

Unbeknownst to Rozetta, the police officer who knocked on her door early that morning would become a very special person in her life. He introduced himself as Deputy Ownby, and he could tell she was very upset. She explained her concerns regarding her son, Nelson, and the new friend he brought home. She also showed the officer the empty box of plastic bags. Officer Ownby began laughing and asked if Nelson had a gorilla mask. She told him yes, and he asked her to go get it because he wanted to see it. Rozetta looked in Nelson's closet and his drawers and could not find it. She told him she couldn't find it, and he started laughing again. She didn't know why he was laughing and asking about Nelson's gorilla mask. She thought this was strange behavior, since she was worried about Nelson.

Officer Ownby asked her the name of the boy Nelson had brought home, and she told him. He stated that he knew this boy and thought they had pulled a prank during the middle of the night. He said one of the female officers almost wrecked to avoid hitting what she thought was a man lying in the middle of U.S. Highway 1, which was directly behind their house. When she stopped her car to check it out she discovered it was pair of pants, shirt and a gorilla mask that were stuffed with blown-up zipper-top bags. He told Rozetta he knew where the mother of this young boy worked and he would go talk to her and come back.

Officer Ownby returned about 20 minutes later and confirmed it was the same boy he thought it was. As he stood talking to Rozetta, Nelson walked through the front door. He was surprised to see a police officer standing in the living room and asked what was going on. Officer Ownby turned to face Nelson and gave him a lecture he never forgot. Nelson didn't like what the officer said but stood frozen listening to him.

Officer Ownby would call to check on Rozetta and Nelson. He became a very important person to her family, because he truly cared. When Nelson was 13 years old, he attempted suicide. He hanged himself in his bedroom closet, and Rozetta found him. Nelson was seconds from being brain dead when she broke the rope that was around his neck. She ran to the other room to call 911. Bud started crying and pounding on Nelson's chest as he lay on his bedroom floor. Nelson started breathing and opened his eyes. The police and paramedics came to her house and transported him to the hospital. Officer Ownby met them at the hospital. Nelson was okay, but his neck had an ugly scar from the rope. It remained that way for over a year and then slowly faded away.

Officer Ownby suggested that Rozetta's children get involved with the Upper Keys Youth Association; he volunteered a lot of his free time to the youth in the community. The children enjoyed being involved with the youth association, but Nelson was angry and began to get into trouble by hanging out with older boys who were a bad influence on him and getting into fights. They would get mad at Nelson and beat him up. He had to have his nose reset several times. Their family doctor finally told him he needed to learn how to "duck." Rozetta was in and out of court because of Nelson, and Officer Ownby was always there for moral support.

Nelson was placed in a group home for boys and eventually court ordered into the Eckerd Wilderness Camp Program in Ocala, Florida. Rozetta was desperate to find the right program for her son. He loved the Eckerd camp and graduated with honors a year later. While Nelson was away at camp, Officer Ownby continued to inquire about Nelson's progress. He also became a mentor for Rozetta. He told Rozetta that she had the perfect personality for a realtor and thought she could be very successful in that profession. She enrolled at the Florida Keys Community College and took the course. Several months later she took the Florida State Board Exam and received her state license. She did not give up her day job, but she worked in the real estate business at night and on weekends and did very well. With the extra money she made from commissions, Rozetta completely remodeled her house inside and out and did new landscaping. Her little house was now one of the prettiest on the street.

After 28 years in the Florida Keys, Rozetta decided to sell her home and leave. She moved to Port St. Lucie, Florida, in 2002. She purchased another home, which was much larger than the one she owned in the Florida Keys, and got a very good job with a large corporation and worked there for four years. When her youngest son turned 21 in 2006, she resigned from her position and sold her home to begin her lifelong quest to find out the truth about her mother's murder.

CHAPTER 36

arcella was placed in the home of Mr. and Mrs. Click in Elizabethton, Tennessee, after she was removed from the Curtis foster home. The Clicks had a teenage son, who was attending college. They had tragically lost their daughter in a house fire many years earlier. They were active members in their local Methodist church and wanted to help a child. They were wonderful Christian people who adored and loved Marcella as though she were their own daughter. They had a beautiful home in a nice neighborhood. They tried to adopt Marcella, but Seig would not sign the adoption papers. This angered Marcella, because she too loved her new family. She did not understand why her natural father, whom she did not know or remember, would not let them adopt her.

Mrs. Click was an excellent seamstress and made Marcella beautiful clothes. She had the best of everything. Mrs. Click was also active with Cub Scout and church activities. Life with the Click family was good, but Marcella had a wild side. She attended Elizabethton High School, but she did not apply herself or strive to improve her grades. She enjoyed her social life and was allowed to have her friends visit at the home. The Clicks had a large swimming pool in their backyard, so she was allowed to have pool parties. She began sneaking out of school or would not go to school. She only wanted to socialize with her friends. She met a young man by the name of Travis, who was several years older than her. She thought he was gorgeous. He was tall and had blond hair and blue eyes. She was always attracted to those types of men. Marcella also started socializing with the wrong kind of young people who introduced her to alcohol and marijuana. She was always fighting with herself to keep her figure. She started taking lots of diet pills and became addicted to them, too.

The Clicks had a difficult time controlling Marcella. She was determined to be with Gary. She would climb out of her bedroom window to sneak off and be with him. This hurt the Clicks deeply; they loved Marcella and did not want her to get into trouble or get hurt. Their punishment and groundings did not work. They were very concerned about her wellbeing and did not know what to do.

Travis and Marcella's courtship led to an unplanned pregnancy and a quick marriage. The Clicks were not happy about the situation Marcella had gotten into, but they were supportive of her decision to marry Travis and arranged a small church wedding for them. It is not known whether she and Travis were in love or thrown into an unhappy situation that neither of them were ready for.

Their daughter was born on May 1, 1971. Marcella was only 17 years old and had no experience with children and did not know how to be a mother. The marriage did not last, and Travis filed for divorce. Marcella left Elizabethton. She was so confused, she did not know what to do. She lived in subsidy housing and collected welfare. She would have affairs with men and would leave her daughter with whomever she could find to watch her. On one occasion it was reported that a group of children had been left alone without an adult being present, and Marcella's daughter was involved. She was taken away from Marcella and placed in a foster home. Marcella neglected her little girl and put her own needs and desires before anything else. She would smoke marijuana and drink in front of the child. Marcella's daughter did not have a normal childhood, and Marcella blamed her for having such a terrible life. Marcella would tell her daughter as she got older that if it hadn't been for her Marcella could have gone to college and had a better life. Being only a child, the daughter was made to feel guilty for something that was not her fault. As she grew older she could never get close to Marcella. They would argue constantly. The situation became a jealousy thing instead of a mother-daughter conflict. Marcella made her daughter's life miserable because of her drinking and drug abuse. She did not want her to be happy because she herself was not happy. After years of moving from place to place she returned to Elizabethton and asked Mr. and Mrs. Click for help. They, of course, could not turn her away. They bought a small house for her and eventually put the deed into her name. Marcella's drinking and marijuana smoking continued.

A friend of Marcella's introduced her to a man by the name of Rick Parlier whom she would eventually marry. He was a nice man who was very shy and was several years younger than Marcella. She seemed to enjoy his company, and they had a good time together.

He was also very good to her daughter. She got a job working in a nursing home and had a steady income until she injured her back and had to have major surgery. After she recovered from her surgery she was addicted to her pain medication. Her family doctor refused to prescribe anymore medication for her. She became so addicted and so desperate that she began buying it off the street wherever she could find it.

Marcella's weight became an obsession with her once again. She underwent gastric bypass surgery to lose weight. She slimmed down and looked better than she had in years, and she and Rick got married. Shortly after her marriage to Rick, she became depressed and was very unhappy. She would cry all the time. She probably didn't know why she was depressed, because of the drug and alcohol abuse that she could not control. She refused to get the help she desperately needed. To her she did not have a problem.

Rick, leaving a super bowl party at his brother's house, was involved in a serious traffic accident and became a paraplegic. Marcella was so upset, she would not go to the hospital to see him for several days. She had been told about his serious injuries, but she was afraid to face the truth. Her daughter eventually insisted that she go to the hospital to visit Rick because he was asking for her and desperately wanted to see her.

It devastated Marcella when she saw Rick and the seriousness of his condition became a reality. She became more depressed and drank even more. When Rick was eventually released from the hospital because there was nothing more that could be done for him, Marcella agreed to be his caregiver even though she really didn't want to. She knew she would never be able to leave him alone and her freedom to come and go as she pleased would have to cease.

Rick was a veteran and could have stayed in the VA hospital indefinitely. She had to convert the second bedroom into a hospital room for Rick. She had to take care of his every need 24 hours a day. She was not physically or mentally able to do this and soon began using his medication for her own pain.

On March 17, 2000, Marcella kissed Rick goodnight and went to her bedroom. The next morning, as Rick called her name she did not come to his room as she usually did. There was no answer and no response to his calls. He immediately knew something was terribly wrong and started screaming in hopes that the neighbors would hear him. He was unable to do anything. He lay in his bed for several days until his in-home care nurse came for her regular weekly visit. As soon as she heard his screams and realized that she could not get inside the house, she called the police for assistance.

The nurse immediately went to Rick, while the police officers searched the house for any signs of Marcella. Rick knew she was dead. He kept telling the police that she must be dead because she never came to his room. He said she did not leave the house because he would have heard her. The police confirmed Rick's fears. They found Marcella in her room lying across her bed with a needle stuck into her arm, and she was pronounced dead. She was only 46 years old. There were empty bottles of Elavil and other pain medications. It is not known whether Marcella deliberately killed herself or if it was an accident, but the autopsy report revealed numerous needle marks on her arms from continuous drug use. Her addictions to drugs and alcohol and her refusal to get the help she desperately needed caused her own death. She spent her entire adult life looking for love that she could not find. She must have thought there was no other way to end her pain and inner suffering. On March 22, 2000, Marcella was buried in the Mountain Home National Cemetery, which was reserved for her husband Rick. After her death, Rick was transported to the VA hospital where he remained until his death. He was buried in the same grave, above Marcella, two years later.

Thanks and Gratitude to the Holston Methodist Home for Children

All of the Mowery children are forever grateful to the Holston Methodist Home who cared for them after their mother's death. Without this wonderful organization to care for them, it is not known what would have happened to them. Although some of the foster homes were not always the best, because they did not have the means to do thorough background screenings in the 1950s and 1960s, their main concern has been and always will be the welfare of the children. Whenever there was a problem they immediately took action to place the children elsewhere. Today their system for screening the foster care program is the best in the country.

Holston Home is a Christian ministry providing hope and healing for children and families struggling with life's challenges. Holston Home strives to be the agency of first choice in serving children and families with special needs in east Tennessee and southwest Virginia. The agency continues be recognized as a regional child and family service leader, with energetic and involved trustees and competent, committed staff and volunteers.

Holston United Methodist Home for Children is, proudly, a ministry of the Holston Conference of the United Methodist Church. That connection is manifested in many ways. The resident Bishop of the Holston Annual Conference is an ex-officio member of their board of trustees, as is the District Superintendent in the Morristown District, and the Health and Welfare Representative of the Conference. Several of their board members have church connections as well. And this ministry of helping children has a heart-felt as well as a monetary connection with every member of a United Methodist Church in the Conference, and that includes more than 915 churches in an area covering all of east Tennessee, the 17 western-most counties of Virginia and a small portion of northern Georgia. To fulfill their mission, they work to build meaningful, trusting relationships which result in wholeness and permanency for children and families.

The Holston United Methodist Home for Children is an extension of the church. The children helped by their ministry often tell them, years after they leave, that the introduction to the church they received at Holston Home has had a meaningful and lasting role in their lives. This was also true for the Mowery children.

Anyone who is interested in more information regarding the Holston Methodist Home, or those who wish to make a donation, please visit their website: www.holstonhome.org or contact: Rev. Charles Hutchins,P.O.Box188,Greeneville,TN37744
charleshutchins@holstonhome.org
(423) 787-8723 to discuss how you may be able to help the children.

Or read the following book:
"Haven in the Hills" by Eva Grey Hutchins

CONCLUSION

When I began my research, I never envisioned that I would be introduced to so many wonderful, caring individuals who willingly and eagerly volunteered their time to help me. A year before I began traveling to Tennessee to get the information I needed, I made telephone calls and inquiries into my past via the Internet and was greeted by cheerful voices of angels who opened up their hearts to assist me.

My heart wanted to let the world know that my mother was a wonderful person and a decent human being who dug herself into a hole that she could not get out of, and she had no family support to help her climb out, so she continued to stay with my father and had more children. The lies and distorted truths that were told by my father to save himself from life in prison or execution became an obsession. The lies he told from the day he was arrested until he had his day in court were picked up by the local news media, which got him the sympathy he desperately needed. My father, who was a monster and a hardcore racist, killed my mother because of a rumor and only served two years in prison for killing her in cold blood. He wasn't born a monster ... his mother turned him into one when he was only a child, as her father did her.

In my attempts to locate the bodies of all the men my grandmother killed, I was turned away by the Tennessee Bureau of Investigations and the Southeastern Timberland Company, which now owns Brickell Ridge behind her property in Meigs County. The TBI agents graciously informed me that there were no missing person reports during the time the killings occurred and they would not be able to identify who they were. I was not allowed access to the property to search for the deep hole by the current owners, due to liability reasons. I was desperate to know the truth of their whereabouts so their souls could be put to rest.

I contracted the services of Annette Martin, a well-known psychic detective, who has worked with law enforcement in California for more than 30 years solving crimes, to corroborate the stories I had been told. That she did ... as was told by my dad on his deathbed. My grandmother threw 25-30 mutilated male bodies into that deep hole on Brickell Ridge. There may be more, besides the men Grace killed ... because Grace was not the only person who knew about the deep hole! Although I had been given this information, there was nothing I could do to put those souls to rest. I informed the current owners to beware as they begin excavating the area for a future housing development. This will remain an unsolved mystery.

As I began to write my story, reminiscing about my childhood days with my mother and her singing and playing her guitar, a mysterious occurrence happened to me. I can't explain it, nor can anyone else. A guitar pick appeared on the floor by my left foot where I always sat with my laptop and worked. I do not own a guitar ... where had this guitar pick come from? I took this as a sign from my mother. I know in my heart that she wanted me to have her guitar. Months later, as I was being interviewed by the Daily Post Athenian newspaper in Athens, I asked the reporter to please put a picture of my mother's guitar in the article, too, and let the residents know I am searching for it. I felt in my heart that someone knew who had my mother's guitar, but the search continues ... the mystery and the lies of who had her guitar and who gave it to whom will never be solved until the person who is in possession of it has a change of heart and brings it forward. The sentimental value of my mother's guitar can only be appreciated by those for whom she played ... her children.

After I discovered the truth about my real grandfather, Harry Evans, and the life of luxury he lived, seeing the mansion he once owned that is now in need of many repairs, and how he took my grandmother's farm away from my dad and his brothers when she clearly wanted to keep the farm in the family, made me very sad. I was not sad because he deprived me and my siblings of our rightful inheritance due to his greed and negligent mismanagement, or that we had to live in poverty as children in a place called Tin Can Holler, but that he did not have any desire to know or paternally bond with me or my siblings.

Our lives would have been completely different and could have been much happier had he been man enough to step up to the plate and admit he was our grandfather and offered to help us, rather than having us sent to an orphanage home to be raised by strangers. He befriended my brother Billy, as Uncle Harry, but he could have made a big difference in my brother's life had he admitted to Billy that he was his grandfather. He could have helped and encouraged Billy to get his contractor's license and start his own roofing company had he not been too proud and had he thought more of his public image than his grandchildren.

My sister, Beulah, needed him the most, and he was not there for her either. If she had known he was her grandfather, she could have gone to him for help rather than give her children away for adoption ... a pain she has lived with her entire life. I promised my sister that I would do my best to find all her children, and I continue to search for two of them. They need to know the truth. Whether they want to meet the family is their choice. They probably don't realize they were actually the lucky ones.

On February 14, 1969, my grandfather passed away at the age of 86, alone and penniless, living off his social security. Someone wrote the following article in the Daily Post Athenian newspaper honoring him. No name was published with the following article:

> A life of service came to an end in the passing of Harry Evans last Friday night. Failing health had been his lot in recent years, but for seven decades the term, "Mr. Harry," was a household word in McMinn County. He began his career as a mere lad assisting his father, the late Tom Evans, a mortician in the 1880s. After his father's death he and his mother continued the mortuary work as Evans and Son. Before he became incapacitated, Mr. Harry could recall and relive moments of various sorts through the years. His span of life saw burial services move from the undertaking label to trained morticians, bearing the proud brand of funeral directors. Horse drawn wagons with coffins in the bed became drawn hearses and presently the beautiful funeral cars. Cemetery custodians have replaced voluntary grave diggers, and lovely chapels have succeeded crowded home rooms for funeral rites. Mr. Harry lived a full life. Sympathetic understanding was his trademark in his profession. He was generous to a fault and through the years individuals, families and small churches have received succor and sustenance from him. His death takes another of the old guard from ranks already depleted. He wrought well in his time.

It gives me a good feeling knowing that my grandfather touched so many lives within his community, because he was a kind and generous man, but it also saddens me to know that he couldn't acknowledge and love his own grandchildren. Nothing more can be said about him ... his legacy will live on in the hearts of many ... as it should; even though he was not there for us, he was there for a lot of other people.

I firmly believe that my family spirits wanted me to see the other side of the story. This is most important, because all the things we do, think and feel are placed into the consciousness. I want to heal the consciousness from all the damage that was done in the past. As I was writing this story I felt that things were being brought into balance, that the truth was coming out and the darkness was being lit with light. My story is a major opportunity to right the wrongs that were done within the energy of my family. We can experience time ... we can go backward and forward into time and correct and heal some of the things that occurred in the past, which then changes the future, and that's part of what this is about. This is very important to me and the wellbeing of my family. It's critical that this fear-based cycle doesn't get carried on and doesn't become a self-fulfilling prophecy for my family members, because there were many circumstances that came together that created Grace and Seig's hate, and most of these circumstances are now gone.

Our challenge is not to let self-fulfilling prophecies come into play. We're not separate here … we are all one, and our energies are all connected and linked within this consciousness. We must not let our fears of our children and grandchildren inheriting this illness overcome us. It's important to release the fear, because it's going to be picked up by others. When we release this fear and come to an understanding … (that's what love is about: understanding, compassion and joy) … then we won't continue with those thoughts that are literally projecting energy out into the consciousness sometimes and directed toward specific people.

I wasn't sure if I believed in family curses, but there have been many things that have occurred in my family that have led me to believe otherwise since finding out the truth about my grandmother, Grace Sims. Many families have dealt with similar problems. Ours is not unique or one of a kind. There are unexplained reasons why four grandchildren and seven great-grandchildren of Grace Sims have similar traits and characteristics; unknown anger problems, mental problems and depression, abuse, low self-esteem, addiction problems (alcohol and drugs), attempted suicides, committing crimes and/or breaking the law, and serving time in prison lead one to believe this cycle continues and needs to be broken. These were not learned or copied behaviors. Our family has been separated for decades with years passing without any contact.

Being the perfect, loving and nurturing parent, having the perfect home life, going to the perfect schools, attending church and being involved with the youth activities, actually does nothing to keep evil out of your life … it's what we have in our genetic DNA that makes us who and what we are, but there are other factors that come into play. The energy surrounding my family needs to be in balance. We live in a world of duality: the fear and love, the dark and light, man and woman. What I gained from my research helped me to better understand the circumstances that came together and created the actions of Grace, Seig and Harry even though it does not excuse or condone them. All this has shown me the other side of the story.

When there are as many fear-based actions as what took place within my family (because that is the epitome of fear), then we also have an opposite ... there's always another side. This helped me to see all the sides of the story, so I could give a more accurate understanding of what happened. Fear feeds on itself. We only have two basic responses to life, one is fear and the other is love. We are using fear as love's opposite, and there's a lot of fear in the world, but there's also a lot of love. Love is a more powerful expression.

Everything vibrates at a certain vibration level, and love has the highest vibration. Whenever there is fear-based energy, we can shift that energy, and this is what I hope to achieve within my family. I'm sure there have been and will continue to be many other people and many other families who have had similar experiences, and only seeing one side of the story literally enhances the fear. Only when we heal that hate will we be able to stop that cycle and perpetuate the positive energy from one generation to the next.

We have guides and angels ... all kinds of people who help and protect us. Because of this, I was separated from my family's belief system, and I developed my own. When we fit in, we adopt that system, and when we don't fit into society or whatever, we are able to stand and create a different one if we choose. This is what happened to me. I want to be able to bring a new way of seeing things, whether it is more spiritual or a realistic way to other people. We have to develop that ... we are sometimes forced to develop it.

I want to send a message to everyone regarding domestic violence and its devastating aftermath if there is no intervention. Intervention can be from any person who is aware of it. Today, in America, domestic violence is escalating even though it has always been in our society. For decades it was ignored and people looked the other way. This is what happened with my mother as she screamed her last breath. Her unnerving screams were heard throughout Tin Can Holler, but no one came to help her ... not even the two men who stood less that 10 feet away and listened as my father stomped her to death! Please report domestic abuse and scream from the highest mountain if you have to in order to get someone's attention. My mother, during the 1950s, had no place to go with seven children. Today there are shelters and safe havens in every city across America. There are countless numbers of organizations that help the victims of domestic abuse whether it be children or adults.

During the 1950s there were no laws protecting my mother, but today it is a crime. Americans need a wakeup call. This type of cruelty is not labeled and has no discrimination. It occurs in poor families and wealthy families and every race on the planet. My family had every type of domestic violence imagined from my great-grandfather's sexual attacks on my grandmother to child and spousal abuse.

Rozetta Mowery

My siblings and I were abused as children and as wives. I hope my story can help others find the root of their family problems or family curses and work to overcome them through love, prayers, counseling or whatever means it takes to break the cycle, because we are still working on ours ... six generations past my great-grandfather, Tyre Houston Sims, where it all began.

DOMESTIC ABUSE HOTLINE: **1-800-799-7233**

CHILD ABUSE HOTLINE: **1-800-422-4453**

Discovering the truth about her family changed Rozetta's life completely and sent her on a mission she never dreamed was possible. Today she is an advocate speaker against domestic violence and assists with fundraisers to promote and support domestic violence programs and shelters. She is a motivational speaker for young people and a spokesperson for CASA (Court Appointed Special Advocates) for children in the states foster care programs and the Holston United Methodist Home for Children. She has made it her life's mission to bring awareness to the public regarding the dangers of domestic violence and how it destroys lives and families. She also has a special place in her heart for foster children and the Holston United Methodist Home for Children, because she was a foster child. She encourages people to get involved in their local communities and support their local CASA chapters. The foster children need a voice and through the wonderful volunteers that work for CASA they have many voices.

Please visit Rozetta's websites and sign her guest books:
www.tragedyintincanholler.com
www.myspace.com/rozettamowery
www.facebook.com

ACKNOWLEDGMENTS and CREDITS

I wish to thank and extend my deepest gratitude to the following people and to those who wished to remain anonymous for their compassion, kindness and contributions, which made this all possible:

➢ Charles and Eva Gray Hutchins and the Holston Methodist Home for Children in Greenville, Tennessee, for the care my siblings and I received and for providing me with documents and letters from my parents that I never knew existed.

➢ The Tennessee Department of Corrections, for all their diligent research in locating my father's prison records.

➢ My two cousins who answered my questions and inquiries regarding the Robinson family history.

➢ Arnold Harrod, a lifetime resident of Athens, Tennessee, who answered my personal ad for information about my mother. Many thanks are extended to Arnold for his kindness. Arnold's numerous contacts within the local McMinn County area were invaluable. He took hours of his own time researching and mailed the information to me before my relocation to Tennessee. Arnold also took me to the exact location where my mother was murdered. Thank you, Arnold.

➢ Gloria Schouggins, Catherine Ricker, Paulette Jones and all the lovely ladies at the Meigs County Historical Museum. They located the records I had searched assiduously for years to find. Gloria and Catherine were also my tour guides and arranged for me to meet and interview many prominent historians from that area. Thanks to their kindness, I now have many new friends there.

➢ Many thanks and appreciation are also extended to Willie Ashley, a very lovely lady and lifetime resident and local historian in Meigs County. All the information provided by her was pertinent for my book.

➢ The nice young couple who now own my grandmother's farm in Meigs County, who welcomed me into their home. They answered all my questions pertaining to the property and provided unknown information to me that was relevant to my research.

➢ Mr. White and his sister, who gave me a quilt that was handmade by my grandmother while she served time in prison.

➢ Special thanks and gratitude are extended to the Register of Deeds for Meigs County and her two assistants. Without their assistance I could not have located the old deeds and records I needed for my story.

➢ Many heartfelt thanks are extended to all those who met with me on several occasions to discuss my research about families who once lived in Tin Can Holler.

➤ The McMinn County Historical Society for providing me with information on the history of Tin Can Holler.

➤ Mrs. Huff, a lifetime resident of Athens, Tennessee, and former neighbor in Tin Can Holler. Her insight and enthusiasm was uplifting as was her knowledge of Tin Can Holler. She enlightened me about life in Tin Can Holler.

➤ Estelle Gennoe-Cole, a lifetime resident of Athens, Tennessee, and former neighbor in Tin Can Holler. Thank you, Estelle, for being there for me and my sisters when no one else was. Estelle's daughter and my childhood playmate, Dorothy, was instrumental in arranging a reunion for me and Estelle. Thank you, Dorothy, for reconnecting me with your wonderful mother.

➤ Mrs. McGhee, my mother's best friend from Tin Can Holler. Her wonderful memories of my mother lifted my spirits as she spoke very fondly of my mother.

➤ Harold Hunter, a lifetime resident of Athens, Tennessee, and the Community Development Director for the City of Athens for discussing and recalling his memories of Tin Can Holler and for arranging the meeting I had with agents from the Tennessee Bureau of Investigations. I am honored to have had the opportunity to meet such a highly respected and dedicated community servant.

➤ My brother's best childhood friend from Tin Can Holler, for all the memories he recalled with my brother, Billy, during the 1950s.

➤ Many thanks and appreciation to all the employees at the Daily Post-Athenian newspaper in Athens, Tennessee, for the research and assistance they provided.

➤ Mr. and Mrs. Wade for talking to me about my parents, whom they had known as children and young adults.

➤ National Archives-Central Plains Region and the NARA SE Region for researching the Federal Archives of the FBI files and locating my grandmother's federal prison records.

➤ The top Geologist with the Tennessee Division of Geology, who spoke with me and searched their topography maps of the Brickell Ridge area in Meigs County.

➤ A special thank you is extended to Sandra Deacon and Annette Martin for their retrospection and spirituality regarding my family's past transgressions.

➤ My sister Cindy's children for sharing their mother's life story with me.

➤ Much appreciation is extended to all the other people whom I cannot name and who spoke with me regarding my parents, life in

Tin Can Holler, my mother's murder and the possible whereabouts of her guitar.

>   My gratitude is also extended to my remaining siblings: Shelia and Beulah and all my nieces and nephews. Thank you for your love and encouragement for me to complete this book, so the loving memory of our mother and grandmother, Eliza Mae, will never be forgotten.

>   A very special thank you is extended to my dear friends Ken and Diane Hiscoe from Port St. Lucie, Florida, for their love and encouragement that kept my spirits up as I was discovering the truth about my family. They traveled from Florida to check on me to make sure I was okay.

>   And to all my friends at Liberty Medical Supply Pharmacy in Port St. Lucie, Florida, I want to say thank you for all the e-mails with well wishes and congratulations that flooded my yahoo account. God bless all of you for your kindness and prayers.

Author's Biography

Rozetta Mowery is a survivor. As a single, 54 year old mother of three and grandmother of four she has always seen life as a challenge. Her life struggles began the day she was born and was taken home to a shack in a place called Tin Can Holler where her mother was brutally murdered when Rozetta was only seven years old.

As a child she was always curious about the people and the world around her and asked a lot of questions. She never wanted to be labeled "one of those kids", whether it was because she came from a place called Tin Can Holler or because she was a foster child. Rozetta always wanted to be different and needed to have her own little sparkle. Although obstacles and hurdles were always thrown into her pathway she was determined to prove that no matter where you came from you could be whatever you choose. There are no brick walls, only those you build for yourself.

When Rozetta was a child in the foster care system in Tennessee, she knew that no one really cared about her and loved her like her mother had. She promised herself that she would someday find out the truth about her mother's vicious murder. Rozetta's childhood hardships never made her bitter. She was a loving child with an outgoing personality who made friends everywhere she went. As she matured into a young lady her friendships were her mainstay that kept her focused. Her many girlfriends were her support team and remain so even today.

After graduating with honors in 1970 from Polk County High School in Benton, Tennessee, Rozetta was on her own at the age of eighteen. The U.S. Forestry Service was her first real employer. She then entered into the corporate world and eventually became a very successful realtor in the Florida Keys where she lived for over twenty-eight years. In 2002 she relocated to Port St. Lucie, Florida to pursue other interests. When her youngest child turned twenty-one in 2006 Rozetta sold her home and quit her job with a major corporation in Port St. Lucie to begin her quest to find out the truth about her mother's murder. Her mother's spirit was calling her to return to the place of her birth and to Tin Can Holler where it all began in 1959. This is her story.

Grace Sims

J. Cornelius Sims

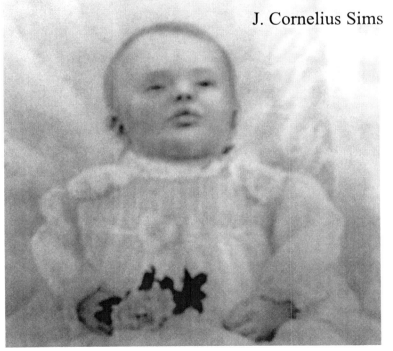

EVANS & SON ONE OF OLDEST STATE UNDERTAKERS

Established 57 Years Ago By Harry Evans' Father

Widow, Son Continue Business Well Started

Fifty-seven years ago the late T. M. Evans, an Englishman by birth, established the first funeral and embalming business in Athens. He is the late husband of Mrs. L. C. Evans and father of Harry Evans, who have carried on the work after his death 40 years ago. The business is now known as Evans & Son Burial Association.

The Evans establishment is the oldest in McMinn county and among the oldest in the State of Tennessee. The Evans Funeral Home, which is a modern addition to the business, is located on West Washington street.

T. M. Evans, a native of Wallsall, England, came to the United States when a youth of 16. He was in St. Louis, Mo., for a while, later coming to Athens. He followed the work of a painter, but soon took up the profession of embalming.

He was married to Miss Lillian Edgemon, daughter of the late Mr. and Mrs. Thomas R. Edgemon, in Meigs county, on Christmas day, 1878. Mr. Evans was building up a splendid business when he was taken ill. He was practically an invalid for eight years prior to his death.

That was the way Mrs. Evans started in the work, and with the assistance of her son, Harry, they carried on and today the establishment is one of the most outstanding in East Tennessee.

Harry Evans conducted his first funeral when only 12 years of age. Mrs. Evans, who is now 82, and her associates, are members of the National Funeral Directors association and a member of the Directors and Embalmers Association of the state of Tennessee.

Mrs. Evans was the first licensed woman in Tennessee and up to the present time, there has been few women who have taken up the work. A daughter, Mrs. H. Ross Bridges, assists with the work.

INHERITS WORK

MRS. L. C. EVANS

MORTICIAN

HARRY EVANS

was the principal trading point for the product, and it would take several weeks for the wagons to get the product to market and return.

The finished castor oil was put into tin containers, holding from one-half to one-gallon of oil each. The sale of the oil enabled Metcalf to purchase the necessary article for his retail trade, and afforded an opportunity for the growers of the bean to exchange their crop for groceries.

Charles W. Metcalf was a cousin

in an envelope properly stamped, and addressed to Mr. Louis

Milner, Groom Creek Route, Prescott, Arizona, said letter

being as follows, to wit:

                            "Decatur, Tennessee
                             Aut. 7th 1931.

"Dear Pal",
          Your letter came O.K. Was pleased to here
from you am very buisy trying to sell my peaches getting
40 cts. per bu. And have to haul them 16 to 30 miles and
pay 19 cts. for gas. I have been selling around home
and taking work for fall that helps out. I have worked
so hard trying to get some money and I have got my fare -
I leave Chattanooga, Tenn. to Chicago then to Billings,
Mont through the Parks leave by Cody - to Seattle Wash.
then to Portland then to Los Angeles and we will meet
there if you wish as I want you to visit and meet my
people and friends and we will come to your place and
arrange things and come home by Salt Lake City, Denver
and Colo. Springs Wonder trip now you let me know at
once if Los Angeles will be O.K. I can wire you when &
what R.R.I will come on as I have not got my ticket yet -
You could meet me at Sta. or if you miss me call at P.O.
and I will drop you line Gen. Del. where to find me now
we want to meet and not make a blunder I am asking a
favor please send me $20.00 to help me out for eats and
expense money on train I hate to be short - I never have
seen times like they are in this country Can't get money
Banks closing and people starving Can't pay for what you
have to sell - I am ready to roll Aug. 20th please rush
letter and tell me what to do and don't forget put me in
$20.00 and be sure to register your letter am going to
depend and trust in you please rush and tell me what to
do and be there to meet me please rush am waiting

                       Your Pal
                          (Signed) Grace V. Sims.
                                                 R.1.

P.S. I am coming alone Dad stay home. "

Tin Can Holler During the 1950's

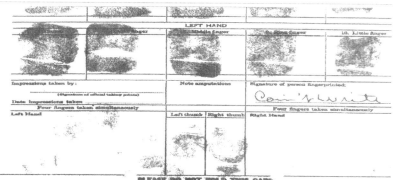

STATE OF TENNESSEE

DEPARTMENT OF PUBLIC WELFARE

July 10, 1957
Athens, Tennessee
McMinn County

FRANK G. CLEMENT
GOVERNOR
CHRISTINE C. REYNOLDS
COMMISSIONER

Mr. Ralph V. Barrett, Director Social Service
Holston Methodist Home
Greenville, Tennessee

Re: Mowery, Mrs. Eliza Mae

ATT: Miss Mary B. Flenniken, Caseworker

Dear Mr. Barrett:

I discussed the possibility of the 3 oldest children visiting with their mother for a short vacation yesterday. Mrs. Mowery is now living in her home alone and would certainly have room for the children for a visit. She is not employed regular, but has been doing some laundry work and assured me that she would be able to provide food for the children without having to ask for help. I had not been in the home for sometime and it is possible that it was in order because of my visit. However I noticed several things such as neatness of the yard, flowers and canning which made me feel that she was doing some better. I feel sure that Mrs. Mowery would hardly be able to cope with the children on a full time basis but I believe that she can do quite well during a short visiting period. She was less emotional yesterday and talked more sensible about the future of the children than I have ever noticed. Mrs. Mowery, however, is an unpredictable person and it would be impossible for me to be absolutely sure that things would go well. She understands that the children are coming only for a visit and must return on the date designated by your agency. She mentioned herself that it would be unwise if she ever expects to get the children back or to visit them in the home to disregard this.

I do think it will have meaning for the children and she especially wants to take them to see their father. For this reason it might be better to plan it for them to leave during the week so they could visit their father on the week-end. I do not believe it would be wise for them to spend a long vacation due to the neighborhood she lives in and her inability to control the children.

If vacation leave is granted she plans now to come after the children and either bring them back or send money for their bus tickets.

Mrs. Mowery understands that you are to notify her what decision is made about this. She also understands that the decision is up to the home and we are only giving the information you asked for.

Yours sincerely,

(Mrs.) Ruth Garrett
County Director

RG/ds   CC: Miss Elizabeth Freeman, Regional Director

Dear Miss Flemister   September 25, 1957.
I thought I would drop you a few
lines to let you no why we
dident get to come up Sunday to see
the children Sig went on a
trip & dident get Back he Coleed
Me Monday night he were in
Suay Toia Said he Coued make
it Back entil Thursday of this
week, I were disiponited to to.
I dont no hardly what to say
about Coming after the children
I ll Call you Friday Morning
or Saturday if he get Back. and
let you no for sur if we Can
Come Sunday are Not I Coued
Come By my Self but he thought
Moby he had to Com to.
My Brother ore Brother Inlow
   woued Bring me one time
after them But I thought it
woued Be wise to wait until I
herd from Sig are intil he got
Back off this trip there Pictures
we Made when they were at Home
I woued like for you to giv

I woued like to no if she
is still at the Home with
Billy & Borbora ore not
I were set to Houing the childrun
with us & I Just cont stay
Home ot night we howe
Ben stay ot my Brothus
where I work I Hope to hure
from you toow
I no it wont Be over two wecke
Befoe 3 Con Come oftr them
I thmik you for what
you howe done for my
childrun but I could Bon Home
Befoe I did But they got my
Popers oll mest up.
it will sure Mean a lote to Houe them all
Bock Home   Your Very Truley

Mr + mrs Seignoyst Mowery

Cbr D. M. Mowery

Benton Tennm

PS mres Ihruiken we will Be up Sunday to
see all the childrun if you Con get

MOTHER OF 6

MURDER SCENE — Mrs. Seig Mowery, 37, was doused with water but did not respond after allegedly being beaten and kicked to death by her husband at the Ebb Dickson home last night. Officers W. R. Reynolds, Nick Crittenden and Ruel Ware examine the area of the yard where she died (top photo). At bottom, the officers point to blood-stains in the Dickson shanty where the woman was first attacked.

Athenian

ID mEIGS COUNTIE.

WLAR 1450

August 17, 1959

SIX CENTS

KICKED TO DEATH

Husband Held In Murder Of Mrs. Seig Mowery

A 37-year-old mother of six children was beaten and kicked to death here last night when her husband allegedly "flew into a rage" after finding her in a shanty with two other men.

Mrs. Eliza Mae Mowery was pronounced a victim of murder by a coroner's jury, empaneled by J. Holland Barker. She apparently died of head injuries.

The woman's half-nude body was found by Policemen Nick Crittenden and Ruel Ware in the yard at the home of Ebb Dickson on Railroad Avenue where she was allegedly kicked to death by her husband, Seig Mowery.

W. O. Kennedy, criminal investigator on the staff of Dist. Atty.-Gen. James Watkins, said Mowery first denied being at the Dickson home but later admitted the attack.

Kennedy said the woman's husband reported he had found Mrs. Mowery nude in the house with Dickson and Glen (Coot) Lawson about midnight. "Mowery apparently flew into a rage, struck the woman there and then dragged her into the yard where he stamped her to death," the officer stated.

Family Affair

Chief Deputy Sheriff Howard Thompson, one of the investigating officers, said Mowery's car struck a ditch near the Dickson home late last night and while her husband went for help, Mrs. Mowery reportedly walked over to Dickson's. When Seig returned and found his wife had left the car he began a search which ended at the shanty.

During questioning at the county jail, Dickson said Mowery struck his wife several times in the house, knocking her to the floor from a box on which she had been sitting. He said when he told Mowery to leave the house that the man dragged the woman into the yard and stamped and kicked her "25 or 30 times."

Dickson said the attack on the woman and her screams unnerved both he and Lawson but that they did not interfere other than to order Mowery from his house. Asked by Kennedy why he had not intervened and stopped the attack, Dickson replied, "I just thought it was a family affair."

After Mrs. Mowery lay prostrate and unconscious in the yard, Dickson said Mowery asked Lawson to bring him some water and when the man returned with a bucketfull, he doused her heavily. The woman did not respond.

Officers had been unable to determine if Mowery was attempting to wash the blood from his wife's body or revive her. Dickson said Mowery and Lawson carried the woman's body to the shoulder of the road where her spouse apparently intended to load it into the car. Lawson then fled and is still being sought by police.

Reports Wife Dead

Jim McSpadden, a civil defense officer serving a weekly shift as radio operator at the county jail, said he received a call from a man identifying himself as Seig Mowery about midnight and was advised by the caller "I think my wife is lying dead near the road at Ebb Dickson's house." McSpadden said Mowery left a telephone number for him to call back.

Officers Crittenden and Ware were immediately dispatched to the scene and other officers arrived soon thereafter. The policeman said the woman's body was nude from the waist up and her face and head badly smashed. Later they arrested Mowery at his home on Howard Street.

Dickson said after beating the woman, Seig left the house, returning later and then left again. It was after the second trip that officers arrived.

Thompson said a blood stained shirt was found in Mowery's car and Deputy Sheriff W. R. Reynolds said other heavily stained clothing was found at the man's home this morning.

Socks Give-Away

The chief deputy said Mowery had washed his shoes and changed clothing but had failed to change his blood stained socks. After first denying the attack on his wife, Mowery was asked to explain how his socks had become stained. "I don't know . . . it's just one of those things," Thompson quoted the man as saying.

It was later in the night, during questioning by Kennedy, Thompson and other officers, that Mowery allegedly admitted the attack on his wife.

At the scene, officers found bloodstains in the house and in the yard. There was also evidence of the water having been thrown on Mrs. Mowery where she lay.

On Parole

Kennedy said Mowery is on parole from the state penitentiary where he was serving six to 13 years on charges of larceny. He reportedly was released about a year ago after serving 35 months.

Both Mr. and Mrs. Mowery were reported to have been drinking before the attack at the Dickson house. Officers were not certain whether Mowery was drunk but said he "smelled heavily."

Mowery will face preliminary hearing on murder charges at 10 a.m. Wednesday in Sessions Court.

Mrs. Mowery was a daughter of the late Fred and Anna Robinson.

Survivors other than her husband are five daughters, Beulah Evans, Cleveland; Barbara, Sheilah, Rossita and Marcilla, all of Athens; son, Billy, Athens.

Funeral services will be held at 2:30 p.m. Tuesday in the chapel of Evans Funeral Home. Burial will be in Clearwater Cemetery. The body will remain at the funeral home.

Huge Airliner in Emergency Landing With 82

SYDNEY, Australia (UPI) — A Qantas Boeing-707 jet plane with 82 persons aboard returned to Sydney Airport Sunday night when it developed engine trouble but strong winds prevented a landing and the plane flew on to Brisbane.

The big jet airliner circled the airfield at Sydney for two hours, one of its four engines dead, and authorities finally ordered it to make the one-hour flight to Brisbane where it made a safe emergency landing.

Rain and winds up to 55 miles an hour at Sydney swept the only

(continued on page 8)

Dear Miss Flenniken:

Thank you for referring these four children to us. It has been very enjoyable working with the. I was somewhat apprehensive about trying to see four persons from the same family lest I should get all of my impressions confused. That difficulty has not developed, and the contacts have been very pleasing ones.

I have written you a separate letter concerning each child so that if you have "case files" on your children, the separate reports may facilitate your dealing with them.

As a general statement concerning these four children as a group I suppose my strongest impression is that I am really surprised that there are no greater problems present in their adjustment. What we know of their history certainly leads one to believe that these children would be experiencing very great emotional difficulty. I was struck with the general impression that the degree of emotional and intellectual disturbances in these children relates fairly directly to their age, the youngest child being less disturbed and the oldest and the middle children being at an intermediate point on a rough scale of psychological disorder. This observation may reflect the ages at which the children have been subjected to the undesirable events and the ages at which they were given greater opportunities of group and boarding-home life. In a similar way I felt that the suitability of these children for adoptive placement varies with their age—the youngest child again being more amenable to this approach than the older ones.

These written reports may meet the needs in regard to these children. Should this not be the case, as always we want you to feel free to come back and talk with us about them. If it is your wish to do that, please let us know and we will arrange some time of mutual convenience.

Sincerely yours,
MENTAL HEALTH CENTER

Sheila, Marcie and Rozetta

Re: Mowery Children

Att.: Miss Mary B. Flenniken,
     Case Worker

Dear Mr. Matthews:

I have delayed letting you know about Mr. Mowery's trial since I was trying to find out exactly how long he would be in the penitentiary. To date I am still very uncertain.

He was tried in Criminal Court and was given a sentence of from two to ten years in the State Penitentiary. There seemed to be some question as to whether he would have to serve all of the years left on the other felony charge before starting the two to ten years for this charge. Mr. Mowery immediately filed for a new trial and the decision on this is to come up next week. I have never been able to determine whether he will have to serve approximately two years or whether it will be many years. I do intend to talk with the Judge when he is back in this County next week.

While Mr. Mowery was here I did go to the jail and talk to him about plans for the children. At that time he was real sure that he could get a new trial and not get any time at all. He was under the impression that if he pulled the 'right strings he wouldn't have to serve more than a year and a half. If this were true he would not want to release the children. I was able to get him to say that if he did receive a long term it would be better for the children to have a family and two parents of their own.

The Sheriff assured me that he would probably be here until a decision was made in March, but they took him back to Petros. As soon as I am able to find out about the length of time he will probably have to serve I do plan to see him here or write to him in Petros to make plans for the children.

- 2 -

Cinderella and her husband are up North and Beulah and her husband are living in Monroe County and neither of them came to the hearing. I am very pleased to know that the children are getting along quite well. Hopefully I will be able to give you some more definite information in the near future.

Sincerely yours,

"Uncle Harry" with Billy's daughter

Uncle Ed with Eliza's guitar

Holston Home Top two. Staff at bottom, Charles Hutchins 2nd from left in back row and Miss Flenniken 2nd from left in front row.

Billy's funeral with the high school football team pallbearers.

Breinigsville, PA USA
01 December 2009

228438BV00003B/86/P

9 780977 968060